Easy-to-Read
Doctrine and Covenants
and
Pearl of Great Price

Easy-to-Read Doctrine and Covenants and Pearl of Great Price

John C. Duffy

Estes Book Company
67 Old Turnpike Rd.
Port Murray, NJ 07865

The Easy-to-Read Doctrine and Covenants and Pearl of Great Price,
Copyright ©2001 by Estes Book Company. Printed and Bound in the United
States of America. All rights reserved. No part of this book may be reproduced
in any form or by any electronic or mechanical means including information
storage and retrieval systems without the permission in writing from the
publisher, except by a reviewer, who may quote brief passages in a review.
For information, please contact Estes Book Company, 67 Old Turnpike Rd.
Port Murray, NJ 07865

First printing 2000.

Library of Congress Catalog Card Number 00-107205
ISBN 0-9644957-1-6

Dedicated to everyone, no matter how young, who seeks to obtain God's word.

TO THE READER

Like many of you, I was baptized when I was eight years old. Not long after my baptism, I decided I wanted to read The Doctrine and Covenants. It was the one book of scripture we used in the LDS Church that I didn't know much about. I knew lots of stories from the Bible and the Book of Mormon. And my family had read the whole Book of Mormon, little by little, around the dinner table. But no one ever seemed to tell stories from The Doctrine and Covenants.

One winter morning, I got up before everyone else in my family. I went into the living room and took my father's copy of The Doctrine and Covenants off the bookshelf. We lived in Idaho, where it gets very cold in the winter. So I sat in front of the hot air vent to read. I started to read Section 1 of The Doctrine and Covenants. I didn't know a lot of the words. But I forced myself to keep going until I'd read the whole section. When I was done, I had no idea what I'd just read. There didn't seem to be any kind of a story to follow. But I wanted to be able to say I'd read the whole Doctrine and Covenants. So I decided to keep at it.

Every morning for a week, I got up early, sat in front of the hot air vent, and read a little from The Doctrine and Covenants. Some days I was able to read just one section. Other days I was able to read two sections, they were so short. But I still didn't understand what I was reading. At the end of the week, after I'd gotten halfway through Section 10, I gave up.

Now I am 28 years old. I have learned to read and understand the language used in the scriptures. But I still remember how I felt when I was just eight. I was tired of reading storybooks based on the scriptures. I wanted to read the scriptures themselves. But the language in the scriptures was too hard for me to understand at that time.

Have you ever felt that way? If you have, then this book is for you. The scriptures were written in a form of English that is beautiful but very old. In this book, I have put the whole Doctrine and Covenants and the Pearl of Great Price into simple modern English. That means the English that you and I use when we talk. If you are in the fourth grade, you should be able to understand most of the words I have used in this book.

If you see a word you don't understand, try looking it up in the "Words to Know" pages at the back of the book. You may find the word explained there.

I believe that God speaks to us through The Doctrine and Covenants and the Pearl of Great Price. Those books teach us how much God loves us. They teach us how important it is to help other people, the way Jesus did. They teach us what we need to do to keep our earth from being destroyed. They teach us how we can be happy.

I believe it is important for people of all ages to be able to read the messages in The Doctrine and Covenants and the Pearl of Great Price. As you read them, and as you think about what they mean, the Spirit will speak to your heart. The Spirit will help you know what is true. It will help you know what God wants you to do.

I hope this book helps you be close to God. If you read it with a member of your family, it could help you be close to them, too.

TO PARENTS

Why This Book Was Written

The *Easy-to-Read Doctrine and Covenants and Pearl of Great Price* is meant to help children, or beginning readers of English, transition from reading storybooks based on the scriptures to reading the scriptures themselves. As many of us know from our own experience, the King James English of LDS scripture is a challenge even for adults. Our children will eventually learn to meet that challenge, as we have. But of course, that takes time. Meanwhile, our older children are left with no means of engaging the scriptural texts on their own, except through storybooks designed for children younger than themselves.

In this book, I provide a verse-by-verse paraphrase of the Doctrine and Covenants and the Pearl of Great Price in simple modern English. I emphasize that this book is a *paraphrase*. It does not pretend to be a new, modernized "translation" of LDS scripture. A translation attempts to fully reproduce the meaning of the original text, so that the translation can be used in place of the original. A paraphrase—and a simplified paraphrase at that—is much more modest. A paraphrase attempts to capture only the gist of the original in order to achieve basic understanding. The complexity and nuances of the original language are lost. This means that a paraphrase can never hope to replace the original text, nor should it try to.

Again, the *Easy-to-Read Doctrine and Covenants and Pearl of Great Price* is designed to help people transition into reading the scriptures. *It is not meant to replace the scriptures.* Nothing could replace the scriptures. No paraphrase—indeed, no translation—could say everything the original texts say.

Verse by verse, clause by clause, these texts are packed with meaning. In creating the paraphrase, I have had to (1) sort out the multiple ideas or meanings worked into a single verse and (2) decide which of those ideas to include for the purposes of this book. That is, naturally, a judgment call on my part. In this process, I have been guided by scriptural commentaries and by my sense of the reasons for which we quote particular passages (i.e., what points we tend to make when we expound on a certain verse). Still, it is possible you will not always be entirely satisfied with the way I have opted to paraphrase a verse. By all means, let your children know that. Discussion between parents and children about the meaning of the scriptures, and enthusiasm on the part of children to grapple with the original texts, is precisely what this book aims to accomplish.

How This Book Was Written

The *Easy-to-Read Doctrine and Covenants and Pearl of Great Price* was written at a fourth-grade reading level. It has taken nearly five years to complete; most of that time was spent in revision. In producing the paraphrase, I followed these guidelines:

(1) With a few exceptions, I have confined myself to the vocabulary found in the Dale list (a list of 3,000 words known to fourth graders, compiled by researcher Edgar Dale) and to religious terms that a Latter-day Saint child would likely know from their Primary experience. Words used in the paraphrase, but not found on the Dale list, are listed in the "Words to Know" section at the back of the book.

(2) The average sentence length has been kept to 8-10 words. Active voice is preferred to passive voice.

(3) Because I am dealing with scripture, I have aimed for a simple yet dignified style. I have not used words which strike me as overly informal or juvenile. I generally avoid contractions (can't, isn't, I've, it's, etc.)

(4) For stylistic reasons, the scriptures are often deliberately redundant. For simplicity's sake, I have generally edited redundancies out of the paraphrase.

(5) I aimed to make each verse a self-contained unit, so that verses could be excerpted and read individually. Since in the original text, one long sentence may run across several verses, this guideline has required some rearrangement of material in a few places (see, for instance, D&C 20:2-3).

(6) While I wanted each verse to be readable as an independent unit, I also wanted the revelations to flow smoothly as a whole, since this is how they were originally written. (In the first editions of The Doctrine and Covenants and the Pearl of Great Price, the revelations are divided into long prose paragraphs. These paragraphs were later chopped up into the smaller verses we know today.) Preserving this sense of flow has required trimming some tangential or parenthetical material out of the paraphrase.

(7) Because children tend to be literal-minded, I have avoided figurative language in the paraphrase. For stock metaphors like harvesting the field or pruning the vineyard, I usually provide literal interpretations. Muted Biblical allusions in the original are spelled out in full in the paraphrase.

(8) The scriptures of the Restoration often speak of God as angry or vengeful. When adults encounter this language, we are able to read it in light of a sophisticated understanding of a God who is both merciful and just, who loves us and seeks our happiness but is bound by eternal law to let the natural consequences of our choices run their course. Children may not be in a position to perform this kind of interpretation. So I have been careful not to say anything in the paraphrase that might give the impression that the Lord is capricious or vindictive, or that he becomes angry in the same way people become angry.

(9) While I aim for a paraphrase that clearly lays out the meaning of the original language, there are passages in the revelations that are unclear or ambiguous—that could be read to mean different things. In such cases, I have tried to preserve the ambiguity in the paraphrase.

How This Book Might Be Used

The book has been written in such a way that children can read it on their own. But, of course, reading from the book with your child can be a way to enjoy quality time together, and a way for you to nurture your child spiritually. Talk about the scriptures with your child. Help your child begin to see how adults apply the scriptures to their own lives. Let your child see what role the scriptures play in your own spirituality. Help your child create a plan for reading the entire book within a certain period—say, a year. Try reading a passage first from the original text, then from the paraphrase. Use the paraphrase as a resource during family home evenings and family scripture study.

Once children have reached the age of accountability, there is no reason that they cannot begin to develop their personal spirituality. It is my hope that you will find this book useful in helping your children expand their appreciation of the scriptures of the Restoration.

ABOUT THE DOCTRINE AND COVENANTS

Members of The Church of Jesus Christ of Latter-day Saints believe that Joseph Smith was a prophet. He received revelations from Jesus Christ. Through these revelations, Jesus taught church members the gospel. He taught them how to build up his restored church and carry out his work.

Doctrine and Covenants is a collection of many of Joseph Smith's revelations. Most of these are written as the words of Jesus Christ himself. The book also includes teachings that Joseph Smith received from the Spirit, but which he wrote in his own words. There are a few revelations and teachings in the book from prophets who lived after Joseph Smith, too.

The word "doctrine" means church teachings. The word "covenants" means holy promises. In Joseph Smith's day, that could mean promises God makes to people. Or it could mean the rules that members of a church promised to keep. So in the book of Doctrine and Covenants, we find the teachings of Jesus Christ's restored church and the rules that church members should live by.

Many of the revelations were given for certain people. Many revelations were given to help church members with problems they were facing at that time. Before each section of the *Easy-to-Read Doctrine and Covenants*, I explain what was happening to the members of the church when each revelation was given. The people the revelations were given to died long ago. The problems they faced are not the same ones we face today. But we can still learn many things from those revelations about how God works in people's lives. We can learn how he wants us to live to be truly happy.

Doctrine and Covenants

SECTION 1

Joseph Smith received many revelations from the Lord. At one of the church's first general conferences, church leaders decided to publish some of the revelations in a book. The Lord gave Joseph a new revelation to put at the beginning of the book, so people would know what the book was about. Section 1 is that revelation.

1 These are the words of the Lord. He looks down from heaven on all the people of the world. He says: Listen, people of my church. Listen, people from faraway lands and islands. Listen, all of you.

2 These words are for all people. Someday, everyone on earth will see the Lord and hear his voice. They will feel the power of his words deep in their hearts.

3 When that day comes, no one will be able to hide their sins anymore. People who have not kept the commandments will be filled with sorrow.

4 I have sent my followers to warn everyone that the end of the world is coming.

5 No one can keep my followers from doing what I have told them to do.

6 That is because I have given my servants my power. I have also given them this book of commandments to share with the whole world. This revelation is the beginning of that book.

7 Read the book carefully and do what it tells you, because everything I have said in it will come true.

8 When my servants go out to share my words with the world, I give them power to perform gospel ordinances. People need to receive gospel ordinances so God can save them.

9 People who do not accept the gospel or keep my commandments cannot receive these ordinances. They will be punished for their sins.

10 When the Lord comes, he will give everyone the reward or punishment they have earned. If you have done good things for other people, the Lord will give good things to you.

11 That is why the Lord calls to everyone on earth who will listen—

12 Get ready to be judged, because the Lord is almost here.

13 The wicked will suffer if they do not repent. Terrible things are going to happen on earth. Many people are going to die.

14 The Lord will show the world his strength. People who want to live with God need to listen to the Lord and his servants. They need to follow the teachings of the prophets and apostles.

15 The people of the world have turned away from my ordinances. They have broken the holy promise I made with them.

16 Instead of doing what the Lord wants, people do whatever they want. They worship the things of the world—things they themselves have made. But when the world is destroyed, all the things they worship will be destroyed, too.

17 I, the Lord, knew about the terrible things that are going to happen on earth. So I talked to my servant Joseph Smith. I gave him commandments.

18 I gave commandments to other people, too. I told them to teach my words to everyone. I did this so that the words the prophets wrote long ago would come true.

19 Things people say are weak will turn out to be more powerful than things people say are strong. This will show people that they should stop teaching their own ideas instead of God's. They should stop trusting their own strength.

20 God wants everyone to be able to speak in his name.

21 Then there will be more faith in the world.

22 Then I can restore my gospel—my holy promise with the world.

23 If you have my power, you do not need a fancy education to teach people the restored gospel. Even kings and rulers will listen to what you say.

24 I, God, have said this. These commandments come from me. I gave them to my servants, even though my servants were weak. I did it in their own language, so they could understand.

25 If my servants make mistakes, I will show them what they are doing wrong.

26 If they want to learn, I will teach them.

27 If they sin, I will correct them, so they can repent.

28 If they are humble, I will make them strong. I will bless them. I will send them revelations now and then, to teach them.

29 I gave my servant, Joseph Smith, the golden plates which the Nephites wrote. I gave him power to translate the Book of Mormon.

30 When I gave these commandments to my servants, I also gave them power to start my church. Because of their work, my church will be well-known. It is the only church in the whole world that has my authority. As a whole, I am very happy with this church, though not with all of its members.

31 That is because I, the Lord, cannot overlook even the smallest amount of sin.

32 Still, I will forgive those who repent and keep my commandments.

33 Those who do not repent will lose the blessings I have already given them. My Spirit cannot stay with people who will not repent.

34 I want everyone on earth to know what I have said.

35 I love everyone equally. I want everyone to know that very soon, there will be great trouble on earth. Satan will have power over those who follow him.

36 At the same time, the Lord will have power over the righteous. He will live among them, as their king. He will come down to judge the world.

37 Study these commandments, because they are true. Everything I have said about what will happen in the future will come true. Every promise that I have given you will come true.

38 I have said some things that may make people angry, but they needed to be said. Nothing can keep my words from coming true. It does not matter if I myself say them, or if my servants say them for me—the words are just as true.

39 The Spirit will testify to you that these are really God's words and that they will all come true. Amen.

SECTION 2

When Joseph Smith was 17 years old, the angel Moroni appeared to him and said that God wanted Joseph to translate the Book of Mormon. (See "Joseph Smith's Story" in the Easy-to-Read Book of Mormon, *or Joseph Smith—History 1:27-54.) Moroni also taught Joseph about what God was going to do in the future. Section 2 is a small part of what Moroni taught. Moroni is quoting something the Lord said to the prophet Malachi.*

1 Before the Second Coming, I will reveal the priesthood to you through the prophet Elijah.

2 Elijah will remind people of the promises made to their ancestors. People's hearts will turn to their ancestors.

3 If this did not happen, the whole world would be destroyed during the Second Coming.

SECTION 3

After Joseph Smith had translated part of the Book of Mormon, Martin Harris asked if he could show the translation to his family. Three times, the Lord told Martin "no." But Martin kept asking. Finally, the Lord said Martin could take the translation home if he promised to show it only to certain people. Martin broke that promise, and someone stole the translation. Joseph was very upset. He was afraid God would not let him keep translating the Book of Mormon. Section 3 is a revelation the Lord gave to Joseph during this time.

1 When God plans to do something, nothing can keep him from doing it.

2 God marches straight ahead, without turning left or right. This means he always does what he says he will. His ways never change.

3 Remember—people's plans may fail. But God's work never fails.

4 It does not matter how many revelations you receive, or how much power God gives you. If you brag about yourself, you will suffer because of it. If you do what you want instead of listening to God, you will suffer because of it.

5 I trusted you with important things. But I also gave you strict commandments about them. Remember what I promised you if you kept those commandments.

6 Time after time, you did what other people wanted instead of what God wanted.

7 I know there are people who hate God's words and want to hurt you. But you should have been more worried about keeping God's commandments than about what other people might do.

8 If you had kept God's commandments, he would have protected you from anything Satan tried to do to stop you. He would have helped you during all your troubles.

9 Joseph, the Lord chose you to do his work. But if you are not careful about keeping God's commandments, you will lose that calling.

10 Remember God's mercy. If you repent of what you did wrong, I

will let you keep your calling. I will let you keep doing my work.

11 If you do not repent, you will lose the special power I gave you.

12 God gave you the power to translate holy writings. But then you gave those writings to a wicked man.

13 That man disobeyed God. He made holy promises to God and then broke them. He trusted his own ideas. He bragged about how smart he was.

14 That is why you have lost your power to translate for a while.

15 From the start, you have let God's commandments be broken.

16 Still, my work will go forward. Just as the world learned about the Savior through the Bible, so my people will learn about the Savior through the Book of Mormon.

17 The Nephites, Jacobites, Josephites, and Zoramites will learn about the Savior through the testimony of their own ancestors.

18 The Lamanites, Lemuelites, and Ishmaelites will also learn from their ancestors' testimony. The Lamanites became weak and stopped believing in the truth because of their ancestors' sins. The Lord let the Lamanites destroy the Nephites because the Nephites became wicked.

19 That is why the golden plates where their ancestors' testimony is written have been kept safe—so that the Lord can keep the promise he made to his people.

20 The Lord wants the Lamanites to learn about their ancestors and about the Lord's promises. He wants them to believe the gospel and trust Jesus Christ to save them. If they have faith in Jesus Christ and repent, they will be saved. Amen.

SECTION 4

One day, Joseph Smith's father came to visit him. He believed that Joseph was a prophet. He wanted to know what God wanted him to do. He asked Joseph for a revelation. Section 4 is the revelation the Lord gave for Joseph Smith's father.

1 An amazing work is about to begin among the people of the world.

2 Those of you who set out to serve God need to work as hard as you can. Then, at the Last Judgment, you will know that God is happy with the work you did.

3 If you have the desire to serve God, you are called to do his work.

4 The people of the world are ready to receive the restored gospel. If you work hard to spread the gospel, you will receive many blessings. You will be saved.

5 <u>If you have faith, hope, and love, you are worthy to do God's work</u>. God's glory must be your only goal.

6 <u>Remember to have faith.</u> <u>Keep the commandments.</u> <u>Study.</u> <u>Show self-control.</u> <u>Be patient.</u> <u>Be kind.</u> <u>Follow the Savior's example.</u> <u>Love others.</u> <u>Be humble.</u> <u>Work hard.</u>

7 If you ask, God will give. If you knock, God will open the door. Amen.

SECTION 5

While Joseph Smith was translating the Book of Mormon, the Lord told him not to let other people see the golden plates. But Martin Harris wanted to see them, so he could know for certain that they were real. Joseph asked the Lord if Martin could see the golden plates. Section 5 is the Lord's answer.

1 My servant Martin Harris wants me to show him that you really have the golden plates you told him about.

2 This is what you will say to Martin. Tell him: I am God. I gave the golden plates to you, Joseph Smith. I commanded you to testify about them.

3 I made you promise not to show the golden plates to anyone unless I told you to. You cannot do anything with the plates unless I give you the power to do it.

4 You have the power to translate the golden plates. This is my first gift to you. I told you not to pretend to have any other gifts. I will give you more gifts later, but not until you finish translating the golden plates.

5 Terrible things will happen to the people of the world if they do not listen to my words.

6 I will send you to teach people my words. You will be ordained to this calling later.

7 If someone will not believe my words, they will not believe your testimony about the golden plates either. Even if you could show them the golden plates, they still would not believe you.

8 People will suffer if they do not accept my words.

9 The fact that I will not let you show anyone the golden plates is part of a wise plan. Someday, people will understand why I did it this way.

10 You are the one who will teach my word to the people of today.

11 I will choose three of my servants to testify with you. They will see the golden plates. They will teach people the revelations I give you.

12 These three witnesses will know for certain that everything you have said about the golden plates is true. I myself will tell them that it is true.

13 I will give them power to see the golden plates for themselves.

14 No one else will have this power. This is a new time. I am starting to restore my church. It will be as bright as the moon and sun. It will be like an army with flags.

15 I will command the three witnesses to share their testimony with the world.

16 I will send my Spirit to everyone who believes my words. They will be born again through baptism and the gift of the Holy Ghost.

17 But you must wait a while for all this to happen. First you have to be ordained.

18 People will suffer if they do not listen to the three witnesses' testimony.

19 That is because a terrible destruction is coming if people do not change their ways. It will come again and again until the Second Coming. Then everyone who will not repent will be destroyed.

20 I warn you about this, just like I warned the people of Jerusalem long ago that their city was going to be destroyed. These words will come true, just as my words have come true in the past.

21 Joseph, I command you to repent and do better. Stop doing what other people want you to do instead of what God commands you to do.

22 Do not be afraid of people wanting to kill you. If you stay strong and keep my commandments, I will give you eternal life.

23 Now, this is what I have to say about Martin Harris.

24 He is too proud. Tell him to be more humble. He must pray very hard, with faith. His heart must be true. If he does all this, I will let him see the golden plates.

25 Then he will tell the world: "I have seen the same things the Lord showed Joseph Smith. Because I have seen them, I know for certain they are true. Only God's power could show them to me."

26 The only thing Martin Harris should say about the golden plates is, "I have seen them, and God's power showed them to me." I command him not to say anything else.

27 If he says more than what I have told him to, he will be guilty of breaking a holy promise with me.

28 He must be humble. He must admit that he has made mistakes. He must promise to keep my commandments. He must show faith in me. If he does not do all these things, I will not let him see the golden plates.

29 If that happens, you must tell Martin not to bother me anymore about this.

30 If it turns out that Martin cannot see the golden plates, then you must stop translating until I tell you to start again.

31 If you do not do this, I will take away your power to translate. I will also take away the golden plates.

32 I know that people are trying to kill you. I know that Martin Harris will turn against you if he does not get to see the golden plates.

33 There are many people trying to destroy you. I have given you these commandments to save your life.

34 That is why I said: Stand still until I tell you what to do. I will give you everything you need to carry out my work.

35 If you keep my commandments, I will bring you to live with me in heaven. Amen.

SECTION 6

Oliver Cowdery worked as a schoolteacher in the place where Joseph Smith's father lived. Oliver learned about the golden plates from Joseph's father. He became very interested. He visited Joseph. He felt that Joseph was telling the truth about the golden plates. Joseph and Oliver began to work together, translating the Book of Mormon. After they had been working together for a while, the Lord gave Joseph a revelation for Oliver. Section 6 is that revelation.

1 An amazing work is about to begin among the people of the world.
2 I am God. Listen to my words, and you will feel their power deep inside you.
3 The people of the world are ready to receive the restored gospel. If you want to help spread the gospel, now is the time. Work as hard as you can, and you will be saved in God's kingdom.
4 God will give a calling to everyone who is willing to help.
5 If you ask me for help, I will help you. Whenever you pray, I will listen.
6 Here is the advice you asked me to give you. Keep my commandments and help build Zion.
7 Do not work to get money. Work to become wise. God himself will teach you. Then you will be truly rich. To be truly rich means to have eternal life.
8 I will give you whatever you ask me for. If you want, I will use you to do many good things in the world.
9 Teach people to repent. If you keep my commandments and help carry out my work, I will bless you.
10 You have a gift. It is a blessing to you. Remember that it is holy and comes from God.
11 If you ask, God will teach you many important and wonderful things. He will reveal these things to you through your gift. Then you can help others learn the truth and see their mistakes.
12 Talk about your gift only with people who share your beliefs. Do not treat holy things lightly.
13 If you do good in the world and endure to the end, you will be saved in God's kingdom. Salvation is God's greatest gift.
14 Asking me to tell you what to do was the right thing. I will bless you for it. Every time you have asked, my Spirit has told you what to do. It was the Spirit that led you to this place.
15 You know that every time you have asked me what to do, thoughts have come into your mind. Those thoughts came from the Spirit.
16 Only God could know your private thoughts. That is why I am telling you this—so you will know it is God who is speaking to you now.
17 I testify to you that the words you have been writing down from the Book of Mormon are true.
18 Work hard. Help my servant Joseph. He will have many troubles as he tries to teach people my word.
19 Correct his weaknesses, and let him correct yours. Be patient. Be serious. Show self-control. Have faith, hope, and love.
20 Oliver, I have given you this revelation because you wanted it. These words are important—treat them that way. If you work hard at keeping God's commandments, you will feel my arms wrapped around you in love.
21 I am Jesus Christ, God's Son. I came to my own people, but they would not listen to me. I am the shining light which the darkness cannot overcome.
22 If you want further proof that these are God's words, remember the night you prayed to know if the things Joseph had told you were true.

23 Remember how peaceful I made you feel. Is that not a revelation from God? What more can you ask for?
24 If I have told you things no one else knows, doesn't that show you that these are really God's words?
25 If you want, I will give you power to translate, just like Joseph.
26 Many parts of my gospel are written down in books which I have kept hidden. I had to hide them because people were too wicked to be trusted with them.
27 If your goal is to help God's work, not to get rich, then I will reveal to you the parts of the scriptures I have kept hidden. I will reveal them to you through your gift.
28 I now give you and Joseph the authority to carry out this work. The two of you will be witnesses for me. There must always be two or three witnesses of the truth.
29 Even if people will not listen when you try to teach them my words, I will bless you. Remember, they cannot do anything worse to you than what they did to me.
30 Even if they kill you, like they killed me, I will bless you. I will bring you to heaven to live with me.
31 But if people listen to your testimonies and accept my words, I will bless them. Then you will rejoice because of the good that has come from your hard work.
32 I tell you the same thing I told my followers long ago: If two or three people come together to do my work, I will be there with them. In the same way, I am with you.
33 Do not be afraid to do good, my children. What you plant, you later harvest. If you do something good, you will receive something good as a reward.
34 Do not be afraid, even though there are just a few of you. Do good. All the powers of earth and hell may come together to fight you. But they cannot win, as long as you do what I have taught you.
35 I forgive your sins. Go on with your lives and keep my commandments. Take the work I have given you seriously.
36 Always remember me. Do not doubt or be afraid.
37 See the spear wound in my side. See the nail prints in my hands and feet. If you keep my commandments, you will live in God's heavenly kingdom. Amen.

SECTION 7

While they were working together, Joseph Smith and Oliver Cowdery disagreed about whether the apostle John had died or was still alive. They decided to ask the Lord. The Lord revealed to Joseph something which John himself had written long ago and then hidden. Section 7 is what John wrote.

1 The Lord said to me, "John, my dear friend, what do you want? I will give you anything you ask for."
2 I said to him, "Lord, give me power so that I will not die. Instead, let me go on living, so I can do your work."
3 The Lord said to me, "I will give you what you want. You will go on living until my Second Coming.

You will teach people in many different countries and in many different languages."

⁴ That is why the Lord said to Peter, "If I decide to let John go on living until I come again, that is none of your business. He wanted to keep doing my work. You wanted to come quickly to be with me in heaven.

⁵ "What you wanted was good, Peter. But John wanted to do more. He wanted to do a work greater than anything he had already done.

⁶ "To help him do this greater work, I will give him power like an angel's. He will use that power to teach and serve the righteous people on earth.

⁷ "You have a different calling, Peter. You will be John's teacher. You will also be James' teacher. The three of you will be in charge of my work until the Second Coming.

⁸ "I will give you what you want, and I will give John what he wants, because each of you wanted what will bring you joy."

SECTION 8

In Section 6, the Lord promised Oliver Cowdery that he would have the chance to translate from the Book of Mormon, just like Joseph Smith. Oliver wanted very much to see that promise come true. The Lord gave Joseph another revelation, telling Oliver how he could translate. Section 8 is that revelation.

¹ Oliver Cowdery, I promise you this: If you ask with faith, and if your heart is true, you will be able to translate the ancient writings I told you about—the parts of the scriptures that I had to hide.

² The Holy Ghost will come into your heart. It will give you thoughts and feelings, to tell you what to write.

³ This is how people receive revelation. This is the same power Moses used to split the Red Sea, so the Israelites could walk across on dry ground.

⁴ This is your gift. If you use it, you will be blessed. The gift will save you when your enemies try to kill you, or when Satan tries to tempt you.

⁵ Remember these words. Keep my commandments. Do not forget that this is your gift.

⁶ This is not your only gift. You also have the gift of receiving revelation the same way Aaron received it. This gift has told you many things.

⁷ God's power is what makes that gift work.

⁸ Do not doubt—your gift is from God, and you will do amazing works with it. Because the gift is from God, no one can take it away from you.

⁹ Through this gift, I will teach you whatever you ask me to.

¹⁰ Remember, you cannot do anything without faith. So ask with faith. Do not treat this gift lightly by asking for things you shouldn't.

¹¹ Ask me to teach you. Ask to be able to translate the ancient scrip-

tures which are hidden. If you have faith, I will give you what you ask for.

12 These are the words of God—the same God who has always spoken to you. Amen.

SECTION 9

When Oliver Cowdery tried to translate from the Book of Mormon, he found it much harder than he had thought it would be. He soon gave up trying to translate. Instead, Joseph went back to translating. Oliver went back to being Joseph's scribe. Section 9 is a revelation the Lord gave to help Oliver feel better about not being able to translate.

1 My son, I want you to keep working as Joseph's scribe until the two of you have finished the Book of Mormon. Translating the Book of Mormon is mainly Joseph's calling, anyway.

2 After the Book of Mormon is finished, I will give you the power to help translate other writings.

3 Be patient, my son. It is best that you not translate right now.

4 Instead, your calling is to work as Joseph's scribe.

5 I took the power to translate away from you, because you gave up after you had started.

6 Do not complain, my son. I am treating you this way for a good reason.

7 You did not understand. You thought that all you had to do was ask, and I would tell you what to write.

8 That is not how it works. First you need to think about it on your own. Then you need to ask me if what you have thought is right. If it is, I will give you a warm feeling inside. That is how you will know that you are right.

9 If it is not right, you will not have a warm feeling. Instead, you will feel confused. You will forget whatever it was you were thinking that was wrong. That way, you will write down only words that really come from me.

10 If you had understood this, you would have been able to translate. But I do not need you to translate now.

11 When I first told you to translate, it was because at that time I needed you to translate. But you were afraid, and now the need for you to translate has passed.

12 You have not done anything wrong. Neither has Joseph. I have given Joseph enough strength to make up for your not translating.

13 Keep working as Joseph's scribe, and things will go well for you. Be faithful. Do not give in to temptations.

14 Be strong and keep working in the calling I have given you. If you do this, I will protect you from danger. I will bring you to live with me in heaven. Amen.

SECTION 10

After Martin Harris lost the translation of the first part of the Book of Mormon (see Section 3), the angel Moroni took the golden plates away from Joseph Smith. Moroni also took away the Urim and the Thummim. Joseph was afraid the Lord would never let him translate again. A few days later, though, Moroni brought back the plates and the Urim and Thummim. At the same time, the Lord gave Joseph the revelation we call Section 10.

1 I gave you the Urim and Thummim so you could translate the Book of Mormon. But then you lost the translation, because you gave it to a wicked man.

2 That is why you lost your gift. That is why you could not translate for a while.

3 I now give you back the power to translate. Be sure to keep my commandments from now on. Keep working until you have finished translating the Book of Mormon.

4 Do not work harder than your strength, time, and money allow. But do work hard until the translation is finished.

5 Always remember to pray, so you can overcome Satan and escape his servants.

6 Satan's servants have tried to destroy you. Even Martin Harris, whom you trusted, has tried to destroy you.

7 That is why I called Martin Harris a wicked man—because he has tried to take away the things I gave you. He has tried to destroy your gift.

8 Because you trusted him with the translation, wicked people have been able to steal it.

9 In other words, you let holy writings fall into the hands of wicked people.

10 Satan has given them the idea of changing the words of the translation.

11 Now that they have changed the translation, it does not say the same things that you and Martin Harris wrote down.

12 This is Satan's plan for destroying my work.

13 He wants to make it look like you are only pretending to translate, even if the people who stole the translation have to lie to make it look that way.

14 I will not let Satan carry out his evil plan.

15 Satan's servants want to put God to the test. They want to force you to translate the same part of the Book of Mormon over again.

16 They are saying to themselves, "We will see if God really gave Joseph Smith power to translate. If God really gave him power, then Joseph will be able to translate this part of the Book of Mormon again.

17 "If Joseph really does have God's power, he will be able to make the same translation over again. But that will not matter, because we have already changed the translation.

18 "We will show people that the two translations are different. Then we will say this proves that Joseph has lied, and that he does not really have the power to translate.

19 "That will be the end of Joseph Smith and his work. We will not have to listen to him telling us to repent anymore. The world will praise us for showing that Joseph is a liar."

20 Satan has great control over these people. He has gotten them to fight against what is good.

21 Their hearts have gone bad. They love darkness, not light. Their works are evil. That is why they will not ask me if the work you are doing is true or not.

22 Satan gives them these ideas so he can lead them to hell.

23 He thinks his plan is clever enough to destroy God's work. But the people who are helping Satan carry out his plan will be punished. At the Last Judgment, they will feel shame for what they have done.

24 Satan makes people angry with my work.

25 He gets them to think there is nothing wrong with making secret plans to destroy other people. He tells them there is nothing wrong with telling a lie if they are doing it to catch someone else lying.

26 That is how he makes people feel good about sinning. That is how he leads them along until he can drag them down to hell. He catches them in their own traps.

27 Satan goes all over the world, trying to destroy people this way.

28 Listen to my words: The fact that you think someone else is lying does not make it right for you to lie. You are still sinning when you tell a lie.

29 Satan tells his servants, "Joseph is trying to trick you by pretending to have the power to translate. So it is all right for you to trick him back by stealing the translation and changing what it says." Satan wants these people to sin. He wants them to get you to test the Lord.

30 That is why I do not want you to make another translation of that part of the golden plates.

31 I will not let these people carry out their evil plan. If you translate the same words again, they will make it look like you are only pretending to have the power to translate. They will tell people you were not able to translate the same words twice.

32 They will publish their lies. Then people will be angry with you. They will not believe my words.

33 In this way, Satan hopes to overpower your testimony. He hopes to keep you from carrying out my work.

34 I will now tell you how to stop Satan's plan. But you must not show this revelation to anyone until you finish translating the Book of Mormon.

35 I tell you not to show this revelation to anyone, for your own safety.

36 There would not be any problem with showing it to someone you know is righteous.

37 But you cannot always tell who is righteous and who is not. So keep quiet about this revelation until I tell you the time is right to share it with the world.

38 There is another part of the golden plates which talks about the same things that were in the translation that got stolen.

39 The part of the Book of Mormon that you already translated men-

tioned something called "the plates of Nephi." It said that the plates of Nephi talked about the same things, but in more detail.

40 The plates of Nephi are part of the golden plates. I want the people of the world to know what is in the plates of Nephi.

41 Translate the plates of Nephi until you get to the part about king Benjamin. Then you will have made up for losing the first translation.

42 Publish the new translation as "Nephi's record." That is how I will keep the people who changed the first translation from carrying out their evil plan.

43 I will not let these people destroy my work. I will show them that I am wiser than Satan.

44 The translation they stole has only part of the things you will find in the plates of Nephi.

45 There are things written in the plates of Nephi which will help people understand my gospel better. That is why I want you to publish the plates of Nephi as part of the Book of Mormon.

46 All through the Book of Mormon, there are important gospel truths. My followers from long ago prayed that I would share these truths with the people of today.

47 I promised I would answer their prayers, because they prayed with faith.

48 They had faith that my gospel would someday be preached to the Lamanites, and to all the Nephite rebels who became Lamanites.

49 They prayed that if anyone else ever came to live in this land, the gospel would be preached to them, too.

50 They blessed this land. They prayed that everyone in this land who accepted the gospel would have eternal life.

51 They blessed this land so that everybody who lived here would be free. They would be free no matter where they came from, what race they belonged to, or what language they spoke.

52 I will answer all these prayers. I am bringing forth the Book of Mormon, so people can read the gospel truths that are in it. This does not mean that people do not already have truth. But the Book of Mormon will add to the truth they already have.

53 That is why I have said, "If the people of today will listen to me, I will build my church among them."

54 I want my church to grow and become strong.

55 The members of my church do not need to be afraid. They will be given a place in God's heavenly kingdom.

56 The people who should be afraid are the ones who start churches just to make money. These people are part of Satan's kingdom. They do not listen to me or keep my commandments. I will throw down their false churches, along with everyone else who does evil.

57 I am Jesus Christ, God's Son. I came to my own people, but they would not listen to me.

58 I am the shining light which the darkness cannot overcome.

59 I said to my followers in Bible times, "I have other sheep who do not belong to this fold." People did not understand what I meant.

⁶⁰ The Book of Mormon will show that the "other sheep" I talked about were the Nephites and Lamanites.

⁶¹ I want the people of today to know about the wonderful things the Nephites and Lamanites did long ago, through my power.

⁶² I want the people of today to know the gospel truths I taught to the Nephites and Lamanites. That does not mean people have not already learned gospel truths. But the Book of Mormon will make my teachings clearer.

⁶³ Then people will not argue so much about my teachings, the way Satan makes them do. People make mistakes when they try to explain my teachings without really understanding them.

⁶⁴ The Book of Mormon will help people understand what confuses them.

⁶⁵ If they accept my teachings, I will bring them to me like a hen brings her chicks together under her wings.

⁶⁶ If they come, I will let them drink the waters of life freely.

⁶⁷ This is my true teaching—everyone who repents and comes to me is part of my church.

⁶⁸ If someone teaches more or less than this, you can know that I did not send them. That person is not part of my church.

⁶⁹ <u>Everyone who is part of my church, and endures to the end,</u> will be safe with me. Satan's power will not overcome them.

⁷⁰ Remember my words. I bring life and light to the world. I am your Savior, your Lord, and your God. Amen.

SECTION 11

One day, Joseph Smith's older brother, Hyrum, came to visit him. Hyrum believed that Joseph was a prophet. Hyrum wanted to know what he should do to help God's work. He asked Joseph for a revelation. Section 11 is the revelation the Lord gave for Hyrum.

¹ An amazing work is about to begin among the people of the world.

² I am God. Listen to my words, and you will feel their power deep inside you.

³ The people of the world are ready to receive the restored gospel. If you want to help spread the gospel, now is the time. Work as hard as you can, and you will be saved in God's kingdom.

⁴ God will give a calling to everyone who is willing to help.

⁵ If you ask me for help, I will help you. Whenever you pray, I will listen.

⁶ Here is the advice you asked me to give you. Keep my commandments and help build Zion.

⁷ Do not work to get money. Work to become wise. God himself will teach you. Then you will be truly rich. To be truly rich means to have eternal life.

8 I will give you whatever you ask me for. If you want, I will use you to do many good things in the world.

9 Teach people to repent. If you keep my commandments and help carry out my work, I will bless you.

10 If you pray with faith, and if your heart is true, I will give you a gift. But you must believe in my power—the power of Jesus Christ.

11 Jesus Christ is the one speaking to you. I am the light which shines in darkness. I give you these words through my power.

12 Trust in the Spirit. My Spirit teaches people to do good. It teaches them to be just, humble, and righteous judges. That is how you will know you are being guided by my Spirit.

13 I will give you my Spirit. It will teach you. It will fill you with joy.

14 Have faith that I will answer your prayers. Then the Spirit will teach you every righteous thing you want to know.

15 But before you can start preaching, you need to be ordained.

16 Wait a little longer, until you have learned more about my gospel. That way, when you do start preaching, you can be sure that you really know my teachings.

17 Then, if you have faith, you will receive everything you want.

18 Keep my commandments. Do not preach yet. Instead, ask my Spirit to teach you.

19 Stay close to me, so you can be a witness of the Book of Mormon. Be patient until the translation is finished.

20 For now, this is your calling—to work as hard as you can to keep my commandments.

21 Do not try to preach. First you must learn my word. Then you will be able to preach. Then, if you want, you will have my Spirit—God's power to convince people of the truth.

22 For now, keep waiting. Study the revelations I have already given. When the Book of Mormon is finished, study that too. Anything else I reveal in modern times will be an addition to that.

23 Hyrum, you are my son. Keep yourself worthy to help build my kingdom.

Then I will give you everything that is right for you.

24 Stay close to me, and you will be safe.

25 Do not say that the Spirit does not really give people revelations. People who say this cannot receive my blessings.

26 Keep studying until I decide the time is right for you to go out preaching.

27 These words are for everyone who wants to share my gospel with others.

28 I am Jesus Christ, God's Son. I bring life and light to the world.

29 I came to my own people, but they would not listen to me.

30 Whoever will listen to me will have the power to be born again. Amen.

SECTION 12

A man named Joseph Knight wanted to help the Lord's work. While Joseph Smith was translating the Book of Mormon, Joseph Knight brought him the things he needed. Joseph Knight asked to know what else he could do to help. Section 12 is a revelation from the Lord for Joseph Knight.

1 An amazing work is about to begin among the people of the world.

2 I am God. Listen to my words, and you will feel their power deep inside you.

3 The people of the world are ready to receive the restored gospel. If you want to help spread the gospel, now is the time. Work as hard as you can, and you will be saved in God's kingdom.

4 God will give a calling to everyone who is willing to help.

5 If you ask me for help, I will help you. Whenever you pray, I will listen.

6 Here is the advice you asked me to give you. Keep my commandments and help build Zion.

7 These words I am giving you are for everyone who wants to help carry out my work.

8 No one can help carry out my work unless they are humble and full of love. They must have faith and hope. They must be careful with whatever I trust them to take care of.

9 I am Jesus Christ. I bring light and life to the world. If you do what I have told you, I will give you a calling. Amen.

SECTION 13

Joseph Smith and Oliver Cowdery were translating a part of the Book of Mormon that talked about baptism. They wondered how people should be baptized. They went into the woods, near a river, to pray. John the Baptist appeared and gave them the Aaronic priesthood. Then he told them to baptize each other in the river. Section 13 is what John the Baptist said when he gave Joseph and Oliver the Aaronic priesthood.

1 In the name of Messiah, I give you, my fellow servants, the Aaronic priesthood. It gives you the power to receive visits from angels. It gives you the authority to teach people to repent. It also gives you the authority to baptize them, to take away their sins. This priesthood will stay on the earth until the Levites again make a righteous sacrifice to the Lord.

SECTION 14

A man named Peter Whitmer let Joseph Smith live in his house while he was translating the Book of Mormon. Peter had a son named David. David wanted to know how he could help the Lord's work. Section 14 is a revelation from the Lord for David Whitmer.

1 An amazing work is about to begin among the people of the world.
2 I am God. Listen to my words, and you will feel their power deep inside you.
3 The people of the world are ready to receive the restored gospel. If you want to help spread the gospel, now is the time. Work as hard as you can, and you will be saved in God's kingdom.
4 God will give a calling to everyone who is willing to help.
5 If you ask me for help, I will help you. Whenever you pray, I will listen.
6 Work to build Zion. Keep all my commandments.
7 If you keep my commandments and endure to the end, you will have eternal life. Eternal life is God's greatest gift.
8 If you pray with faith, you will receive the Holy Ghost. It will help you preach. You will testify about the things you see and hear. You will teach people to repent.
9 I am Jesus Christ, God's Son. I created heaven and earth. I am a light which cannot be hidden.
10 I will send my restored gospel to every people on earth.
11 David, you are called to help carry out my work. If you are faithful, I will give you many blessings. Amen.

SECTION 15

While he was translating the Book of Mormon, Joseph lived in the house of a man named Peter Whitmer (see section 14). Peter had a son named John. John wanted to know how he could help the Lord's work. Section 15 is a revelation from the Lord for John Whitmer.

1 Listen, my servant John. These are the words of Jesus Christ.
2 I have power over the whole world. Listen very carefully to what I have to say.
3 I will tell you something which nobody knows except you and me.
4 You have prayed many times to know what is the most important thing you could do.
5 That was a good thing to pray for. I will bless you for it. I will also bless you for speaking my words, as I commanded you to.
6 The most important thing you can do is teach people to repent, so they can come to me. Then you will be able to live with them in my Father's kingdom. Amen.

SECTION 16

While he was translating the Book of Mormon, Joseph lived in the house of a man named Peter Whitmer (see section 14). Peter had a son who was also named Peter. Section 16 is a revelation from the Lord for Peter Whitmer, Junior.

1 Listen, my servant Peter. These are the words of Jesus Christ.
2 I have power over the whole world. Listen very carefully to what I have to say.
3 I will tell you something which nobody knows except you and me.
4 You have prayed many times to know what is the most important thing you could do.
5 That was a good thing to pray for. I will bless you for it. I will also bless you for speaking my words, as I commanded you to.
6 The most important thing you can do is teach people to repent, so they can come to me. Then you will be able to live with them in my Father's kingdom. Amen.

SECTION 17

The Book of Mormon said that the Lord would choose three witnesses. God would let these witnesses see the golden plates, so they could testify about them. Oliver Cowdery, David Whitmer, and Martin Harris wanted to be the three witnesses. Section 17 is a revelation the Lord gave for them. (You can find the three witnesses' testimony in the Book of Mormon.)

1 You must trust my word with all your heart. If you do, I will let you see the golden plates. I will also let you see the breastplate, Laban's sword, the Urim and Thummim, and the Liahona. (The Urim and Thummim Joseph Smith has is the same one I gave to Jared's brother.)
2 If you want to see these things, you must have faith, just like the prophets of long ago.
3 After you have seen them, you will testify about them through God's power.
4 Your testimony will show Joseph's enemies that he has been telling the truth. Your testimony will help me bring the Book of Mormon to the world.
5 You need to explain to people that it was through my power that you were able to see the golden plates. If you did not have faith, you would not have been able to see them. Neither would Joseph Smith.
6 He has translated the parts of the Book of Mormon I commanded him to. I, the Lord, testify that what he has written is true.
7 You have the same power, faith, and gift that he has.
8 If you keep the commandments I have just given you, Satan's power will not overcome you. My grace will protect you. I will bring you to live with me in heaven.
9 I am Jesus Christ. I have given you this revelation as part of my righteous plan for the people of the world. Amen.

SECTION 18

Joseph and Oliver received the Aaronic priesthood from John the Baptist (see Section 13). John the Baptist told them that later they would receive the Melchizedek priesthood from Peter, James, and John. Joseph and Oliver wanted to know more about receiving the Melchizedek priesthood and restoring the church. The Lord gave them this revelation. We now call it Section 18.

1 I give these words to my servant Oliver Cowdery.

2 You know that the things you have been writing are true, because my Spirit has told you many times that they are.

3. If you know the words are true, then you should do what they say.

4 The things you have been writing explain everything you need to know about starting my church and restoring my gospel.

5 Build up my church the way I teach you to. Then Satan's power will not be able to overcome you.

6 The world is becoming more and more wicked. Someone needs to tell people to repent. Everyone on earth needs to repent.

7 When Joseph Smith baptized you, he was doing what I commanded him to.

8 Do not be surprised that I have given him another work to do. This is all part of my plan. If Joseph keeps my commandments, I will bless him with eternal life.

9 These next words, Oliver, are for you and David Whitmer both. I command everyone, everywhere, to repent. I give you two the same calling I gave my apostle Paul.

10 Remember that every person on earth is important to God.

11 The Savior suffered everyone's pain and died, so they could repent and come to him.

12 Because he came back from the dead, he is able to bring everyone who repents to heaven to live with him.

13 How happy he is when someone repents!

14 That is why he wants you to teach people to repent.

15 Even if you bring just one person to me during your whole life, think how happy you and that person will be in my Father's kingdom!

16 And if you would be that happy bringing just one person to me, think how happy you will be if you can bring many people!

17 You have my gospel. You know what people need to do to be saved.

18 If you pray to the Father with faith, you will receive the Holy Ghost. The Holy Ghost teaches people everything they need to know.

19 But you cannot do anything unless you have faith, hope, and love.

20 Do not fight with any other church (unless it is the devil's church).

21 Take on Christ's name. Teach the truth. Take your work seriously.

22 Everyone who repents, is baptized in Jesus Christ's name, and endures to the end, will be saved.

23 The Father has said that Jesus Christ's name is the only name that can save people.

24 That is why everyone must be baptized in Jesus Christ's name. At

the Last Judgment, people will be called by that name.

25 If they have not been baptized in Jesus Christ's name, they cannot live in my Father's kingdom.

26 I will call others to teach my gospel, besides you two. They will teach it to everyone on earth.

27 I will call twelve others, to be exact. They will be my apostles. They will be people who want with all their hearts to take on my name.

28 I will send these twelve people to preach my gospel to everyone on earth.

29 I will ordain them so they can baptize people in my name, the way the scriptures teach.

30 You have the scriptures. Baptize people the way the scriptures tell you to.

31 These next words are for my twelve apostles. My grace is all you need. <u>Do what is right. Do not sin.</u>

32 I give you the authority to ordain priests and teachers. I give you the authority to teach my gospel through the Holy Ghost's power. <u>God gives everybody different callings and gifts.</u>

33 It is Jesus Christ who has said this. I am your Lord and your God.

34 These words were not made up by someone on earth. They are my words. You will testify that they are my words

35 My voice speaks these words to you. My Spirit gives them to you. My power makes it possible for you to read them to each other. Without my power, you could not have these words.

36 That is why you can testify that you have heard my voice and know my words.

37 Now, Oliver Cowdery, I give you and David Whitmer the job of choosing the twelve apostles. Remember that you need to choose people who want with all their hearts to be my servants.

38 Choose people who are doing things that show they want to serve me.

39 When you find the right people, show them this revelation.

40 Then kneel down and worship the Father in my name.

41 Tell the people of the world: "Repent and be baptized in Jesus Christ's name."

42 Everyone must repent and be baptized—men and women. Children who are old enough to know right and wrong need to be baptized, too.

43 Do everything I have commanded you.

44 I will use you to carry out my work. Because of what you do, many people will see that they need to change their lives. Because of you, many people will repent and come to my Father's kingdom.

45 I will give you my greatest blessings.

46 But if you do not do what I have commanded you, you cannot be saved in my Father's kingdom.

47 I, Jesus Christ, have given you these words through my Spirit's power. Amen.

SECTION 19

When it came time to publish the Book of Mormon, Martin Harris was very worried. He had given a lot of money to help publish the book, and he was afraid people would not buy it. Also, he was not sure if God would forgive his sins. He asked Joseph Smith for a revelation. Section 19 is the revelation the Lord gave for Martin Harris.

1 I am Christ the Lord, the Savior of the world. I am the beginning and the end.

2 I have done everything the Father wanted me to. He has given me power over the whole universe.

3 At the end of the world, I will destroy Satan and all his works. I will judge everyone on earth based on what they did during their lives.

4 Everyone must repent or suffer, because I, God, am endless.

5 That means I am not going to change my mind after I have judged people. Everyone who was wicked will have to be punished for their sins.

6 That does not mean they will suffer forever and ever, though, the way some people think. The scriptures do not say their suffering will never end. Instead, the scriptures talk about "endless suffering."

7 The scriptures also talk about "eternal punishment." These words are meant to touch people strongly, as part of my plan to save them.

8 I will teach you what these words really mean, the way I taught my apostles long ago.

9 I am revealing this to you, to give you peace.

10 See how wonderful the true meaning of these words is! "Endless" is one of my names. So when the scriptures talk about "endless punishment," they do not mean a punishment that never ends. They just mean the punishment that comes from me.

11 "Eternal punishment" means "God's punishment."

12 "Endless punishment" means "God's punishment."

13 So, I command you to repent and keep the commandments I have revealed for you through Joseph Smith.

14 You received those commandments through my power.

15 Repent, or you will have to be punished for your sins. You cannot imagine how terrible that punishment will be. You cannot imagine how much you will have to suffer.

16 I suffered the punishment for everyone's sins, so they would not have to. But people still have to repent.

17 If they do not repent, then they will have to suffer the way I did.

18. My suffering was so intense that even though I was God—the most powerful of all—I shook from the pain. I sweat blood. My body and my spirit suffered so much that I wanted to quit.

19 But I did not quit. I finished the work the Father gave me to do. I suffered the punishment for everyone's sins so they could be saved.

20 Again, I command you—repent and confess your sins. If you do not, you will have to suffer the punishments I have told you about.

Remember how much you suffered when I took my Spirit away from you? The punishment for your sins will be much, much worse.

21 These things I have taught you about eternal punishment are for you only. Do not teach them to other people until I decide the time is right. For now, just teach people to repent.

22 The people you teach are not ready to understand this revelation yet. If you teach it to them now, it might do them harm.

23 Learn about me. Listen to my words. Be gentle, the way my Spirit teaches, and I will give you peace.

24 I am Jesus Christ. I came to earth to carry out the Father's work. I do what the Father commands me.

25 I command you not to lust after another man's wife. I command you not to try to hurt other people.

26 I command you not to be selfish. Give your money freely to help publish the Book of Mormon. It is God's word.

27 After it goes to the Gentiles, the Book of Mormon will go to the Jews and the Lamanites. It will teach them the gospel. It will teach the Jews that the Messiah has already come.

28 I command you to pray. You should pray not only in private, but also at meetings, in front of other people.

29 You should share the gospel wherever you go. Do not be shy or afraid. Let people hear God's good news.

30 At the same time, be humble. Trust in me. Do not argue with people who try to argue with you.

31 Do not talk about points of doctrine. Just teach people to repent, to have faith in the Savior, to be baptized, and to receive the gift of the Holy Ghost.

32 This is the last revelation I will give you on this subject. I have told you enough things in this revelation to guide you your whole life.

33 If you do not follow the advice I have given you, you will suffer. You and everything you own will be destroyed.

34 Sell as much of your land as you can—everything your family does not need. Use the money to pay for publishing the Book of Mormon.

35 Pay off your debt to the printer. Being in debt is like being someone's slave.

36 Leave home and go preach the gospel. You can go back home to visit your family if you want to, though.

37 Talk freely to everyone. Teach the truth openly and joyfully. Shout, "Hosanna! Hosanna! Praise to God's name!"

38 Always remember to pray, and I will give you my Spirit. I will give you blessings that are worth more than any treasure on earth. Treasures rust, but my blessings last forever.

39 Doesn't reading this make you want to shout for joy?

40 You have a choice now. You can keep running around like a blind man trying to tell others where to walk.

41 Or you can be humble and gentle, and follow the advice I have given you. Make the right choice. Come to me, your Savior. Amen.

SECTION 20

Joseph Smith and Oliver Cowdery received revelations telling them how to restore the church. The revelations also told them what day to restore the church on. The first meeting of the church was held on April 6, 1830. It was held in Peter Whitmer's house. At first, there were only six members. Section 20 tells how the church should be run, based on the revelations Joseph and Oliver received.

1 Jesus Christ's church was restored on April 6, 1830. When we started the church, we followed all the steps our country's laws said we needed to follow. We also followed the commandments we received from God.

2 God revealed his commandments to Joseph Smith and Oliver Cowdery.

3. Joseph Smith was ordained to be the first elder of this church. Oliver Cowdery was ordained to be the second elder.

4 This was done through the grace of Jesus Christ. Glory to him, now and forever. Amen.

5 God gave Joseph Smith a witness that his sins were forgiven. But then Joseph became tangled in worldly things again.

6 Joseph repented. He asked God to forgive him. God sent an angel to visit Joseph. The angel's face was like lightning. His clothing was pure white.

7 The angel gave Joseph commandments from God.

8. He also gave Joseph the Urim and Thummim, so Joseph would have power to translate the Book of Mormon.

9 The Book of Mormon tells about a people who sinned and were destroyed. It teaches the full gospel of Jesus Christ to everyone on earth.

10 Joseph translated the Book of Mormon through God's power. Angels appeared to other people, too, so they could testify that the Book of Mormon is true.

11 The Book of Mormon proves to the world that the Bible is true. It shows that God still gives people revelation. It shows that God calls people to do his work in modern times, just as he did long ago.

12 This shows the world that God's ways never change. Amen.

13 God has given powerful witnesses of this work. Everyone who learns about these witnesses will be judged based on whether or not they accept them.

14 Those who accept the work with faith and do good works will receive eternal life.

15 Those who reject the work will not be able to enjoy the blessings it offers.

16 The Lord has said this. We, the elders of the church, testify that we have heard God's words. Glory to God, forever and ever. Amen.

17 Because of these things, we know there is a God in heaven. He is all-powerful and neverending. He created the earth and sky and everything in them.

18 He created men and women to look like him.

19 He commanded them to love and serve him. He told them that because he is the only true God, he is the only being they should worship.

20 But people disobeyed God's laws. They became worldly and wicked. They could not be with God anymore.

21 That is why God sacrificed his only Son, as the scriptures say.

22 Jesus was tempted, but he did not give in to the temptations.

23 He was crucified and died. He came back from the dead three days later.

24 He went up into heaven to sit on a throne next to the Father. He rules with all power. He does whatever the Father commands.

25 He did all this so that everyone who has faith, and is baptized, and endures to the end, can be saved.

26 People who lived before Jesus came to earth, who had faith in the prophets' words, will be saved, too. The prophets were inspired by the Holy Ghost to teach about Jesus Christ.

27 People who were born after Jesus came to earth need to believe in the gifts and callings that come from the Holy Ghost. The Holy Ghost testifies about the Father and the Son.

28 The Father, the Son, and the Holy Ghost form one neverending Godhead. Amen.

29 We know that everyone must repent, believe in Jesus Christ, worship the Father in Jesus' name, and endure to the end. Unless they do these things, they cannot be saved in God's kingdom.

30 We know that people's sins are justly and truly forgiven through the grace of Jesus Christ.

31 We also know that people who love and serve God with all their hearts are made holy through the grace of Jesus Christ.

32 It is possible, though, for people to lose God's grace. Then they cannot be with him.

33 That is why the members of the church should always remember to pray, so they will not give in to temptation.

34 There is no one who does not need to watch out for temptation.

35 We know that everything we have said here is true. We have not said anything that does not agree with the Bible. We believe God will give more revelation in the future.

36 The Lord has said this. Glory to God, now and forever. Amen.

37 *A commandment to the church about how to baptize:* People who want to be baptized need to feel sorry for their sins. They need to pray for God's forgiveness. They must show the church that they have truly repented. They must show that they want to follow Jesus Christ and serve him all their lives. They must show by their actions that the Spirit is with them. Then they can be baptized to have their sins forgiven and to become members of Christ's church.

38 *The duties of elders, priests, teachers, deacons, and members:* Apostles are elders. Elders are called to baptize.

39 They can ordain other elders, priests, teachers, and deacons.

40 They can bless the sacrament.

41 They can give people who have been baptized the gift of the Holy Ghost.

42 Their calling is to teach from the scriptures, baptize new members, and watch over the church.

43 They can also give people the gift of the Holy Ghost.

44 They should take charge of meetings.
45 When they direct a meeting, they should do it the way the Spirit leads them to, in keeping with God's commandments.
46 Priests are called to teach from the scriptures, baptize new members, and bless the sacrament.
47. They should visit the members' homes. They should remind the members to pray and carry out their family duties.
48 They may ordain other priests, teachers, and deacons.
49 If there isn't an elder at a meeting, a priest should take charge.
50 If there is an elder there, a priest can only teach from the scriptures and baptize new members.
51 Also, a priest can visit the members' homes.
52 By doing these things, the priests will be helping the elders.
53 Teachers are called to watch over the members of the church. The teachers should always be with the members, to help them be strong.
54 They should make sure there is no wickedness in the church. They should make sure members are not lying, gossiping, or treating each other badly.
55 Teachers should make sure that members of the church meet together often. They should make sure the members carry out their church duties.
56 A teacher can take charge of a meeting if there isn't an elder or a priest there.
57 If the teachers need help carrying out their duties, they can get it from the deacons.
58 Teachers and deacons do not have the authority to baptize, to bless the sacrament, or to lay on hands.
59 Instead, their calling is to warn people to keep the commandments, teach from the scriptures, and invite everyone to come to Christ.
60 Elders, priests, teachers, and deacons are called by God. They are ordained through the power of the Holy Ghost. They each have different gifts.
61 Every three months, all the elders should hold a general conference. The elders can decide later if it would be better to hold general conferences more or less often than that.
62 At general conference, the elders will take care of church business.
63 Every elder needs to get a license from another elder. Church members need to vote on whether or not a certain person should become an elder. This can be done in the person's branch, or at general conference.
64 Priests, teachers, and deacons need licenses, too. If they were ordained by a priest, they need to get a certificate from the priest who ordained them. Then they can take that certificate to one of the elders, or to general conference, and receive their license. The license lets them carry out their calling.
65 Someone who lives in a branch cannot be ordained to a church office unless the members of the branch vote in favor.
66 But where there isn't a branch yet, presiding elders, traveling bishops, high councilors, high priests, and elders can ordain someone without a vote.

67 A high council or general conference has to vote before a presiding elder, a bishop, a high councilor, or a high priest can be ordained.

68 *The duties of baptized members:* New members should not take the sacrament or be confirmed until they have had time to learn all about the church.

69 New members must show the elders that they are worthy to take the sacrament and be confirmed. This is to make sure that all the members of the church "walk in holiness before the Lord," as the scriptures say.

70 Members should bring their children to church to be blessed. The elders will lay their hands on the children and bless them in Jesus Christ's name.

71 No one can become a member of Christ's church until they are old enough to know right from wrong. If they are not old enough to know right from wrong, they cannot really repent.

72 This is how people who repent should be baptized.

73 The person who has authority to baptize will go down into the water with the person who wants to be baptized. The person baptizing will call the person being baptized by name, and say: Having received authority from Jesus Christ, I baptize you in the name of the Father, and of the Son, and of the Holy Ghost. Amen.

74 After this, the person baptizing will put the person being baptized all the way under the water, and then bring them back out of the water.

75 It is very important for members to meet together often to take the sacrament.

76 The sacrament needs to be blessed by an elder or a priest. The elder or priest will kneel down and pray, using these words.

77 O God, Eternal Father, in the name of your Son, Jesus Christ, we ask you to bless this bread. Make it holy for everyone who eats it, so they can eat it in memory of your Son's body. This will show you that they want to take on your Son's name. It will show that they want to remember him always and to keep his commandments, so his Spirit will always be with them. Amen.

78 To bless the wine, the elder or priest will take the cup and say:

79 O God, Eternal Father, in the name of your Son, Jesus Christ, we ask you to bless this wine. Make it holy for everyone who drinks it, so they can drink it in memory of your Son's blood, which was sacrificed for them. This will show you that they always remember him, so his Spirit will be with them. Amen.

80 If a member commits a serious sin, handle it the way the scriptures teach.

81 Every branch in the church should send at least one teacher (or priest) to general conference.

82 Each teacher (or priest) will bring a list of members who have joined the church since the last general conference. One of the elders should be called to keep all these lists in a book.

83 The teachers should also bring a list of any people who are not members of the church anymore. That way their names can be crossed off the church's records.

84 When members move from one branch of the church to another, they can take along a letter saying they are worthy members. This letter can be signed by any elder or priest who knows them, or by the teachers and deacons of their branch.

SECTION 21

During the first church meeting on April 6, 1830, Joseph Smith and Oliver Cowdery ordained each other elders. Then they blessed the sacrament and confirmed the other members of the church. Everyone at the meeting could feel the Holy Ghost. While the meeting was still going on, the Lord gave Joseph Smith the revelation we now call Section 21.

1 The church should keep a record. The record will say that God has called you to be a prophet and an apostle, as well as an elder. God has given you the power to receive visions and to translate.

2 The Holy Ghost led you to restore my church. It will teach you how to make the church stronger and holier.

3 The church was restored on April 6, 1830.

4 Now I am speaking to the members of the church. I will give you my commandments through Joseph Smith. Listen to what he tells you. Be holy. Do what is right.

5 Treat what Joseph says to you as if I myself had said it. Be patient with him. Have faith.

6 If you do all this, Satan will not be able to overcome you. The Lord will scatter Satan's army in front of you. God would make the whole sky shake if that would help you carry out his work.

7 I, have filled Joseph with a desire to build Zion. He will help make Zion a powerful force for good. I know how hard he has worked. I have heard his prayers.

8 I have seen him crying because he wants so much to help Zion. I will make it so that he does not have to cry anymore. It is time for him to rejoice. I have forgiven his sins. He will begin to see my blessings.

9 I will bless everyone who helps carry out my work. Believe the things Joseph teaches, because he receives them from the Spirit. The Spirit testifies that Jesus died on the cross. He died so that people's sins can be forgiven, if they repent.

10 Oliver Cowdery, I want you to ordain Joseph Smith.

11 Joseph will be the first elder in my church. He will ordain you to be the second elder.

12 He will also ordain you to be the church's first preacher. You will preach not only to church members, but to everyone on earth. Amen.

SECTION 22

Many of the church's first members had already been baptized in other churches. They did not understand why they had to be baptized again when they joined the restored church. Section 22 is a revelation from the Lord, explaining why the new members needed to be baptized again.

1 Any promises you made with me before I restored my church have ended. I have made a new promise—the same promise I made at the beginning of the world.

2 So even if you had already been baptized 100 times, it would not matter. After Jesus came, people could not be saved by obeying the Law of Moses anymore. In the same way, your old baptism does not count, now that I have restored my church.

3 The churches that baptized you did not have my authority. That is why I restored my church—so you could be baptized by someone with my authority.

4 If you want to come into my kingdom, you need to be baptized the way I have commanded. Stop trying to tell God what to do. Amen.

SECTION 23

After the church was restored, Oliver Cowdery, Hyrum Smith, Samuel H. Smith, Joseph Smith's father, and Joseph Knight asked Joseph for a revelation. They asked what the Lord wanted each of them to do to help the church. Section 23 is the Lord's answer to them.

1 These words are for Oliver. I am pleased with you. I am not saying you have done anything wrong, but you need to watch out for pride.

2 Let people in the church and in the world know about your calling. I will open your heart, so you can preach the truth forever. Amen.

3 These words are for Hyrum. I am pleased with you. I call you to preach. Teach people to do what is right. Help make my church strong. Because of your family, your duty will always be to serve the church. Amen.

4 These words are for Samuel. I am pleased with you. Your calling is to make the church strong and to remind church members to do what is right. I have not yet called you to go out preaching to the world. Amen.

5 These words are for Joseph Smith, Senior. I am pleased with you. Your calling is to make the church strong and to remind church members to do what is right. This will be your duty forever. Amen.

6 These words are for Joseph Knight. Even though it is hard, you need to follow me. You need to pray in public, not just in private. You should pray with your family, your friends, and everywhere.

7 Your duty is to join the true church. In everything you say, remind others to do what is right. Then I can reward you for doing my work. Amen.

SECTION 24

Many people became angry when Joseph Smith began teaching about the Book of Mormon and the restored church. Joseph was arrested because people said he was causing trouble. In the end, he was set free. But because of all this trouble, and because of the work he had been doing for the church, Joseph had not been able to plant his crops. He worried about how he would take care of his family. Section 24 is a revelation the Lord gave to help Joseph stop worrying.

1 I called you to translate the Book of Mormon and to serve me. I helped you during all your troubles. I told you how to escape your enemies. I have saved you from Satan's power.

2 That does not mean I excuse your sins. But I forgive you. Do not sin anymore.

3 Do your best to carry out your calling. As soon as your crops are planted, go to the branches of the church in Colesville, Fayette, and Manchester. The members there will give you what you need to live. I will bless them for doing this.

4 If they do not take care of you, I will not give them my blessings.

5 Keep praying. Write the things which the Spirit reveals to you. Explain the scriptures to the members of the church.

6 I will tell you what to say or write the moment you go to say or write it. The members of the church need to listen to you if they want my blessings.

7 I will make you strong so you can serve Zion. Serving Zion is your only job.

8 You will have many troubles. But be patient and carry on. I will be with you as long as you live.

9 I will not give you strength to do anything except the work I have called you to do. Your calling is to explain the scriptures and to keep confirming the members of the church. I will give you everything you need to carry out this calling.

10 Oliver should keep preaching my gospel to the members of the church and to the world. He should never think that he has said enough to help my work. I will be with him all his life.

11 He will have my glory wherever he goes, even if he gets put in jail. It will be my glory, not his own. So it will not matter whether he himself is weak or strong.

12 He should preach my gospel openly, everywhere, day and night. I will give him strength like you have never seen before.

13 Do not try to do miracles unless I tell you to. The scriptures do say, though, that my servants will have power to send away devils and to heal people. The scriptures also say my servants will be protected from snakes and poison.

14 You need to do what the scriptures say. But do not do these miracles unless people ask you to.

15 If you go to a place where no one will listen to you, shake the dust off your shoes and wash your feet by the road. This shows that those people have rejected the Lord's messengers. Someday they will be judged for rejecting you.

16 If someone tries to hurt you, tell them, in my name, that they are

going to be punished. Someday, they will be punished like you said.

¹⁷ If someone tries to get you in trouble with the law, the law will punish them.

¹⁸ Do not take money or extra clothes with you. If you need food, clothes, shoes, or money, the members of the church will give it to you, at the very moment you need it.

¹⁹ This is the last time my gospel will be preached before the end of the world. You and everyone else who is called to preach my gospel need to follow these directions. Amen.

SECTION 25

Joseph Smith's wife was named Emma. She married Joseph even though her parents did not want her to. They did not believe he was really a prophet. But Emma believed. Emma's life was very hard because of the work Joseph had to do as prophet and because of the trouble he often had. Section 25 is a revelation the Lord gave for Emma.

¹ These are the words of the Lord for Emma Smith. You are my daughter. Everyone who accepts my gospel is my son or daughter.

² I am giving you this revelation so you will know what I want you to do. If you are faithful and do what is right, I will keep you safe. I will give you a home in Zion.

³ Your sins are forgiven. You are a chosen woman. I have a calling for you.

⁴ Do not complain because I have not shown you certain things. I have not shown them to the rest of the world, either. Later, you will see there was a good reason for that.

⁵ Your calling is to comfort Joseph Smith when he is in trouble. Use gentle words and a gentle spirit.

⁶ You will go with Joseph when he travels. You will work as his scribe when he does not have one. That way I can send Oliver Cowdery to other places.

⁷ Joseph will ordain you to teach from the scriptures and to preach to the members of the church. You will preach whatever my Spirit tells you to.

⁸ He will lay his hands on you so you can receive the Holy Ghost. You will spend your time writing and studying.

⁹ You do not need to be afraid. The members of the church will give Joseph the things you need to live. They will do this because his calling is to serve them and to receive revelations for them.

¹⁰ Let go of worldly things. Worry about spiritual things instead.

¹¹ I want you to put together a hymnbook for the church. The Spirit will help you.

¹² It makes me happy to hear people sing from their hearts. A righteous person's song is like a prayer. I will answer it by sending them blessings.

¹³ Be happy. Keep the promises you made to me.

¹⁴ Be gentle. Watch out for pride. Enjoy being with your husband.

The glory he will receive is for both of you.

¹⁵ Always keep my commandments, and I will make you a ruler in my kingdom. If you do not keep my commandments, you will not be able to come live with me.

¹⁶ The words I have said to you are for everyone. Amen.

SECTION 26

Joseph Smith's enemies had him arrested, so he had to go to court. The judge decided Joseph had done nothing wrong and let him go (see Section 24). Joseph went back home to Emma in Pennsylvania. While he was there, he received a revelation from the Lord. The revelation was for Joseph, Oliver Cowdery, and John Whitmer. It told them what to do next. Section 26 is that revelation.

¹ Spend your time studying the scriptures, preaching, and confirming the members of the church in Colesville. Also, do whatever work you need to on the farm. Then go west for the next conference. After that, I will tell you what to do next.

² Everything that is done in the church must be agreed to by everyone. Use prayer and faith to decide what to do. Through faith, everything will come to you. Amen.

SECTION 27

At first, after the church was restored, wine was used in the sacrament as a symbol of Christ's blood. One day, as Joseph Smith was going to buy wine for a sacrament meeting, he was met by an angel. The angel gave him the revelation which is now Section 27. Partly because of this revelation, church members today use water in the sacrament instead of wine.

¹ Listen to the voice of Jesus Christ, your Lord and Savior. Feel the power of his word.

² It does not matter what you eat or drink when you take the sacrament. All that matters is that you do it to show the Father that you remember my body and my blood. My body and my blood were sacrificed for you, so your sins could be forgiven.

³ I command you not to buy wine or alcohol from your enemies.

⁴ Use only new wine, made by members of the church.

⁵ Do not be surprised. This is part of my wise plan. Soon I will return to earth to hold a sacrament meeting with you. Moroni will be there—the one I sent to give you the Book of Mormon, which contains my full gospel.

⁶ Elias will be there—the one I put in charge of restoring everything the prophets told about.

⁷ Elias was the angel who promised Zacharias he would have a son named John. John would be filled with the spirit of Elias.

⁸ John the Baptist will be there—the one I sent to ordain you, Joseph Smith and Oliver Cowdery, to the Aaronic priesthood.

9 Elijah will be there—the one I gave power to unite people with their ancestors.

10 Joseph, Jacob, Isaac, and Abraham will be there—the ones through whom I made my promises to all people.

11 Michael, or Adam, will be there—the first man and prince of the whole world. Michael is the one the scriptures call "ancient of days."

12 Peter, James, and John will be there—the ones I sent to ordain you to be apostles and special witnesses of me. The same authority I gave to them, they gave to you.

13 I gave them the authority to build my kingdom and to teach my gospel for the last time before the Second Coming. That time is now. It is the time when I will bring together everything in heaven and on earth.

14 Everyone the Father gives me to save will be at that special sacrament meeting when I come again.

15 So rejoice and prepare yourselves! Put on my armor, so that you can stand up against the difficult times that are coming.

16 Put on the belt of truth and the breastplate of righteousness. Boot yourselves up with the preparation that comes from living the restored gospel.

17 Take the shield of faith to protect yourself from Satan's fiery arrows.

18 Salvation will be your helmet. My Spirit will be your sword. If you agree among yourselves about what to ask me, I will send you revelations. If you are faithful until I come again, you will be lifted up to be with me. Amen.

SECTION 28

A member of the church named Hiram Page used to receive revelations through a stone, the same way Joseph Smith received revelations through the Urim and Thummim. Some of Hiram's revelations were about where the city of Zion should be built. Many church members, including Oliver Cowdery, believed in Hiram's revelations. The Lord told Joseph Smith to warn Oliver that Hiram's revelations were not from God. Section 28 is the revelation the Lord gave for Oliver.

1 Oliver, your calling is to teach the members of the church through the Spirit. You should teach them about the revelations I have given.

2 But the only person in this church who is called to receive revelations is Joseph Smith. He receives revelations from me, just like Moses did.

3 Your calling is to teach church members the comandments I reveal to Joseph Smith, just like Aaron taught the commandments I revealed to Moses.

4 If you are ever speaking or teaching, and the Spirit tells you to give church members a commandment, you can do it.

5 But you cannot give a commandment to church members in writing. You can only give them advice.

6 You also cannot give commandments to Joseph Smith. That is be-

cause he is the leader of the whole church.

7 Joseph Smith is the only person who will have the authority to receive revelations for the church, until I call someone else to take his place.

8 I now send you to teach my gospel to the Lamanites. If they accept your teachings, build up branches of my church among them. You will receive revelations during your mission, but you should not write them down as commandments.

9 No one knows where the city of Zion will be built, because I have not revealed it yet. For now, I tell you only that it will be built near the Lamanites' lands.

10 Do not leave for your mission until after the conference. The elders will vote to have Joseph Smith lead the conference. He will tell you what to do then.

11 Meet with Hiram Page privately. Tell him that the revelations he has received through that stone are not from me. Satan is fooling him.

12 Hiram Page has not been called to receive revelations for the church. No member of this church will be called to do anything not in keeping with church law.

13 Everything in the church must be done properly, with prayer and by vote.

14 Help to clear up this confusion about Hiram Page's stone, in keeping with church law. Clear it up before you leave for your mission to the Lamanites.

15 From the time you leave until the time you come back, I will tell you what to do.

16 Use every chance you have to tell people about my gospel. Let them hear how happy it makes you. Amen.

SECTION 29

In September 1830, the church held a general conference. A few days before the conference, the Lord gave Joseph Smith a revelation. The revelation was to help church members better understand the plan of salvation and the Second Coming. Section 29 is that revelation.

1 Listen to the voice of your Savior, Jesus Christ. I am the one who spoke to Moses. I am the one who paid the price for your sins.

2 I will gather my people like a hen gathers her chicks under her wings. My people are all those who listen to me, repent, and pray.

3 I now forgive your sins. That is why you are able to receive this revelation. But if you sin again, you may find yourselves in danger.

4 Out of all the world, you have been chosen to teach my gospel. Teach with joy, for everyone to hear.

5 Cheer up! I am with you. I ask the Father to send you his blessings. He has promised to build his kingdom among you.

6 The scriptures say, "You will be given whatever you ask for, if you have faith and pray together as one."

7 Your calling is to gather my chosen people. My chosen people are those who open their hearts and listen to me.

8 The Father has commanded that my people be gathered together in one place. There they can prepare themselves for the terrible time when the wicked will be destroyed.

9 The day is coming soon when everyone who is proud and wicked will be burned up like dry grass. Then wickedness will finally disappear from the earth.

10 Everything my apostles said long ago will soon come to pass.

11 I will come down from heaven with power and glory, for everyone to see. All the angels will come with me. I will live on earth for 1000 years. All the wicked will be destroyed.

12 The Father has said that my twelve apostles, who were with me in Jerusalem, will come down with me. They will have the same glory I will. They will judge the people of Israel—those who have loved me and kept my commandments.

13 A trumpet will give a long, loud blast, just like when I appeared at Mount Sinai. The earth will shake. All the righteous people who have died will be brought back from the dead. They will have the same glory I do. They will live with me forever.

14 But before that happens, the sun will go dark. The moon will turn blood-red. The stars will fall from the sky. Terrible things will be seen in the sky and on the earth.

15 People will cry and howl.

16 A huge hailstorm will be sent to destroy people's crops.

17 The wicked will suffer if they do not repent. If they will not listen to me, I will not be able to wash away their sins.

18 Flies will cover the earth. They will eat people's skin and lay eggs in their bodies.

19 People will be so sick they will not even be able to curse me. Their skin will fall off their bones. Their eyes will drop out of their heads.

20 Wild animals and birds will eat them up.

21 Then the devil's church will be destroyed with fire, just like Ezekiel said it would. The things Ezekiel wrote have not come true yet. But they will. Wickedness cannot rule the world forever.

22 I will rule on earth for 1000 years. Then there will come a time when people again stop believing in God.

23 Not long after that, the world will end. The earth and sky will be completely destroyed. A new earth and sky will be created.

24 Everything old will give way to something new. The earth and sky will be made new. So will everything in them—people, animals, birds, and fish.

25 Nothing, no matter how small, will be lost, because I made them all.

26 But before the end of the world, Michael, my chief angel, will blow his trumpet. Then everyone who has died will be brought back to life.

27 I will bring the righteous to me. They will receive eternal life. But I cannot bring the wicked into the Father's kingdom.

28 I will have to say to them, "You

cannot be with me. You must go away, to live with the devil and his angels."

29 I have never said that the wicked will come back. That is because they do not have the power to be where I am.

30 But remember that I have not revealed all my judgments yet. Remember what I have said—the first will be last and the last will be first. This is true for everything I have created.

31 I created everything through the power of the Spirit. I created both spiritual things and earthly things.

32 When I started my work, spiritual things came first, then earthly things. When I finish my work, earthly things will come first, then spiritual things.

33 I am saying this in a way that you will be able to understand. The way I understand them, my works do not have an end or a beginning. But I talk about endings and beginnings so I can help you understand the thing you asked me about.

34 To me, everything is spiritual. I have never given a law that was not spiritual—not to you or to anyone else, including Adam.

35 I gave Adam the power to make his own choices. I gave him commandments that had to do with spiritual things, just as all my commandments have to do with spiritual things.

36 Adam was tempted by Satan. Satan was the one who fought against me before the world was created. He wanted my power. He turned one third of everyone in heaven against me.

37 Satan and his followers were thrown out of heaven. That is how the devil and his angels came to be.

38 Since the beginning of the world, there has been a place ready for them. It is called hell.

39 There needs to be a devil to tempt people, so they can choose between right and wrong. If people never tasted what is bitter, they could never know what is sweet.

40 That is why the devil was allowed to tempt Adam. Adam gave in to the temptation. He disobeyed my commandment by eating the forbidden fruit. He fell into the devil's power.

41 Because Adam sinned, he could not be with me anymore. That is why I had to make him leave the Garden of Eden. In the same way, at the Last Judgment, I will have to tell the wicked, "You cannot be with me. You must go away."

42 But I did not let Adam and his family die until I sent angels to teach them. The angels taught them about the atonement. The angels taught them to repent and have faith in my only Son.

43 Life became a time of testing. Death became the way that everyone who had faith in the Savior could receive eternal life.

44 People who refuse to put their faith in the Savior will not be able to have eternal life with me. They will have to be punished for their sins, because they did not repent.

45 They love darkness instead of light. They do evil. They will have to receive their reward from the one they chose to follow—the devil.

46 But small children are saved from the beginning, through my only Son's atonement.

⁴⁷ Small children cannot sin, because Satan does not have power to tempt them. He cannot tempt them until they are old enough to know right from wrong.

⁴⁸ Because I do not give small children the power to know right from wrong, their parents need to teach them. I will judge parents based on how well they teach their children.

⁴⁹ Everyone who knows right and wrong is commanded to repent.

⁵⁰ If there are grown people who cannot understand the gospel, I will judge them in keeping with what the scriptures say about this. That is all I have to tell you for now. Amen.

SECTION 30

The people who went to general conference in September 1830 felt the Spirit very strongly. During the conference, Hiram Page agreed to give up the stone he had been using to receive false revelations (see Section 28). After the conference, but before everyone had gone back home, Joseph Smith received revelations for the Whitmer brothers—David, Peter Junior, and John. Those revelations were published together as Section 30.

¹ David, you have been too afraid of other people. You have not trusted me to make you strong, the way you should have.

² You have paid more attention to earthly things than to spiritual things. You have not paid enough attention to your calling. You have not listened to my Spirit or to the people I chose to be your leaders. You have listened to other people instead.

³ I leave you to pray and think about what you have been given.

⁴ Live in your father's house until I tell you differently. Give more time to your calling in the church and among the people who live around you. Amen.

⁵ Peter, you will travel with Oliver Cowdery. The time has come for you to preach my gospel. Do not be afraid. Listen to Oliver's advice.

⁶ Share each other's troubles. Always pray that the two of you will be kept safe. I have given Oliver power to start my church among the Lamanites.

⁷ The only person in the church who has more authority than Oliver Cowdery is Joseph Smith.

⁸ If you do what I have told you, and work hard to keep my commandments, I will bless you with eternal life. Amen.

⁹ John, the time has come for you, too, to preach my gospel. Let everyone hear what you have to say.

¹⁰ Work in the area around Philip Burroughs' home. Preach wherever people will listen to you, until I tell you to go somewhere else.

¹¹ From now on, your only job is to do everything you can to build Zion. Never be afraid to speak up for my work. Do not worry about what other people might do, because I will always be with you. Amen.

SECTION 31

A man named Thomas Marsh was one of the first converts to the church. The rest of his family—his wife and children—did not believe in the restored gospel. After Thomas was baptized, the Lord gave Joseph Smith a revelation for him. Section 31 is that revelation. Thomas' family joined the church later. Thomas went on to become the first president of the Quorum of the Twelve.

1 Thomas, my son, I bless you for your faith in my work.

2 You have suffered because of your family. But I will bless you and your family. Someday they, like you, will accept the restored gospel. They will join my church.

3 Cheer up! The time has come for you to serve a mission. You will teach God's good news to the people of today. The Spirit will help you know what to say.

4 Teach people the revelations I gave to Joseph Smith. Start preaching now, because the Second Coming will be here soon.

5 If you work as hard as you can, your sins will be forgiven. You will receive a great reward. Do not worry about your family. I will make sure they have the things they need to live.

6 You do not need to be away from your family for long. I will have a place ready for them while you are out preaching.

7 I will open people's hearts, so they will listen to you. Through you, I will start a branch of my church.

8 You will make the members of that branch strong. You will help them get ready to move to live with the rest of the members of the church.

9 Things may be hard. But be patient. If people try to argue with you, do not argue back. Lead your family gently. Be strong.

10 You will help to heal church members, even if people outside the church will not accept you.

11 Go wherever I tell you. The Spirit will tell you what to do and where to go.

12 Always remember to pray, so you do not give in to temptation and lose your blessings.

13 Endure to the end, and I will be with you. These words did not come from someone on earth. They are the words of Jesus Christ, your Savior. Amen.

SECTION 32 -

Many elders wanted to send missionaries to the Native Americans. They wanted to help the promises the Lord had made to the Lamanites in the Book of Mormon start to come true. They asked the Lord if it was time to send missionaries. Section 32 is the Lord's answer. In the end, the United States government kept the missionaries from teaching many Native Americans. But the work the missionaries did made it possible for church members to move west later.

¹ This is what I have to say to Parley P. Pratt: I want him to preach my gospel. I want him to learn about me. I want him to be gentle and humble.
² His calling is to go with Oliver Cowdery and Peter Whitmer, Junior. Together they will go preach to the Lamanites.
³ Ziba Peterson should go with them, too. I will be with them as they travel. I will ask the Father to bless them, so that nothing can stop them.
⁴ They should not pretend that they have received any revelations besides those found in the scriptures. They should pray that I will help them understand the scriptures.
⁵ If they do everything I have told them, I will bless them. Amen.

SECTION 33

After the missionaries left to preach to the Lamanites, a man named Ezra Thayre and a man named Northrop Sweet joined the church. Soon after Ezra and Northrop were baptized, the Lord gave them a revelation through Joseph Smith. Section 33 is that revelation.

¹ Ezra and Northrop, listen to this revelation from the Lord. He knows all your thoughts. Feel the power of the Lord's words deep inside you.
² I call you to preach the gospel to the people of today. Tell them openly what they are doing wrong.
³ The Second Coming is very close. This is the last time I will call people to do my work.
⁴ The whole world has gone wrong. Only a few people are still righteous. Even they make mistakes because of false teachings.
⁵ That is why I restored my church. I want it to become well-known.
⁶ I will gather together everyone who believes in me and listens to what I say. I will gather them from all over the world.
⁷ The time to do my work is now. Work as hard as you can.
⁸ Start talking to people, and I will tell you what to say. You will be like Nephi of long ago.
⁹ Do not be afraid to talk to people about the gospel. I am with you. I will bless you.
¹⁰ Tell people to repent. Tell them to get ready, because the Lord is coming soon.
¹¹ Tell everyone to repent and be baptized so their sins can be forgiven. If they will be baptized, I will send them the Holy Ghost.
¹² This is my gospel. Remember that unless people have faith in me, they cannot be saved.
¹³ These are the teachings my church is built on. These are the teachings you have chosen to build your own lives on. If you stay true to them, Satan's power will not overcome you.
¹⁴ Remember to keep the laws of the church.
¹⁵ You have the authority to confirm members of the church. Lay your hands on them, and I will give them the gift of the Holy Ghost.
¹⁶ Study the Book of Mormon and

the Bible. Remember that the Spirit is what gives you power.
¹⁷ So be faithful. Always remember to pray. Be like the wise women who kept extra oil for their lamps.
¹⁸ I am coming soon. Amen.

SECTION 34

Parley P. Pratt was one of the missionaries to the Lamanites (see Section 32). Parley had a 19-year-old brother named Orson. Parley taught Orson the restored gospel. Orson accepted the gospel and was baptized. Orson then traveled 200 miles to visit Joseph Smith. Orson asked Joseph what the Lord wanted him to do. Section 34 is the Lord's answer.

¹ Orson, my son, hear what the Lord Jesus Christ has to say to you.
² I give the world light and life. I am the shining light which the darkness cannot overcome.
³ I loved the world so much that I gave up my life. That way everyone who believed in me could be born again. Because you have been born again, I call you my son.
⁴ I bless you for your faith.
⁵ Your greatest blessing is that I have called you to preach my gospel.
⁶ Preach openly, for everyone to hear. Tell the people of today to repent. In this way, you will help prepare the world for the Second Coming.
⁷ I will be coming soon. I will come in a cloud, with power and glory.
⁸ All the peoples of the world will shake when they see me coming.
⁹ Before I come, the sun will go dark. The moon will turn blood-red. The stars will stop shining. Some of them will fall from the sky. Many wicked people will be destroyed.
¹⁰ That is why you must not be afraid to preach the gospel boldly. The Holy Ghost will tell you what to say.
¹¹ If you are faithful, I will be with you to the end.
¹² Again, I am coming soon. I am your Lord and Savior. Amen.

SECTION 35

Parley P. Pratt and the other missionaries to the Lamanites travelled to Ohio. There they met a preacher for another church. The preacher's name was Sidney Rigdon. Sidney believed what the missionaries taught him about the restored gospel. He and many other members of his church were baptized. Sidney then traveled to visit Joseph Smith. He asked Joseph what the Lord wanted him to do. Section 35 is the Lord's answer.

¹ These are the words of the Lord: I am the beginning and the end. I am the same forever.
² I am Jesus Christ, God's son. I died on the cross so that everyone who has faith in me could be born again. When people are born again, they become one with me, just as I am one with the Father.
³ Sidney, I have seen the good

works you have done. I have heard your prayers. I have a greater work for you to do.

4 You have my blessings. You will do important things. You did not know it, but I sent you to be a preacher in Ohio. I did it so that the people in your church would be ready to accept the restored gospel when the missionaries came.

5 You baptized the people of your church in water to help them repent. But you did not have the authority to give them the gift of the Holy Ghost.

6 From now on, you will have not just the authority to baptize. You will also have the authority to give people the gift of the Holy Ghost, just like the apostles did long ago.

7 An important work will be carried out in this land. Everyone will see how foolish and wicked the people of this land are.

8 I am God. I have all power. I will show amazing things to those who have faith in me.

9 People who have faith in me will be able to throw out devils. They will be able to heal people who are sick. They will be able to heal people who cannot see, or hear, or speak, or walk.

10 Soon you will see great things happen.

11 But those who refuse to put their faith in me will see only terrible things happen. They will see the devil's kingdom destroyed.

12 There are not many people in the world who do good anymore. But those who do are the ones whose hearts are ready to receive my restored gospel.

13 People the world thinks of as weak are the ones I call to preach my gospel—people who do not have a fancy education, and people who are hated. The Spirit will give these people power over the world.

14 I will use these people to do my work. I will protect them from their enemies. No one will be able to stop them.

15 The gospel will be preached to the poor and the humble. They are the ones who will be looking forward to my Second Coming.

16 They are the ones who will know how to tell when the Second Coming is almost here.

17 I have restored my gospel through Joseph Smith. He is weak. But I have blessed him.

18 I gave Joseph Smith power to reveal things that have been kept secret since the world began. He also has power to receive revelations about the future. He will have that power as long as he keeps my commandments. If he does not keep my commandments, I will give his calling to someone else.

19 Watch over him. Help him stay faithful. That way the Spirit can keep giving him revelations.

20 I command you to be Joseph's scribe. You will write down his new translation of the Bible. By doing this, you will be serving my people in a very important way.

21 Through this new translation of the Bible, I will reveal important truths to my people. Knowing these truths will help them prepare for the Second Coming. It will help them become more like me.

22 Stay with Joseph Smith wherever he goes, and everything I have promised here will come true.

23 When you are not working as his scribe, the two of you will preach my gospel. I will tell Joseph what to say. You will use the scriptures to show that what he says is true.

24 Keep the commandments and the promises you have made, and I will use all my power to help you. Satan will shake with fear. But Zion will grow and be filled with joy.

25 When the time comes, I will save my people Israel. They will be led by priesthood authority. Their enemies will never have power over them again.

26 Be happy! I am coming to save you.

27 Do not be afraid, little flock. My kingdom is yours until I come again. I am coming soon. Amen.

SECTION 36

When Sidney Rigdon traveled to visit Joseph Smith (see Section 35), a man named Edward Partridge went with him. Edward believed Joseph's teachings. He asked Joseph to baptize him. The Lord gave a revelation for Edward after he was baptized. That revelation is Section 36.

1 These are the words of the Lord: Edward, your sins are forgiven. I call you to preach my gospel.

2 Sidney Rigdon will lay his hands on you, to give you my Spirit. The Spirit will teach you about my kingdom.

3 Preach with a loud voice. Say, "Hosanna, praise to God's name!"

4 This calling is not just for you.

5 Anyone who comes to Sidney Rigdon and Joseph Smith to be ordained to preach the gospel will receive the same calling.

6 A missionary's calling is to teach people to repent. People need to stop living the way the world teaches, if they want to save themselves from being destroyed.

7 This commandment is for all the elders in my church. Everyone who accepts this commandment with all their heart can be ordained and sent to preach the gospel.

8 I am Jesus Christ, God's Son. Prepare yourselves, and I will come to you. Amen.

SECTION 37

Sidney Rigdon began to help Joseph Smith work on a new translation of the Bible. This new translation would correct changes that had been made to the Bible over time. Around the same time, church members in New York were having lots of trouble from their enemies. Finally, the Lord told Joseph the members needed to move away from New York. They should move to Ohio, where Sidney was from. Section 37 is a revelation to Joseph and Sidney about that move.

1 Because of your enemies, you should stop working on the translation of the Bible. You can start again once you move to Ohio.

2 But you should not move to Ohio until you have preached my gospel some more. You also need to visit the different branches of the church.

You especially need to visit the Colesville branch—their prayers show great faith. The branches need to be stronger before they move.

3 I need the members of the church to gather in Ohio, so they can be ready for Oliver Cowdery's return.

4 Everyone is free to choose for themselves. But if you are wise, you will take my advice. I am coming soon. Amen.

SECTION 38

During a general conference in New York, Joseph Smith received a revelation for all the members of the church there. The revelation explained why it was so important for the members to move to Ohio. The revelation also told them how to set about making the move. Section 38 is that revelation.

1 These are the words of the Lord Jesus Christ: I am the beginning and the end. Before the world was created, I looked out over all space. I looked out over all the angels.

2 I know everything, because I see it all.

3 I gave the word, and the earth was created. Everything was made through me.

4 I took Enoch's Zion into heaven. I have begged the Father to save everyone who has faith in me, because of the blood I sacrificed for them.

5 But the wicked must sit in a dark prison until the Last Judgment.

6 Everyone who refuses to listen to me, or to open their hearts, must go to this prison. They will suffer terribly.

7 I am watching over you. You cannot see me, but I am among you.

8 You will see me with your own eyes on the day when I show myself to the whole world. That day is coming soon. Only those who have been made holy will be able to stand that day.

9 So prepare yourselves. I have given you my kingdom. Satan will not be able to destroy it.

10 I am pleased with you—not with all of you, but as a whole. You are trying to do what is right.

11 The rest of the world has become wicked. When the angels look down from heaven, they see that the forces of evil rule the earth.

12 The angels are so upset by this, they have stopped singing. They are waiting for God to give the order to go down and free the world from evil. Satan knows this. He has gathered together his forces.

13 Now I will tell you the secret plans your enemies have made to destroy you.

14 I will bless you. Some of you have sinned. Others have not had enough faith. But I will forgive your weaknesses.

15 Be strong from now on. Do not be afraid. I have given you my kingdom.

16 I will tell you what to do to be saved. I have heard the poor praying for help. I have power over the rich, because I created them. To me, all people are equal.

17 I have filled the earth with riches. The earth is my footstool. That means I will stand on it again someday.
18 I will give you a land of your own. It will be a land of riches and plenty. That land will be kept safe during the Second Coming.
19 I will let you live in that land forever, if you work for it with all your heart.
20 I will make you a promise. The promise is that you and your descendants will own the land forever. You will own it both in this life and in the next.
21 Someday there will be no more earthly rulers. Instead, I will be your ruler. I will watch over you.
22 If you do what I tell you, you will be a free people. When I come again, you will have no laws but my laws. That is because I am the most powerful of all.
23 Teach one another, in keeping with the callings I have given you.
24 Treat each other as equals. Do what is good and holy.
25 I say again, treat each other as equals.
26 A man had twelve sons. All his sons obeyed him. He said to one of his sons, "Wear these beautiful robes and sit here by me." He said to another son, "Wear these old rags and sit somewhere else." Can this man say he treated his sons justly?
27 I tell you this story to teach you that you must be equal. If you are not equal, you are not my people.
28 Again, your enemy is making secret plans to kill you.
29 You talk about how there will soon be wars in far-off countries. But you do not know what people in your own country are planning.
30 I am telling you this because you have prayed to me. Pay attention to my warnings. Follow my advice. Unless you do, your enemies will carry out their wicked plans. But if you prepare yourselves, you have no need to be afraid.
31 I want you to escape your enemies. I want you to become a holy people.
32 This is why I told you to move to Ohio. In Ohio, I will reveal my law to you. I will give you power from heaven.
33 From Ohio, I will send people all over the world to do my work. I will save my people Israel. I will lead them wherever I want. Nothing can stop me.
34 The branches of the church in New York need to choose some people for a special calling.
35 Those people will be called to look after the poor. They will make sure the poor have everything they need to move to Ohio.
36 They will also be called to take care of church property.
37 If people cannot sell their farms before they move, they should leave them or rent them out, whichever seems best.
38 If you leave anything behind, make sure it is kept safe. After I send people out from Ohio with heavenly power, you will get it all back again.
39 If you work for the riches which the Father wants to give you, you will be the richest people in the world. That is because you will have the riches of heaven. I can give you earthly riches, too. But be

careful that you do not become proud, like the Nephites did long ago.

40 Everyone needs to work hard—elders, priests, teachers, and members. They need to prepare the things I have commanded.

41 Everyone should warn their neighbors about what will happen to the wicked. But they should do this gently and humbly.

42. Move away from the wicked. Save yourselves. My servants must be holy. Amen.

SECTION 39

A man named James Covill came to visit Joseph Smith. James had been a preacher for another church for 40 years. He believed that Joseph was a prophet. He promised the Lord that if Joseph received a revelation for him, he would do whatever the revelation said. Section 39 is the revelation the Lord gave for James Colville.

1 These are the words of Jesus Christ, the eternal God.

2 I give the world light and life. I am the shining light which the darkness cannot overcome.

3 I came to my own people long ago. But they would not accept me.

4 Those people who did accept me received power to be born again. I will give that same power to everyone who accepts me in modern times.

5 Accepting me means accepting my gospel.

6 My gospel teaches that people need to be repent and be baptized. Then they can receive the gift of the Holy Ghost. The Holy Ghost tells people everything they need to know. It teaches them about my kingdom.

7 I know you, James. I have seen all your works.

8 I see that you want to do the right thing. I have given you great blessings.

9 I know that you have suffered often, because you let pride and worldly concerns turn you away from me.

10 Still, you will be saved if you do what I tell you. Be baptized. Then pray, and I will give you my Spirit. I will bless you more than you have ever been blessed before.

11 I have a work for you. I want you to preach my restored gospel.

12 I will give you power and faith. I will be with you. I will prepare the way for you.

13 Your calling is to build up my church. Help Zion grow and rejoice.

14 I do not want you to go east to preach. Instead, I want you to go to Ohio.

15 As my people gather in Ohio, I will give them a blessing like no one has ever seen before. After they receive this blessing, people will go out from Ohio to every country of the world.

16 People in Ohio are praying that the wicked will not be destroyed. But nothing can keep that from happening now.

17 Work hard. Call others to help you. This is the last time I will call people to do my work.

18 People who repent, accept my restored gospel, and become holy will be saved.

19 So go out, shouting "God's kingdom is coming!" Shout, "Hosanna! Praise to God's name!"

20 Baptize people. Prepare the way for the Second Coming.

21 I am coming soon. No one knows exactly when. But I am sure to come.

22 Whoever accepts what I have said here, accepts me. They will be with me, both in this life and in the next.

23 Lay your hands on everyone you baptize, and they will receive the gift of the Holy Ghost. Tell them to watch for the signs that I am coming. When I come, they will know me.

24 I am coming soon. Amen.

SECTION 40

In Section 39, the Lord told James Covill to be baptized into the restored church. But right away, James began to have second thoughts. Instead of doing what the revelation told him, he decided to go back to his old church. Section 40 is a revelation the Lord gave Joseph Smith to explain why James made the choice he did.

1 My servant James Covill wanted to do what was right. I know that, because he promised me that he would obey my word.

2 At first, he accepted my word. It made him happy. But right away, Satan began to tempt him. He was afraid of what other people might think, or what they might do to him. So in the end, his worrying about worldly things kept him from accepting my word.

3 He broke his promise to me. Now I will do with him whatever seems best to me. Amen.

SECTION 41

As the Lord had commanded in Section 37, Joseph and Emma Smith moved to Ohio. They did not have their own home in Ohio, so they lived for a while with a church member named Newel K. Whitney and his family. Newel owned a store in a town called Kirtland. There were about 100 members of the church in Kirtland. The members in Kirtland were trying hard to do what God wanted. Section 41 is a revelation for the members in Kirtland.

1 These are the words of the Lord: To you who listen, I am happy to give my greatest blessings. Those of you who will not listen will suffer. You call yourselves my people. But you cannot receive my blessings.

2 Listen, elders of my church—I need you to come together for a special meeting.

3 Pray with faith, and I will reveal my law to you. I will tell you how I want you to lead my church.

4 I will be your ruler when I come. I

am coming soon. So be sure to keep my law.

5 Those who keep my law are my true followers. Those who say they accept my law, but do not keep it, are not truly my followers. They cannot go on being members of my church.

6 People who are not willing to keep my law cannot receive the blessings that come from being part of my kingdom.

7 A house needs to be built for Joseph Smith. That way he will have a place to live and to work on the new translation of the Bible.

8 Sidney Rigdon can live wherever he thinks best, as long as he keeps my commandments.

9 I want Edward Partridge to be ordained, by vote, to the calling of bishop. He should leave his business and spend all his time working for the church.

10 Once I reveal my law, he will know how to carry out his calling.

11 I have chosen him because he has a good heart, like Nathanael of long ago.

12 These are my words, so be careful how you treat them. You will be judged based on whether or not you do what these words tell you. Amen.

SECTION 42

When the Lord told the members of the church in New York to move to Ohio, he promised that he would reveal his law to them. This was a very important promise for the members of the church. After Joseph Smith moved to Ohio, the Lord told him to hold a special meeting with the elders in Kirtland (see Section 41). Joseph and twelve elders came together for the meeting. At the meeting, the Lord revealed to Joseph Smith the law he had promised. Section 42 is that revelation. It is also called "The Law of the Lord."

1 Listen, elders of my church: You have met in my name, the name of Jesus Christ, the Savior.

2 Listen to the law I am about to give you. Listen and obey.

3 I am giving you this law because you did what I commanded you. You met together and agreed to ask the Father, in my name, to reveal this law to you.

4 So, this is my first commandment for you. All of you will go out to preach in my name, except Joseph Smith and Sidney Rigdon.

5 Those two should only go out for a little while, until the Spirit tells them to come back.

6 The rest of you will go out two by two to preach my gospel. You will have the power of my Spirit. You will be like angels, sent to teach people my word.

7 You will baptize people. You will tell them to repent, because God's kingdom is coming.

8 You will go west, starting branches of the church wherever people will accept you.

9 You will keep preaching until I reveal when the city of New Jerusalem should be built. Then all the members of the church will gather together. You will be my people, and I will be your God.

10 Edward Partridge will serve as bishop of the church. If he sins, someone else will be called to take his place. Amen.

11 No one can go out preaching my gospel, or building up my church, unless they have been ordained by someone with the right authority. The members of the church need to know that the person has been properly ordained.

12 The elders, priests, and teachers of this church will teach the truths found in the Bible and the Book of Mormon.

13 They should also teach the revelations and laws given to the church. Whenever they teach, they should let the Spirit guide them.

14 If you pray with faith, you will receive the Spirit. You should not try to teach without the Spirit.

15 This is how I want you to teach. Later, I will reveal more scriptures for you to teach.

16 If you teach through the Spirit, you will be saying the things I want you to say.

17 The Spirit knows everything. It testifies about the Father and the Son.

18 Now I am talking to all the members of the church. Do not murder. Someone who murders will be punished for it both in this life and in the next.

19 I repeat, do not commit murder. People who murder will be put to death.

20 Do not steal. People who steal, and will not repent, cannot be members of my church.

21 Do not lie. People who lie, and will not repent, cannot be members of my church.

22 Love your spouse with all your heart. Do not give yourself to anyone else the same way you give yourself to your spouse.

23 People who look at others with lust are not being true to their faith. They cannot have the Spirit. If they do not repent, they cannot go on being members of my church.

24 Do not commit adultery. People who commit adultery, and will not repent, cannot be members of my church.

25 But if someone who committed adultery repents with all their heart, and does not do it again, you will forgive them.

26 If they commit adultery again, then they cannot go on being members of my church.

27 Do not talk badly about others. Do not hurt them in any way.

28 You know what the scriptures teach. Someone who sins, and will not repent, cannot be a member of my church.

29 If you love me, you will serve me and keep all my commandments.

30 Make a holy promise to donate your property to help care for the poor.

31 Donating what you have to the poor is the same as donating it to me. You will bring your donations to the bishop and his counselors.

32 You will tell the bishop that you want to donate your property to the church. Your property will become the church's property. Then the bishop will make you caretaker over the property you donated—or over as much of it as your family needs.

33 If your property is more than what you and your family need,

49

the bishop will keep whatever you do not need. The bishop will use the leftover property to help the poor. This way everyone will have enough to meet their needs.

34 The bishop will keep the leftover property in my storehouse. The leaders of the church will decide how to use it. Mainly it will be used to help the poor.

35 It could also be used to buy land—land for building churches, or for the New Jerusalem.

36 This will make it possible for my people to gather together in time for the Second Coming. It will help me save my people.

37 Someone who stops being a member of the church will not be able to get their property back. That is because it is no longer their property. It is the church's property.

38 Remember that when you donate to the poor, it is the same as if you donated it to me.

39 What the prophets wrote will come true: I will take the riches of those who accept my gospel and give them to the poor.

40 Do not be proud. Your clothes should be simple, but nice. You should make them yourselves.

41 Be clean in everything you do.

42 Do not be lazy. People need to work if they want food to eat and clothes to wear.

43 When church members get sick, take good care of them. Give them herbs and soft foods. Members who are sick should be taken care of by other members.

44 Two or more elders should be called to give the sick member a priesthood blessing. I will then decide whether it is better for the person to come home to me or to get well.

45 Live together in love. If you love someone, it is normal to cry when they die. Being sad because the person is gone does not mean you do not have faith there is a life after this one.

46 For the righteous, death will be sweet.

47 For the wicked, death will be bitter.

48 If someone has a special kind of faith, and if it is my will that they be healed, then they will be healed.

49 Someone who is blind could be made to see again.

50 Someone who is deaf could be made to hear again.

51 Someone who is lame could be made to walk again.

52 But if someone does not have that special kind of faith, or if it is not my will that they be healed, that does not mean I am punishing them. Church members should help them out with their troubles.

53 Take good care of the things you have been trusted with.

54 Pay for whatever another person gives you.

55 If you have more than you need, donate it to my storehouse. That way the poor can be taken care of.

56 Pray for my scriptures to be revealed. Once I reveal them, keep them safe.

57 Keep quiet about them for now. Do not teach them to other people until I have revealed them all to you.

58 Then you should teach them to everyone—in every country, from every race, and in every language.

59 Use the scriptures you have received as the law for my church.

60 Those who keep my law will be saved. Those who do not will have to be punished unless they repent.

61 If you ask, I will give you more revelations. I will teach you more and more about the truths which bring peace, joy, and eternal life.

62 When the time is right, I will tell you where to build the New Jerusalem.

63 Send my servants out in every direction—east, west, north, and south.

64 Those who go east should teach people to move west. That way they will escape the terrible things that are going to happen to the wicked.

65 If you do all these things, I will reward you. I will teach you truths which have not been revealed to the rest of the world.

66 Keep the laws you have received. Be faithful.

67 Later, I will give you more laws, to help you build up the church both here and in the New Jerusalem.

68 If you need to know something, do not be afraid to ask me. I will answer freely.

69 Rejoice! I have given you my kingdom—in other words, the authority to run my church. Amen.

70 Priests and teachers should be made caretakers just like any other member.

71 The people who serve as the bishop's counselors should get the things their families need to live from the bishop's storehouse.

72 Either that, or they should be paid for their service. One way to pay them would be to make them caretakers.

73 The bishop, too, should either get what he needs from the storehouse or be paid for his service.

74 If you find out that a person left their spouse because the spouse was unfaithful, that person can still be a member of the church.

75 But if you learn that the person, not the spouse, was unfaithful, and that their spouse is still alive, then the person cannot be a member of the church.

76 Be very careful to find out about people like this. Do not let them become members of the church if they are still married.

77 If they are not married, and if they repent of all their sins, then they can become members of the church

78 Every member of the church has to keep the laws of the church.

79 Church members who murder should be arrested and punished in keeping with the laws of your country. They must be punished for what they did. But they must get a fair trial first.

80 Church members who commit adultery will be taken to two or more elders for a church court. Two other church members must be witnesses that the person committed adultery. It is better if there are more than two witnesses.

81 If the elders decide it is true that the person committed adultery, then the case will be handled in keeping with God's law.

82 If possible, the bishop should be at the church court, too.

83 This is how all church courts should be run.

84 If a church member is a robber, turn them over to the law.
85 If a church member steals, turn them over to the law.
86 If a church member lies, turn them over to the law.
87 If a church member commits a serious sin, take them to a church court.
88 If someone does something wrong to you, you should meet with the person in private. If they admit they did wrong, forgive them.
89 If they will not admit they did wrong, only then should you take them to a church court. A church court should be a private meeting.
90 If someone does something that hurts many people, the person should be corrected in front of many people.
91 If someone sins in public, they should be corrected in public. If they still will not admit they did wrong, they should be taken to a church court.
92 Someone who sins in private should be corrected in private. That way the person has a chance to repent, and to say they are sorry to the people they hurt, without other church members talking badly about them.
93 That is how I want you to run my church.

SECTION 43

A woman called Mrs. Hubble told the members in Kirtland that God had given her revelations for them. Mrs. Hubble felt that because she had received these revelations, church members should make her a teacher over them. Several members believed in Mrs. Hubble's revelations. Section 43 is a message from the Lord for those members. Section 43 also has a message for the elders about how they should preach the gospel.

1 Listen to my word, elders of my church.
2 Joseph Smith is the one I have chosen to receive revelations for you. That is why he was the one I revealed my law to.
3 As long as Joseph Smith is alive, and as long as he keeps my commandments, no one else will be called to receive revelations for the church.
4 Not only that, but Joseph Smith is the only one who has authority to choose the person who will receive revelations after he is gone. Even if Joseph Smith sins and loses the power to receive revelation, he will still have the power to choose the person who takes his place.
5 So do not accept anyone else's teachings if that person says they are receiving revelations for the church.
6 If you follow that rule, Satan will not be able to fool you.
7 When I finally call another prophet, it will be in the way I just explained. The new prophet will teach the same things I revealed to Joseph Smith.
8 During your meetings, you should build each other up. You

should teach each other the commandments. You should teach each other how to run my church.

9 If you learn the law of my church, and promise to do holy works, you will be made holy.

10 By doing this, you will bring glory to my kingdom. If you do not do these things, you will lose the blessings I have already given you.

11 I command you to become a holy people, free of sin.

12 If you want me to keep teaching you about my kingdom, you need to help Joseph Smith. He needs your prayers and your faith.

13 You also need to give him the food and clothing he needs. That way he can spend his time doing my work.

14 If you will not help him, he will go be with people who will—people who are willing to do everything God commands them.

15 Listen, elders of my church. I am not sending you out to be taught. I am sending you out to teach the world the things I have revealed to you.

16 I myself will teach you what you need to know. If you make yourselves holy, I will give you the power you need to teach my gospel.

17 Listen to me. The Second Coming is almost here.

18 Soon you will hear the Lord speaking out of heaven. The earth and sky will shake. God's trumpet will blow loud and long. The Lord will say to those who have died, "Saints, get up and live. Sinners, stay in your graves until I call again."

19 If you want to be among the saints, you need to prepare yourselves.

20 Do not be afraid to talk to people. Be bold. Tell everyone to repent—old and young, slaves and free. Tell them, "Prepare yourselves for the Second Coming."

21 Tell them, "If you do not like it when I tell you to repent, what will you say when you hear voices of thunder telling everyone—Repent, because the Lord is on his way?

22 "And what will you say when lightning rips across the sky from east to west, telling everyone, in a voice that makes their ears tingle—Repent, because the Lord is here?"

23 On that day, the Lord will say, "Listen, everyone on earth. Hear what your Creator has to say.

24 "Time and time again, I wanted to bring you to me, like a hen brings her chicks under her wings. But you refused to come.

25 "Time and time again, I warned you to repent. I sent my servants to warn you. I sent angels to warn you. I sent my own voice to warn you. I sent thunder and lightning and storms to warn you. There were earthquakes, and hailstorms, and famine, and disease to warn you. I called to you with the sound of a trumpet. I warned you of punishment. I promised you mercy, glory, and eternal life. I wanted to save you. But you refused to be saved.

26 "Now the time has come when you must be punished."

27 These are the words of the Lord.

28 So go preach my gospel. Work hard. One last time, warn the people of the world to repent.

29 Soon I will come to earth to judge

the world. My people will be saved. They will rule the earth with me.

30 Then will come the thousand years the prophets wrote about.

31 During those thousand years, Satan will be locked up. When he is set free again, it will be for a just little while. Then the world will end.

32 The righteous people who are living at that time will become immortal in the blink of an eye. Then the earth will be destroyed, as if with fire.

33 The wicked will be sent away to be punished. No one knows how long they will be punished. No one will know that until the Last Judgment.

34 Listen to these words. I am Jesus Christ, your Savior. Remember these things I have told you. Think about them often.

35 Be serious. Keep all my commandments. Amen.

SECTION 44

The elders went out from Kirtland to different parts of the country. They taught people the restored gospel. After a while, the Lord told Joseph Smith that the elders needed to come together again for a general conference in Kirtland. The Lord planned to give them important directions at general conference. Section 44 is the revelation in which the Lord told the elders to come back together.

1 This is the word of the Lord: The elders of my church need to be called back from the different places they have gone.

2 They need to hold a meeting. At that meeting, I will give them my Spirit, if they are faithful.

3 Then they will go back out preaching. They will teach the people who live in the places round about to repent.

4 Many people will join the church—enough that you can organize yourselves in keeping with the laws of the country.

5 Then your enemies will not be able to overpower you. Everything they do to try to destroy you will fail. You will be able to keep my laws safely.

6 You must visit the poor. Help them get by until church members are able to donate their property, as I commanded. Amen.

SECTION 45

As the church grew, people in Ohio started to make fun of it. People told untrue stories about church members and their beliefs. Things became hard for members of the church. To help lift their spirits, the Lord gave Joseph Smith a revelation about the Second Coming. Section 45 is that revelation. In his history of the church, Joseph Smith wrote that the members were very happy to receive this revelation.

1 Listen, people of my church: I have given you my kingdom. I created the earth and sky and everything in them.

2 Listen to me, so I can keep you from being destroyed. If you do not listen, I will not be able to save you when the end comes. It will come suddenly.

3 I am the one who defends you to the Father.

4 I tell him, "Father, see how much I suffered for them. See the blood I sacrificed for them.

5 "Father, these are my brothers and sisters. They have faith in me. Let them come share eternal life with me."

6 Listen, people of my church. Listen, elders. Listen to me while you still have time to do my work. Open your hearts.

7 I am the beginning and the end. I give the world light and life. I am the shining light that the darkness cannot overcome.

8 I came to my own people, but they rejected me. I gave everyone who accepted me the power to do miracles. I gave them the power to be born again. I gave them the power to receive eternal life.

9 I have sent my restored gospel into the world. It will lead them and show them the way. It will gather my people together. It will teach them to prepare for the Second Coming.

10 If you accept my gospel, I will teach you, like I taught the prophets long ago. I will show you that the gospel makes sense.

11 Let me teach you my wisdom—the wisdom of the one you call the God of Enoch.

12 I lifted Enoch and his people off the earth. When people become righteous enough, Enoch's city will return. There have been very righteous people in the past who longed to see Enoch's city return. But it did not happen because there was still too much wickedness.

13 The people who were waiting for Enoch's city to return felt like strangers in the world. They knew that there was something better.

14 I promised them that someday they would see Enoch's city.

15 Listen, and I will teach you, like I taught the prophets long ago.

16 I will teach you what I taught my followers when I lived on earth. I said to them, "You have asked me how you will know when my Second Coming is near—when I will come back in glory to keep the promises I made to your ancestors.

17 "You know that you when you die, your spirits will be kept apart from your bodies. You think of death as a kind of prison. So I will tell you how you will be freed. I will tell you how Israel will be gathered together again.

18 "You see the temple here in Jerusalem. Your enemies say that this temple will never be destroyed.

19 "But I tell you that when they least expect it, this people will be destroyed. They will be scattered all over the world.

20 "This temple you see here will be torn down. Not one stone will be left on top of another.

21 "Some of the Jews alive today will live to see this happen.

22 "You say you know that the end of the world is coming. You know

that the earth and sky will someday be destroyed.

23 "You are right. But there are other things that have to happen first.

24 "I told you that when Jerusalem is destroyed, some of its people will escape. They will be scattered all over the world.

25 "The day will come when they will be gathered together again. But first there will be a time for the Gentiles.

26 "There will be wars and talk of wars. There will be trouble all over the world. People will give up hope. They will say that Christ has decided not to return until the earth is completely destroyed.

27 "People's love will turn cold. There will be much wickedness.

28 "When the time for the Gentiles comes, my restored gospel will shine among them. It will be like a light for people sitting in the dark.

29 "But many of the Gentiles will not accept the gospel. They will not see that the gospel is light. Because of false teachings, they will turn away from me.

30 "Then the time of the Gentiles will end.

31 "The people living at that time will see a terrible sickness cover the land.

32 "Those who follow me will be safe in holy places. But the wicked will die, howling and swearing.

33 "There will be earthquakes in many different places. Many people will be destroyed. But still, people will refuse to listen to me. They will go on fighting and killing each other."

34 After I said this to my followers, they were frightened.

35 I told them, "Do not be frightened. When you see all this happening, you will know that you are about to receive the things God promised you.

36 "Listen to this story:

37 "You look at some fig trees. You see that the trees are growing new branches. You see that their leaves are still soft. When you see this, you know that it is almost summer.

38 "In the same way, when people see the things I have just told you about, they will know that it is almost time for the Second Coming.

39 "Those who pay attention to me will be watching for these things. They will know when my Second Coming is almost here.

40 "They will see amazing things on earth and in the sky.

41 "They will see blood, fire, and smoke.

42 "Before the Second Coming, the sun will go dark. The moon will turn blood-red. The stars will fall from the sky.

43 "The Jews who are left will be gathered together here in Jerusalem.

44 "They will be watching for me. They will see me coming to them through the sky with power and glory. All the angels will be with me. Someone who is not watching for me cannot come to me.

45 "An angel will blow his trumpet. Then all the righteous people who have died will be brought back from the dead. They will rise up to meet me in the sky.

46 "They will come from all over the world. So if you die before the Second Coming, and if you are

righteous, you will come to me. You will be saved from death.

47 "Then the Lord will punish the wicked.

48 "He will come down on the Mount of Olives. The mountain will split in two. The earth and sky will shake.

49 "Everyone on earth will hear the Lord's voice. Then they will be sorry they did not repent. They will see how foolish they were.

50 "Those who made fun of my people will be destroyed. Those who looked for ways to sin will be thrown down.

51 "Then the Jews will look at me and say, 'What are these wounds in your hands and feet?'

52 "I will say to them, 'My friends gave me these wounds. I am Jesus, who died on the cross. I am God's Son.' Then they will know that I am the Lord.

53 "They will cry because of their sins. They will cry because they made their king suffer.

54 "Those who have not heard the gospel will also be saved. Because they did not know my law, they will be brought back from the dead along with the righteous.

55 "Satan will be locked up. He will not have power to tempt people anymore.

56 "When I come again, the story I told you about the ten young women will come true.

57 "Those who are wise will accept the truth. They will not be fooled, because they let the Spirit guide them. They are the ones who will not be destroyed.

58 "The whole earth will belong to them. They will become a strong people, with many children. Their children will grow up doing what is right.

59 "The Lord himself will live with them. He will be their king and lawgiver. They will share his glory."

60 That is all I will give you of that chapter for now. You will be able to read the rest once the new translation of the Bible is finished.

61 I now give you the power to start translating the Bible again. The things you learn from the new translation will prepare you for the future.

62 Important things lay ahead of you.

63 You hear about wars in other countries. But war is closer to you than you think. In a few years, you will hear about wars in your own country.

64 That is why I told you to move west. I now tell the elders—go preach even farther west. Teach the people there to repent. Start branches of my church.

65 Make your hearts and minds one. Pool your riches together, so you can buy the land in the place which I will later choose to be your home.

66 That place will be called the New Jerusalem. It will be a land of peace. There the members of God's church can be safe.

67 The Lord's glory will be there to frighten away the wicked. That place will be called Zion.

68 Someday, Zion will be the only place where people who do not want to fight or go to war will be safe.

69 People will come to Zion from all

over the world. The people of Zion will be the only people who are not at war with each other.

70 The wicked will say, "We do not dare go to war against Zion. No one can stand up against the people of Zion."

71 From all over the world, the righteous will come to Zion. They will come singing songs of eternal joy.

72 You must not let the world know about this revelation until I tell you the time is right. That way, your enemies will not know what you are doing. They will not be able to stop my work.

73 When they finally do learn about this revelation, it will make them stop and think.

74 The Lord's coming will seem terrible to them. They will run away from him, shaking with fear.

75 The peoples of the world will be afraid when they see the Lord's power. Amen.

SECTION 46

Because the church was still new, the members were not sure how to run their meetings. Some people thought non-members should not be allowed to attend church meetings. Others thought they should. The members also had questions about the gifts of the Spirit. Section 46 is a revelation the Lord gave Joseph Smith to answer the members' questions.

1 Listen, people of my church. What I am about to say will help you understand.

2 The scriptures and revelations give you directions about how to hold your meetings. Also, the elders are free to lead meetings the way the Spirit tells them to.

3 But you must never throw anyone out of one of your public meetings.

4 You must not throw a church member out of sacrament meeting. If a member has committed a serious sin, they should not take the sacrament. But they can still attend the meeting.

5 If a non-member wants to learn about the church, there is no reason they cannot attend sacrament meeting.

6 There is no reason they cannot attend the meetings where you confirm people, either.

7 Always ask God what to do. Then do what the Spirit tells you. Do everything with a holy heart. Remember that you are trying to become like the Savior. Give thanks for all things. Pray that you will not be tempted by Satan or fooled by false teachings.

8 You will not be fooled if you have the gifts of the Spirit. Look for those gifts. Always remember what they are for.

9 The gifts of the Spirit are for everyone who loves me and tries to keep my commandments. They are not given just to make people feel good about themselves. They should be used to help people.

10 Church members will have different gifts. Always remember that.

11 Everyone has a gift of the Spirit. But not everyone has every gift.

12 One person will get one gift.

Someone else will get a different gift. But the gifts are to help everyone.

13 Some people have the gift of knowing that Jesus Christ is God's Son. They have the gift of knowing that he died on the cross for our sins.

14 Not everyone has that gift. Some people believe in Jesus Christ because of someone else's testimony. That too is a gift. It does not matter which of those gifts you have. As long as you stay faithful, you will receive eternal life.

15 Some people have the gift of knowing the different ways that people can serve. Since people have different needs, the Lord will call people to serve in different ways.

16 Some people have the gift of knowing the different ways that the Spirit carries out God's work. They will be able to tell whether something is really from God or not.

17 Some people have the gift of wisdom.

18 Other people have the gift of knowing how to teach others.

19 Some people are given the faith to be healed.

20 Other people are given the faith to heal.

21 Some people are given the power to do miracles.

22 Other people are given the power to reveal God's word.

23 Other people have the gift of knowing which spirits are good and which are evil.

24 Some people have the gift of speaking other languages.

25 Other people have the gift of understanding other languages.

26 All these gifts come from God. They should be used to help God's children.

27 The bishop and the elders will have the power to tell whether or not a person really has a gift of the Spirit. That way, you will not be fooled.

28 If you have the Spirit when you pray, the Spirit will be able to answer your prayer.

29 Some people will have all the gifts of the Spirit. They will serve as leaders in the church, so they can use their gifts to help all the members.

30 If you have the Spirit when you pray, the things you pray for will be the things God wants you to pray for. So everything you pray for will come true.

31 Anything the Spirit leads you to do must be done in Christ's name.

32 You must thank God for whatever blessing you receive.

33 Do good and holy works always. Amen.

SECTION 47

After the church was restored, Oliver Cowdery was chosen to write the history of the church. After a while, Joseph Smith felt that John Whitmer should take over that calling. John did not want the calling. But he said he would accept it if the Lord told him to. Joseph asked the Lord what John should do. Section 47 is the Lord's answer.

¹ I want John to be the person who writes the history of the church. Until I give him another calling, he should also help write down Joseph Smith's revelations.
² He can also speak in meetings, if he needs to.

³ At first, Oliver Cowdery was called to write the church history. But now Oliver has been given a different calling. So I need John to take Oliver's place.
⁴ If John is faithful, the Spirit will tell him what to write. Amen.

SECTION 48

In Section 37, the Lord had told the members of the church in New York to move to Ohio. No one knew how the members from New York would get land to live on once they moved to Ohio. At the same time, the members in Ohio wondered if they should be getting ready to go build the New Jerusalem. Section 48 is the Lord's answer to the members' questions.

¹ For now, you need to keep living in your homes here in Ohio, if you can.
² Share your land with the church members moving in from New York.
³ If you do not have enough land to share with all the members from New York, they should buy land in the places round about. That way they will have someplace to live for now.
⁴ Save as much money as you can. That way you will be able to buy land for your new home in the New Jerusalem.

⁵ It is not yet time for me to reveal where you should build the New Jerusalem. After the members from New York have all arrived, then I will choose certain people to receive that revelation.
⁶ Those same people will be in charge of buying land and starting to build the city. Then you and your families will begin to move there. The church presidency and the bishop will organize the move in keeping with the revelations I have given. Amen.

SECTION 49

One of the new members of the church was a man named Leman Copley. Before he joined the church, Leman had belonged to a group called the Shakers. Shakers believed that Christ had come back to earth as a woman named Ann Lee. Shakers did not believe in getting married or having children. They would not eat certain kinds of meat. Leman asked Joseph Smith if he could go preach the restored gospel to the Shakers. Joseph asked the Lord about it. Section 49 is the Lord's answer. Leman went with Sidney Rigdon and Parley P. Pratt to read this revelation to the Shakers. The Shakers threw them out, because they felt the missionaries were being rude.

1 I command my servants Sidney, Parley, and Leman to go preach my restored gospel to the Shakers.

2 They have part of the truth, but not all of it. They need to repent of the things they do that are not right.

3 This is why I am sending you, Sidney and Parley, to preach the gospel to them.

4 Leman has been chosen for this work so he can show the Shakers that what you teach them makes sense. If he does what you teach him, I will bless him. If he does not do what you teach him, he will fail.

5 These are God's words. I sent my only Son to earth to save the world. Those who accept my Son will be saved. Those who reject him cannot be saved.

6 People did whatever they wanted to my Son while he was on earth. But now he rules with God in heaven. Soon he will come back to earth. Then he will have power over all his enemies.

7 No one knows when the Second Coming will be, not even the angels. No one will know until it happens.

8 Everyone on earth needs to repent, except for a few holy people you do not know about.

9 I have sent you my restored gospel. It is the same gospel that was preached in the beginning.

10 I have done what I promised. My kingdom is going to fill the whole world. Everything that is proud and lifted up needs to humble itself, or it will be thrown down.

11 I command you to go tell this people the same thing my apostle Peter said long ago—

12 Have faith in the Lord Jesus, who lived on earth and will come again.

13 Repent and be baptized in the name of Jesus Christ, as I have commanded. Then your sins can be forgiven.

14 Whoever does this will receive the gift of the Holy Ghost. They will receive it from the elders, by the laying on of hands.

15 Whoever commands people not to get married is not speaking God's word. That is because marriage is part of God's law.

16 God's law allows a person to have one spouse. It also allows people to have children.

17 The earth was made so that all the people God created before the beginning of the world could be born on it.

18 Whoever commands people not to eat meat is not speaking God's word.

19 God allows people to use animals for food and clothes. He allows them to use as much as they need.

20 But it was not God's plan for one person to have more than another. This is a sin the whole world needs to repent of.

21 It is a sin to waste meat. It is a sin to kill animals when there is no need.

22 When Christ comes again, he will not come as a woman. He will not come as a man travelling from place to place.

23 Do not be fooled. Be faithful and watch for the Second Coming. When the angel blows his trumpet, the earth and sky will shake. Valleys will be lifted up. Mountains

will be made flat. Rough places will become smooth.

24 But before all that happens, the people of Israel will become strong in the desert. The Lamanites will blossom like a rose.

25 Zion will grow strong in the mountains. My people will gather with joy in the place I have chosen.

26 Go where I have commanded you. Repent of all your sins. If you ask, I will give. If you knock, I will open the door.

27 I will be with you as you travel, to keep you safe. I will clear the way in front of you. I will protect you from behind. You will not be put to shame.

28 I am Jesus Christ. I am coming soon. Amen.

SECTION 50

In some branches of the church, members were acting strangely in their meetings. They were shaking and shouting. Some members would fall down as if they had fainted. Some were even running around outside and climbing trees. They believed that God's Spirit made them do these things. Some of the elders came to ask Joseph Smith if these members were really receiving God's Spirit. Section 50 is the Lord's answer.

1 Listen to God's word, elders of my church. I will teach you what you want to know about the church. I will teach you about the spirits that are travelling through the earth.

2 There are many false spirits going around the world fooling people.

3 Satan has tried to fool you, because he wants to destroy you.

4 I have seen people doing terrible things in my church.

5 Those who are faithful and endure to the end—even if that means they have to die—will have eternal life.

6 But those who only pretend to be righteous will be punished.

7 There are people among you who are only pretending to be righteous. That is why Satan has had power over you. Those people can still be saved if they repent.

8 But if they will not repent, they cannot go on being members of my church. They will not be able to live with me after they die. The world will have power over them.

9 So be careful, all of you. Do only what is true and righteous.

10 The Lord says to the elders: Come, let us talk together. Let me help you understand.

11 We will be like people talking face-to-face.

12 I will talk to you the same way you talk to each other. That way you can understand.

13 Let me ask you a question. What were you ordained to do?

14 To preach my gospel through the Spirit, which is sent to teach the truth.

15 So was it right for you to accept spirits you could not understand, as if they came from God?

16 You already know the answer is no. But I will show mercy to you. Those of you are who are weak will become strong.

17 Those of you I sent to preach the gospel—do you teach with the Spirit, or some other way?
18 If you are teaching some other way, you are not doing teaching God's way.
19 Those who are converted to the gospel—are they converted by the Spirit, or some other way?
20 If they are converted some other way, they are not being converted God's way.
21 This is very simple. If you want people to be converted by the Spirit, you need to teach with the Spirit.
22 When you teach with the Spirit, you and the person you are teaching will understand each other. You will both be built up. You will rejoice together.
23 Something that does not build people up is not from God. It is darkness.
24 What comes from God is light. Those who receive God's light, and stay close to God, will receive more light. Their light will grow brighter and brighter until they are made perfect.
25 I tell you this so you will know the truth. I tell you this so you can chase darkness away from you.
26 The people God chooses to do his work are both the highest of people and the lowest of people. They are the lowest of people because they are everyone else's servants.
27 They are the highest of people because God gives them power over everything in heaven and on earth. They have the power of the Spirit. The Father sends the Spirit out into the world through his Son, Jesus Christ.
28 Only someone who has had all their sins taken away can have power over all things.
29 If all your sins have been taken away, then anything you ask in Jesus' name will be done.
30 Because you will have power over everything, you will be able to control the spirits.
31 So if you see a spirit which you cannot understand, ask the Father, in Jesus' name, to give that spirit to you. If God does not give that spirit to you, then you know that the spirit is not from God.
32 If you know a spirit is not from God, tell the people around you that it is not from God.
33 But be calm as you do this. Do not brag or shout. If you do, the evil spirit may be able to overcome you.
34 Remember that whatever power or blessings you have come from God. It should make you happy to know that God finds you worthy.
35 Do everything I have taught you, and the Father will give you his kingdom. You will have power to overcome everything which is not from God.
36 I forgive the sins of those who are now hearing this revelation.
37 I command Joseph Wakefield and Parley P. Pratt to visit the branches of the church. Speak words that will help the members be strong.
38 John Corrill and the rest of the elders should do the same thing. No one must keep them from doing this work.
39 Edward Partridge has tried to keep the elders from doing what I have commanded. That is wrong. If he repents, he will be forgiven.

⁴⁰ You are like little children. There are many things you are still not ready for. You need to learn and grow more.
⁴¹ Do not be afraid, little children. My Father has given me power to save you from the world.
⁴² No one my Father has let me save will be lost.
⁴³ As you accept me, you become one with me, just as I am one with the Father.
⁴⁴ I am with you. I am the Good Shepherd and the Rock. If you build your house on my rock, you will never fall.
⁴⁵ I am coming soon. Then you will hear and see me for yourselves.
⁴⁶ Watch, so you will be ready. Amen.

SECTION 51

In Section 48, the Lord told the members in Ohio to share their land with the members moving in from New York. When the New York members arrived, Bishop Edward Partridge needed to find out more about how the Lord wanted the land divided. He asked Joseph Smith for a revelation. Section 51 is the revelation the Lord gave to answer Bishop Partridge's question.

¹ The Lord says: Listen, and I will tell Edward Partridge how to organize my people.
² They must be organized in keeping with my laws if they want to belong to my people.
³ Edward Partridge and his counselors should give every family an equal share of property, based on the size and needs of each family.
⁴ Whenever he gives someone a share, Edward Partridge also needs to give them a certificate. The certificate will give them the right to keep their share as long as they are worthy members of the church.
⁵ If someone loses the right to belong to the church, they will keep whatever property the certificate says they own. If they donated other property to the church, they will not be able to get it back.
⁶ This is in keeping with the laws of your country.
⁷ What belongs to my people should be given to my people.
⁸ If there is money left over after everyone has their shares, choose someone to take charge of the money. That person will be the church's agent. The agent will use the money to buy food and clothes for church members, if needed.
⁹ Eveyone should be honest. Everyone should have equal shares. Then you will be equal, like I commanded.
¹⁰ What belongs to one branch of the church should not be given to another branch.
¹¹ If another branch wants to receive money from this branch, they need to agree to pay it back.
¹² This agreement should be made through the bishop or through the agent.
¹³ The bishop should keep a church storehouse. If there is money or food left over after my people's needs have been met, it can be kept in the storehouse.

14 Bishop Partridge will not be doing any other work besides his church service. So he can use what is in the storehouse to meet his family's needs.
15 This is how I want my people to be organized.
16 You will not be living in this land long. Soon I will tell you to move to another land.
17 But you do not know when I will command you to move. So it would be best to act as if you were going to have this land for years.
18 What I have commanded here should be done in all the branches of my church.
19 Whoever proves to be a faithful and wise caretaker will receive eternal life. They will share the Lord's joy forever.
20 I am Jesus Christ. I will come soon. I will come when you are not expecting it. Amen.

SECTION 52

As they had been commanded in Section 44, all the elders met for a conference in Kirtland. Important things happened at that conference to prepare the elders for a new work. Some elders were ordained high priests for the first time. Satan tried to show his power at the conference. He made it so that some of the elders lost the power to speak. Joseph Smith used the priesthood to free the elders from Satan's power. Near the end of the conference, the Lord gave a revelation telling the elders about their new work. Section 52 is that revelation.

1 This is what the Lord says to the elders: I have called you through my Spirit.
2 I will tell you what I want you to do between now and the next conference. That conference will be held in Missouri. Missouri is where my people's promised land is.
3 Joseph Smith and Sidney Rigdon should travel to Missouri as soon as they can.
4 If they are faithful, I will tell them what to do there.
5 If they are faithful, I will tell them where your promised land is.
6 If they are not faithful, I will not let them go on doing my work.
7 Lyman Wight and John Corrill should also travel quickly to Missouri.
8 So should John Murdock and Hyrum Smith. They should travel by way of Detroit.
9 On the way, they should preach the gospel. They should preach only what the prophets and apostles have written, and what the Spirit tells them.
10 They should travel two by two. They should preach in every church they find on the way. They should baptize people. They should confirm the people they baptize right there by the water.
11 That is because I am going to cut my work short. Very soon I will come to judge the world.
12 Lyman Wight must be careful, because Satan wants to destroy him.
13 If he is faithful, I will place him in charge of many things.

14 Satan is travelling all over the world, fooling people. But I will teach you how not to be fooled.
15 Someone who prays, repents, and keeps my commandments is one of mine.
16 Someone who speaks humbly, builds people up, and keeps my commandments, is one of mine.
17 Someone who shakes under my power will be made strong. They will do good works, in keeping with the revelations I have given you.
18 Someone who does not do those kinds of works is not one of mine.
19 That is how you can tell whether or not someone has my Spirit.
20 The end is coming. What you receive depends on your faith.
21 I give this commandment to all my elders.
22 Thomas B. Marsh and Ezra Thayre should travel to Missouri. They should preach the gospel on the way.
23 So should Isaac Morley and Ezra Booth.
24 Edward Partridge and Martin Harris should travel with Sidney Rigdon and Joseph Smith.
25 David Whitmer should travel to Missouri with Harvey Whitlock.
26 Parley P. Pratt should travel with Orson Pratt.
27 Solomon Hancock should travel with Simeon Carter.
28 Edson Fuller should travel with Jacob Scott.
29 Levi W. Hancock should travel with Zebedee Coltrin.
30 Reynolds Cahoon should travel with Samuel H. Smith.
31 Wheeler Baldwin should travel with William Carter.
32 Newel Knight and Selah J. Griffin should be ordained and travel together as well.
33 All the elders should take different routes to Missouri. One pair of elders should not follow another. One pair should not build on what another pair has started.
34 Those who are faithful will be kept safe. I will help them do good work.
35 Joseph Wakefield and Solomon Humphrey should travel east.
36 They should work with their families. They should teach using only the scriptures and their own testimonies.
37 Because of his sins, Herman Basset's calling should be given to Simonds Ryder instead.
38 Jared Carter and George James should be ordained priests.
39 The rest of the elders should watch over the branches of the church where they are. Also, they can teach the gospel in places nearby. But the elders should work for a living. Church members should not have to take care of them.
40 Remember to help the poor and the sick. If you do not, you are not truly my followers.
41 Joseph Smith, Sidney Rigdon, and Edward Partridge should carry with them a recommend from the church. Oliver Cowdery needs one as well.
42 If you are faithful, you will all meet again in Missouri. It is your promised land, even though right now it belongs to your enemies.
43 Soon I will help you build the New Jerusalem. The faithful will meet me there when I come again.
44 I am Jesus Christ, God's Son. In the end, I will bring all the faithful to heaven. Amen.

SECTION 53

After the general conference in Kirtland, the elders began preparing to carry out the missions the Lord had given them. A man named Sidney Gilbert asked Joseph Smith what the Lord wanted him to do. Section 53 is the Lord's answer.

1 Sidney Gilbert, I have heard your prayers. You have asked to know what your calling in the church is.
2 I am the Lord. I died on the cross to take away the world's sins. I command you to leave behind worldly things.
3 Accept the calling of an elder. Teach people to have faith and to repent. Teach them to have their sins taken away through baptism, the way I have commanded. Teach them to receive the Holy Ghost by the laying on of hands.
4 Later, I will have the bishop call you to be an agent for the church.
5 You will travel to Missouri with my servants Joseph Smith and Sidney Rigdon.
6 These are the first directions I have for you. Later, if you keep working faithfully, I will tell you what else to do.
7 I want you to know that only those who endure to the end are saved. Amen.

SECTION 54

Leman Copley was a member of the Church in Ohio. He owned a large farm. He promised to donate his farm to the church. That way it could be shared with the members moving in from New York. But then Leman broke his promise. Now the members from New York didn't have anywhere to live. The members sent their branch president, Newel Knight, to ask Joseph Smith what they should do. Section 54 is the Lord's answer.

1 These are the words of the Lord. I died on the cross for the world's sins.
2 Newel Knight, you should keep serving faithfully as branch president.
3 If your brothers and sisters in the church want to escape their enemies, they need to repent of all their sins. They need to become truly humble.
4 The promise they made with me no longer counts, because it was broken.
5 The man who broke it will be punished. What he has done has hurt many people.
6 But those who kept their promises will be blessed. I will help them.
7 Hurry and move, before your enemies attack you. Choose someone to be in charge of the move. Then start your journey.
8 Travel west, to Missouri, near the Lamanites' lands.
9 When you arrive, work for your living, the way people usually do, until I have your home ready.
10 Be patient in your troubles. I am coming soon. When I come, I will reward those who have prepared to meet me. They will find rest from their troubles. Amen.

SECTION 55

While Joseph Smith was getting ready to go on his mission to Missouri, a man named William W. Phelps came to him. William had just moved to Kirtland with his family. Before that, he had lived in New York. In New York, he had helped publish a newspaper. William asked Joseph what the Lord wanted him to do now. Section 55 is the Lord's answer.

1 This is what the Lord says to William: I have a calling for you. After you are baptized, your sins will be forgiven. You will receive the Holy Spirit by the laying on of hands.
2 Then Joseph Smith will ordain you to be an elder. You will teach people to repent. You will teach them to have their sins taken away by being baptized in Jesus Christ's name.
3 You will have the power to lay your hands of people who repent, to give them the Holy Ghost.
4 You will also be called to help Oliver Cowdery as a printer. You and Oliver will make schoolbooks for the children in the church. It pleases me when children are able to learn about me.
5 Travel to Missouri with Joseph Smith and Sidney Rigdon, so you can settle there and do my work.
6 Joseph Coe should travel with Joseph and Sidney, too. I will give you more directions later. Amen.

SECTION 56

In Section 52, the Lord called Thomas B. Marsh and Ezra Thayre to serve a mission together. But after Leman Copley refused to share his land with the members from New York (see Section 54), there were a lot of problems. Because of those problems, Ezra wasn't ready to go with Thomas when it came time to leave. Thomas asked Joseph what he should do. Section 56 is the Lord's answer.

1 Listen, you who call yourselves my people: Those who disobey my commandments will be punished in the day I judge the world.
2 People cannot be saved if they are not willing to make sacrifices when I need them to.
3 If someone breaks a commandment of mine, it is only a matter of time before they will be punished.
4 If I have to, I will take back a commandment. But the people who disobeyed the commandment will still be punished.
5 I take back the commandment I gave Thomas B. Marsh and Ezra Thayre. Instead, I command Thomas to travel with Selah J. Griffin. The two of you need to leave quickly for Missouri.
6 I take back the commandment I gave Selah J. Griffin and Newel Knight. I do this because the members of my church in Thompson disobeyed.
7 Newel Knight will stay with the members in Thompson. Those who repent, he will lead to Missouri.
8 Ezra Thayre has been proud and selfish. I command him to repent.

He needs to obey the commandment I gave him earlier about the place where he is living.

9 If he keeps the commandment I gave him, he can still be chosen to go to Missouri.

10 If he is not willing to keep the commandment, then he should get his money back and leave. He will no longer be a member of my church.

11 I will not take back these words. Nothing can keep them from coming true.

12 If Joseph Smith has to use his own money to pay Ezra Thayre, I will call on the members in Missouri to pay Joseph his money back. Those who help pay Joseph's money back will be rewarded.

13 I will reward them with land they can call their own.

14 This is what I have to say to my people. You have much to do, and much to repent of. I have seen your sins. You have tried to do things your own way instead of keeping my commandments.

15 You are greedy. You enjoy what is wicked instead of doing what is right.

16 You who are rich, and refuse to share with the poor, need to repent. Your riches will be like a disease to you. At the Last Judgment you will cry, "The end has come, and I am not saved!"

17 You who are poor because you refuse to work also need to repent. You must not be proud or greedy. You must not take what does not belong to you.

18 But the poor who are humble and repent will be blessed. God's kingdom will come in power to save them. The riches of the earth will belong to them.

19 The Lord will come to give everyone what they have earned. Then the poor will rejoice.

20 Then they and their descendants will own the earth forever. That is all I have to say for now. Amen.

SECTION 57

As they had been commanded in Section 52, Joseph Smith and the other elders travelled to Missouri. At that time, Missouri was on the western edge of the United States. The elders were very happy to meet again in Missouri. They were eager to know where their promised land would be. They asked the Lord to reveal to them where to build New Jerusalem, or the city of Zion. The Lord answered by giving Joseph Smith the revelation we call Section 57.

1 The Lord says: Listen, elders of my church. You have met in Missouri as I commanded. Missouri is the land I have chosen for gathering the members of my church.

2 This is the promised land. This is where the city of Zion will be built.

3 Listen carefully to what I tell you. The place called Independence is the center for gathering the members of the church. There is a place for building the temple to the west, on a piece of land near the courthouse.

4 The members of the church should buy that piece of land. They

should buy all the land to the west, all the way to where the Lamanites' lands begin.

5 They should buy as much land as they can near the prairies. If they buy it, they will be able to own it forever.

6 Sidney Gilbert will serve as church agent here. He will collect money from church members. He will use the money to buy as much land in the areas round about as seems wise.

7 Edward Partridge and his counselors will divide up the land among the members of the church. They must do it the way I have commanded.

8 Sidney Gilbert should start a store here. That way he can raise more money to buy land for the members of the church. He will also be able to get members the things they need to settle in their new homes.

9 I want him to get a license, so he can hire clerks to help him run the store.

10 That way my people will be able to get everything they need. They will be able to preach my gospel to the people in this dark land.

11 William W. Phelps will settle here as a printer for the church.

12 If he can, he should sell books to non-members, too. He should raise as much money as possible to help the members of the church.

13 Oliver Cowdery will help William run the printshop. The Spirit will help Oliver know how to put together the books they will be publishing.

14 The people I have just named should settle in Zion with their families as quickly as they can. They should start carrying out the work I have given them.

15 As soon as possible, the bishop and the agent should get everything ready for the families who have been chosen to come settle here.

16 I will tell the rest of the elders and members what to do later. Amen.

SECTION 58

Not long after Joseph Smith and the elders left for Missouri, the members from Thompson, Ohio, left as well. The members reached Missouri about a week after Section 57 was revealed. The Lord gave Joseph Smith a revelation telling the members what to do next. Section 58 is that revelation.

1 Listen, elders of my church. I will tell you what I want you to do in this land.

2 Those who keep my commandments will be blessed, either in this life or the next. Those who stay faithful in times of trouble will receive a greater reward in heaven.

3 You are not yet able to see what God is planning to do. You will have many troubles. But wonderful things will come out of it.

4 You will suffer much. But in the end you will be blessed. You will be crowned with glory—not now, but soon.

5 Remember this. I am telling it to you now so you will accept what happens later.

6 I have sent you here to do my will.

I have sent you to prepare yourselves to be my witnesses.

7 You have the honor of starting to build Zion. You will be witnesses of Zion.

8 You will prepare a feast of fine food for the poor. Then the world will see that the prophets' words are going to come true.

9 Everyone on earth will be invited to the Lord's house for the feast.

10 First the rich will be invited—those with titles or a fancy education.

11 Then will come the day of my power. Then the poor, and the lame, and the blind, and the deaf will come to the feast. They will come to celebrate with the Lord.

12 I, the Lord, have said it.

13 My word will go out from Zion, the city of the people of God.

14 That is why I brought you here. That is why I called Edward Partridge to organize my people.

15 But Edward Partridge needs to show more faith. If he does not repent, he will lose his calling.

16 I have told him what his mission is. I will not tell him again.

17 Whoever is called to serve as bishop becomes a judge. They are like the judges who ruled the people of Israel and divided the promised land.

18 The bishop judges God's people in keeping with the laws God has revealed through the prophets. The bishop does this with the help of counselors.

19 My law must be kept in this land.

20 No one should think of themselves as a ruler. God is your only ruler. Those who serve in the church as judges or counselors should do only what God tells them.

21 No one should break the laws of their country. If you keep God's laws, you will have no need to break your country's laws.

22 Someday Christ himself will rule the earth. But until then, you should obey the earthly governments.

23 The laws I have given you are laws for the church They are not laws for making your own government. You should let non-members know that they are laws for the church only. That way non-members will not get the wrong idea.

24 Edward Partridge should make his home in this land. So should his counselors and the person I have chosen to run my storehouse.

25 They should make plans to bring their families here. I will help guide them. But they need to decide for themselves what to do.

26 People should not expect me to always tell them what to do. People who always have to be given orders before they do anything are lazy and foolish servants. They will not be rewarded.

27 People should eagerly become part of good causes. They should make good things happen by their own choice.

28 People have the power to decide for themselves what to do. They will be rewarded for whatever good they do.

29 People should not have to be commanded before they do things. When they are commanded to do something, they should have faith and work hard to do it.

30 What kind of God would I be if I

did not expect people to keep my commandments?

31 What kind of God would I be if I made promises and then did not keep them?

32 The only time I take back my promises is when people do not keep my commandments. People who do not keep my commandments cannot receive my blessings.

33 Then they say to themselves, "This must not be the Lord's work, because he has not kept his promises." People who say this are in danger of being trapped by Satan.

34 I have more directions to give you about this land.

35 Martin Harris should set an example for the members of the church. He should go to the bishop to donate all his money to the church.

36 Everyone who comes to live in this land should do this. That is what my law commands.

37 The church should buy land in Independence for the storehouse and the printshop.

38 The Spirit will tell Martin Harris what else he needs to do to get the land he wants.

39 He needs to repent. He needs to stop looking for the world's praise.

40 William W. Phelps needs to carry out the work I gave him. He should be given land to live on.

41 I am not very pleased with him. He needs to repent. He needs to stop trying to be better than others. He needs to be more humble.

42 When someone repents of their sins, I forgive them. I completely forget about the things they did wrong.

43 Here is how you will know when people have truly repented of their sins. They will admit they have done wrong, and they will stop doing it.

44 It will be many years before it is time for the rest of the elders to move to Missouri. I may let them move earlier if they pray for it with faith. But they cannot move until I tell them to.

45 For now, I need them to bring people together from all over the world.

46 Hold a meeting. Then those who have not been chosen to stay here should go preach the gospel in the areas round about. After that, they should go home.

47 They should keep preaching on the way. They should bear their testimonies everywhere. They should teach everyone to repent—rich and poor, high and low.

48 They should start branches of the church in places where people repent.

49 The members of the church should choose an agent by vote. The agent will collect money from the members in Ohio. The money will be used to buy land in Zion.

50 I want Sidney Rigdon to describe the land of Zion in writing. He should write down everything that God wants done here. The Spirit will tell him what to write.

51 He will write a letter to all the branches of the church. He will ask them to donate money to buy land for God's people. The people should give their money to either the bishop or the agent, whichever the bishop decides is best.

52 The Lord wants his followers—

and all people—to donate enough money that the church can buy this whole area. This should be done as soon as possible.

53 If church members do not buy the land in time, they may not be able to get land at all, except by fighting for it.

54 As long as there is land to buy, workers of all kinds should come get it ready for the members of God's church.

55 Everything must be done in an orderly way. Every now and then, the bishop or the church agent should announce who else is to be given their share of land.

56 The gathering of my people should not be done quickly. It should not be done as if you were running here to escape your enemies. Instead, the elders of the church should decide at the conferences how to carry out the gathering. From time to time, I will give them revelations about what to do.

57 Sidney Rigdon should dedicate this land for the Lord. He should also dedicate the place where the temple will be built.

58 Hold a conference. Then Sidney Rigdon, Joseph Smith, and Oliver Cowdery should go back to their own homes. There they will finish the work I gave them to do. The rest of you will do whatever you decide at the conference.

59 No one should go home without sharing their testimony with the people they meet on the way.

60 The calling I gave Ziba Peterson should be taken away. He will work for his own living, like any other member. He will do this until he has been punished enough for trying to hide his sins.

61 When the rest of the elders who are on their way to this land arrive, they should hold a conference here, too.

62 Then they should return home. On the way, they should preach the gospel. They should testify about the revelations they have received.

63 From here, people will go out to preach the gospel in every part of the world. Everyone needs to hear my gospel. Those who believe will be able to do miracles.

64 Jesus Christ is coming. Amen.

SECTION 59

One of the members moving from Ohio to Missouri was a woman named Polly Knight. Polly was very sick. But she wanted to reach the land of Zion before she died. One week after she reach Zion, she died. The Lord talks about Polly's death at the beginning of Section 59. Section 59 is a revelation for the members of the church who were just settling in the land of Zion.

1 This is what the Lord says: The people who come to this land out of a desire to do my work will be blessed.

2 Those who live will own the earth. Those who die will find rest from their suffering. Their good works will be known. I will make them rulers in heaven.

3 The people in Zion who have obeyed my gospel will be blessed. I will reward them with the good

things of the earth. Their land will be fruitful.

4 They will also receive heavenly blessings. If they are faithful and work hard, I will give them many revelations. I will teach them what I want them to do.

5 I give them this commandment. Love God with all your heart. Serve him in Jesus Christ's name.

6 Love those around you as if they were you. Do not steal. Do not commit adultery. Do not kill. Do not do anything like these things.

7 Thank the Lord for everything you have.

8 Repent. That is the sacrifice the Lord wants you to give him.

9 To help you become more holy, go to church on the Sabbath.

10 I have given you the Sabbath so you have a day to rest from your work and to worship God.

11 Of course, you should serve God all all times and on every day.

12 But on the Sabbath, you will offer God special service. You will take the sacrament. You will confess your sins to your fellow members and to the Lord.

13 You should do nothing else on the Sabbath except prepare your meals. Even then, your thoughts should be on the Lord. Then your fasting will be perfect. In other words, your joy will be full.

14 "To fast and pray" means "to rejoice and pray."

15 Do these things thankfully and cheerfully. But do not laugh in a way that will drive away the Spirit.

16 Then you will receive everything the land can give you. You will have animals for your farms. You will have birds and wild animals to hunt.

17 You will have plants for food and clothes. You will have houses and barns. You will have orchards, gardens, and grapevines.

18 Everything that comes from the earth is for people to use. Some things are made to be beautiful. Some things are made to make people happy.

19 Some things are made to be used as food or clothing. Some things are made to taste good or smell good. Some things are made to give people strong bodies. Some things are made to lift their spirits.

20 God is happy to give people all these things. That is what they were made for. But they should be used wisely. People should not use more than they need. They should not get these things by force.

21 There is only one thing that makes God unhappy. It is when people fail to see that everything is his work and refuse to keep his commandments.

22 The things I just said are the same things the scriptures teach. Do not bother me anymore about this subject.

23 Those who do what is right will be rewarded. I will give them peace on earth and eternal life in heaven.

24 The Spirit testifies that these are truly the Lord's words. Amen.

SECTION 60

The members who had moved to Missouri began to settle in. They were excited about starting to build the city of Zion. It came time for Joseph Smith and the other elders to go back to Ohio. The elders asked the Lord to give them directions for the trip. Section 60 is the Lord's answer.

1 This is what the Lord says to the elders who are about to go back to Ohio: I am pleased that you have come here.

2 But I am unhappy that some of you are afraid to talk to people about my gospel. Because of their fear, they are hiding the gift I gave them. That is what makes me unhappy.

3 If they are not more faithful, they will lose what they have been given.

4 I am the ruler of heaven. I am more powerful than all the armies on earth. Someday I will come to give my people glory. Then everyone will see how God's power is made known.

5 For your trip back to Ohio, you should buy or make a boat. It does not matter to me whether you buy it or make it. Do whichever you think is best. Then travel quickly to St. Louis.

6 From there, Sidney Rigdon, Joseph Smith, and Oliver Cowdery will travel to Cincinnati.

7 There they will preach my gospel. Their preaching should be bold, but not angry. Have faith. I can make you holy. Your sins are forgiven.

8 The rest of the elders will travel in pairs from St. Louis. They should travel slowly. They should preach the gospel on the way, until they reach home.

9 I have sent the elders to do all this because it will help the branches of the church.

10 Edward Partridge should give some of the money I gave him to the elders who are going home.

11 Those who can should pay back that money through the agent. Those who cannot pay it back do not have to.

12 Now I have something to say to the elders who are still on their way to this land.

13 Their calling is to preach my gospel. I say to them: Do not waste your time. Do not hide your gift.

14 After you reach Zion, preach my gospel for a little while. Then go back home. Travel slowly. Preach my gospel on the way. Your preaching should not be angry. You should not argue with people.

15 If people reject you, shake the dirt off your shoes and wash your feet. This is a sign that those people will punished at the Last Judgment. But do this in private, not in front of them. That way you do not make them angry.

16 This is all you need to know for now. It is God's will.

17 I will give Joseph Smith a revelation telling Sidney Rigdon and Oliver Cowdery what to do. I will tell everyone else what to do later. Amen.

SECTION 61

Joseph Smith and the other elders began their trip from Missouri back to Ohio. For three days, they travelled down a river in canoes. On the third day, the river became dangerous. After the elders stopped to camp for the night, William W. Phelps had a terrible vision. He saw Satan riding on the water. The next morning, after the elders prayed, the Lord gave the revelation that is now Section 61.

1 Listen to the voice of God. He has all power. He is eternal. He is the beginning and the end.

2 This is what the Lord says to you who are gathered here: I forgive your sins. I do this because I am kind to those who confess and are humble.

3 You do not all need to be travelling so quickly down the river. There are people living on both sides of this river who need to hear the gospel.

4 I let you come this far so you could see for yourselves how dangerous the water is. It is only going to get more dangerous.

5 That is because water has been given the power to destroy. This river is one of the most dangerous.

6 Still, I am in control of everything that happens to people. So if you are faithful, the water will not be able to destroy you.

7 Sidney Gilbert and William W. Phelps need to hurry on their way. They need to carry out their mission.

8 I did not want them to leave sooner, because I wanted to correct you all for your sins. I wanted you to stay together. That way none of you would be killed before you could repent.

9 But the time has come for you to go your separate ways. Sidney Gilbert and William W. Phelps should go quickly to carry out their mission. If they have faith, nothing will be able to stop them.

10 If they are faithful, they will be kept safe. I will be with them.

11 The rest of you should take all the clothing you need.

12 Whatever you decide you do not need, Sidney Gilbert will take with him.

13 I gave you this commandment for your own good. I will teach you like I taught people long ago.

14 When I created the world, I blessed the water. But as the end of the world began to get closer, I had my servant John put a curse on the water.

15 Because of that curse, there will come a time when no one will be safe on water.

16 A time will come when people will say that only the righteous can travel to Zion by water.

17 The opposite of what happened to the water happened to the land. In the beginning of the world, I cursed the land. But now that the end of the world is coming, I have blessed it. That way the members of my church can enjoy the good things of the land.

18 Warn the other members of the church not to travel on this river. That way, if their faith weakens, Satan will not be able to put them in danger.

19 Because of the curse, Satan has power to ride on this river. I am not

going to undo the curse. So Satan will go on having that power.

20 I was unhappy with you yesterday, but not today.

21 Those I have commanded should hurry on their way.

22 After a little while, if they carry out their mission, they can travel by water again if they want. They should use their best judgment to decide whether to travel by water or by land.

23 But if Sidney Rigdon, Joseph Smith, and Oliver Cowdery travel by water again, it should only be on the canal.

24 When the members of my church travel to Zion, they should go first by canal, then by land.

25 As they travel, they will live in tents, like the Israelites.

26 Teach this commandment to all the members of the church.

27 But if there is someone who has power to make the water obey them, the Spirit will tell that person how to travel.

28 That person can travel by land or by water, depending on what the Spirit tells them.

29 This is how the members of the church should travel. They are the Lord's camp.

30 Sidney Rigdon, Joseph Smith, and Oliver Cowdery should not preach to the wicked until they reach Cincinnati.

31 They should be bold about telling the people of that city to repent. The people need to know how unhappy God is with them. They are so wicked that they are very close to being destroyed.

32 Then Sidney, Joseph, and Oliver should travel on to the branches of the church. Their work is needed there even more than it is among the wicked.

33 The rest of the elders should travel wherever they are directed. They should preach the gospel to the wicked.

34 If they do this, I will make them holy.

35 They can divide themselves up into pairs, however they think best, except for Reynolds Cahoon and Samuel H. Smith. I am pleased with those two. I want them to stay together until they reach home.

36 What I am about to say is for all of you. Cheer up, little children. I am with you. I have not left you alone.

37 Because you have been humble, the blessings of God's kingdom are yours.

38 Be serious. Watch for the Second Coming. Be ready, because I will come when you are not expecting it.

39 Pray that you will not be tempted. That way you will be able to stand with me when I come again. It will not matter whether you are alive or dead when I come. Amen.

SECTION 62

While Joseph Smith was travelling from Missouri back to Ohio, he met a group of elders who were travelling from Ohio to Missouri. Joseph told the elders that the Lord had revealed where Zion would be built. When the elders heard this, they became even more eager to finish their journey. Section 62 is a revelation the Lord gave for the elders travelling to Zion.

1 Listen, elders of my church: I am Jesus Christ, your defender. I myself lived as a human being. So I know to help people when they are tempted.
2 I am watching those of you who have not yet travelled to Zion. You have still not finished your mission.
3 Still, I am pleased with you. The testimonies you have shared have been written down in heaven for the angels to read. They rejoice when they see what you are doing. Your sins are forgiven.
4 Keep travelling. When you reach Zion, hold a sacrament meeting. Rejoice together.
5 Then you can go home to bear your testimonies about everything that happened to you. You can travel all together or in pairs. It does not matter to me which. Just be sure that on the way, you preach the gospel.
6 I have brought you together so I could keep my promise. I promised to protect the faithful. I promised to bring them to Missouri to rejoice together. I cannot lie. When I make a promise, I keep it.
7 If you want, you can ride home on horses, mules, or wagons. But remember that this is a blessing from the Lord. Thank him for everything he gives you.
8 I leave you to decide what to do. Ask the Spirit to guide you.
9 Remember that the kingdom is yours. I am always with the faithful. Amen.

SECTION 63

Joseph Smith, Sidney Rigdon, and Oliver Cowdery travelled from Missouri back to Ohio. They told the members in Ohio that the Lord had revealed where Zion would be built. The members became excited. They asked Joseph what they needed to do to receive homes in the land of Zion. Section 63 is the Lord's answer.

1 Listen, you who call yourselves the Lord's people. Open your hearts, wherever you are. Listen to what the Lord wants you to do.
2 I am not pleased with those who refuse to keep my commandments.
3 I am the one who decides when a person should go on living and when they should die.
4 I build when I think best. I destroy when I think best. I have the power to punish people's sins.
5 When I say something will be done, it will be done.
6 Those who refuse to accept my gospel or keep my commandments will suffer because of it. They will be destroyed, as if by a whirlwind. Then everyone on earth will know that I am God.

7 Then the people who wanted a sign from God will get one. But it will be too late for them to be saved.

8 Some of you are asking for signs. There have been people asking for signs ever since the world began.

9 But faith does not come because of signs. Signs come because of faith.

10 Signs come when God wants, not when people want.

11 Signs come when they are needed to do important works. God will not show signs to someone without faith, except to punish them for not having faith.

12 I am happy to send signs and miracles if they will do people good. But I am not pleased with those of you who look for signs and miracles as a way of getting faith.

13 I gave you commandments. But many of you have not kept them.

14 There are still people among you who have not been faithful to your spouses. Some of those people have already left the church. But others are still trying to hide what they have done. Sooner or later, they will be found out.

15 Those who have committed adultery need to repent quickly, before they are found out. If they are found out, then everyone will know what they have done. Everyone will know how foolish they have been.

16 I repeat what I have said before. People who look at others with lust, or who think about committing adultery, cannot have the Spirit. They are not being true to their faith. Such people ought to be afraid.

17 After they die, they will have to go live with Satan. So will people who reject the gospel, or who love to tell lies, or who use black magic.

18 Those people will not be able to come back from the dead until 1000 years after the righteous come back from the dead. They will not be able to live with God.

19 People who commit these sins cannot be members of my church.

20 Those who endure to the end and keep my commandments will be saved. They will be given a home on earth after the earth has been transformed.

21 The earth will be transformed the same way my apostles saw me transformed on the mountain. I have not yet revealed to you the full story of what happened there.

22 Now I will tell you what I want you to do, like I promised I would. But I will not make it a commandment. That is because there are so many of you who do not keep my commandments.

23 I will bless those who do keep my commandments, though. I will teach them everything they need to know to have eternal life.

24 I want the members of the church to gather together in Zion. But they should not gather quickly. If they try to move too quickly, things will not be organized. That can cause disease.

25 I have power over the land of Zion. It belongs to me.

26 But earthly powers need to have their due.

27 That is why I want you to buy the land. If you buy the land, the law will protect your rights. People will have no reason to be angry with you.

28 Satan wants to make people angry with you. He wants to force you to fight and kill.

29 He knows that there are only two ways you can get a home in Zion. Either you have to buy the land, or you have to fight for it.

30 If you want me to help you, you must buy the land.

31 If you fight for the land, I will not help you. That is because it is against my law for you to kill. Without my help, you will lose. Your enemies will chase you from one place to another, until only a few of you are left.

32 As long as the people of the world refuse to keep my commandments, I cannot give them my Spirit.

33 There are going to be wars on earth. The wicked will destroy each other. Everyone will be afraid.

34 Even the members of the church will almost be destroyed. But I am with them. I will come down from heaven. The wicked will be destroyed as if by fire.

35 It is still not time for this to happen. But the time is coming.

36 It is because all these terrible things are going to happen that I want the members of my church to gather in Zion.

37 Everyone needs to be faithful. They need to do what is right. Warn people that the wicked are going to be destroyed. Warn them by your words, and by the fact that you are moving away.

38 The members who live on this farm in Kirtland should get ready to move.

39 Titus Billing should turn the farm over to someone else. That way he can be ready to move to Zion next spring. Most of the people living on the farm will go with him. A few need to stay here until I tell them.

40 Send all the money you can to Zion, even if it is just a little.

41 The Spirit will tell Joseph Smith who should go to Zion and who should stay here.

42 Newel K. Whitney should keep his store a little while longer.

43 But he should send all the money he can to Zion.

44 He should do whatever seems best to him.

45 He will serve as the agent for the members who stay here in Kirtland.

46 Go quickly to the different branches of the church. Take Oliver Cowdery with you. Teach the members what I have told you about collecting money.

47 Those who are faithful and endure to the end will be saved.

48 Those who send money to Zion will be rewarded. They will be given a home on earth and a reward in heaven.

49 Righteous people who die will also be rewarded. When the Lord comes to make everything new, they will be brought back from the dead. They will never die again. Then they will be given a home in the Lord's holy city.

50 Righteous people who are alive when the Lord comes will be rewarded, too. But they will have to die when they get old, like people normally do.

51 After the Second Coming, children will grow until they get old. Then they will die. But they will

come back from the dead in the blink of an eye. Their bodies will become immortal, instead of having to be buried.

52 That is why the apostles taught about people coming back from the dead.

53 That is what you have to look forward to. From the Lord's point of view, these things are coming very soon.

54 Until then, it will be like the story about the ten young women waiting for the wedding party. Some church members will be foolish. Some will be wise. But when I come, the righteous and the wicked will be separated. I will send my angels to sort out the wicked. They will have to live with Satan.

55 I am not pleased with Sidney Rigdon. He thinks too highly of himself. He has lost the Spirit. That is because he has not listened to other people's advice.

56 I cannot accept the letter he wrote describing Zion. He needs to write it over again. If I cannot accept the new letter, he will lose his calling.

57 If there are people who feel the desire to go out warning people to repent, they should be ordained to do so. But they must be humble and gentle when they preach.

58 People should be warned in as few words as possible. That is because the end of the world is so close.

59 I am in heaven. But I have power over everything on earth. I am everywhere. I know everything that happens. Soon I will be the ruler of all.

60 I am Jesus Christ. I am the beginning and the end.

61 Everyone should be careful how they use my name.

62 People who use my name for no reason, or without authority, will be punished.

63 If the members of the church repent of their sins, I will accept them as my people. If they do not repent, they will not be able to live with me.

64 Remember that the revelations you receive are holy. Be careful when you talk about them. Only talk about them the way the Spirit tells you to. You receive the Spirit by praying.

65 Joseph Smith and Sidney Rigdon should pray for the Spirit to show them where to find a home.

66 Be patient. You will have troubles. But if you do everything I have said here, you will receive a greater reward. If you do not do what I have said here, you will receive a greater punishment. Amen.

SECTION 64

The members in Ohio started to get ready to move to Missouri to help build Zion. Around the same time, some members started to say that Joseph Smith was sinning. Section 64 is a revelation from the Lord answering the things those members said. Section 64 also gives more information about the move to Zion.

1 This is what the Lord says to the elders of my church: Listen to what I want you to do.
2 I will show you my kindness, because I want you to overcome the world.
3 Some of you have sinned. But this one time, I have forgiven you. That is because I want you to be saved, for my glory.
4 I will show mercy to you, because you are the ones I gave my kingdom to.
5 Joseph Smith will have the authority to receive revelations for the church as long as he is alive and keeps my commandments.
6 The people who say Joseph Smith is sinning are wrong.
7 It is true that he has sinned. But if people admit to me that they have sinned, and if they ask me to forgive them, I do. There are only a few sins that cannot be forgiven.
8 My followers long ago used to point fingers at each other. They did not truly forgive each other. This was evil. I had to correct them for it.
9 That is why I say you should forgive each other. Someone who refuses to forgive another person is committing a more serious sin than the one the other person committed.
10 I, the Lord, will forgive whoever I decide to forgive. But you need to forgive everyone.
11 When someone does something wrong to you, you should say to yourself, "I leave it to God to judge you. God will give you whatever you have earned."
12 You need to hold a church court, though, for a member of the church who refuses to repent or confess their sins. You must do what the scriptures and the revelations tell you to.
13 Holding a church court does not mean that you do not love the person. Even if you yourselves forgive the person, you still have to hold a church court in order to keep God's law. You may also need to hold a church court to show that you respect the laws of your country.
14 That is why you need to hold church courts.
15 Ezra Booth is no longer my servant, because he did not keep my law. Isaac Morley did not keep my law either.
16 I took my Spirit away from them because they had evil desires. They said something was evil when in fact it was good. But I have forgiven Isaac Morley.
17 Edward Partridge has sinned, too. Satan is trying to destroy him. But if these men repent of their sins when they hear this revelation, they will be forgiven.
18 I need Sidney Gilbert to go back to his store in a few weeks. I need him to keep serving as church agent in Zion.
19 He should tell the members there about this revelation. That way, they will not be destroyed.
20 I commanded Isaac Morley to sell his farm. I did this so he would not face a temptation he could not overcome. I also did it to keep him from giving you harmful advice.
21 Frederick G. Williams must not sell his farm yet. My people will need a safe home in Kirtland for another five years. During that time, the wicked will not be de-

stroyed. I will be able to save some of them.

22 After those five years, anyone who wants to move to Zion can do so. But their hearts must be open. I need people's hearts.

23 The time between now and the Second Coming, I call "today." "Today" is a time for my people to make sacrifices. They should pay tithing. If they pay tithing, they will not be burned up during the Second Coming.

24 After "today"—remember, the Lord is using these words in a special way—the proud and the wicked will be burned up like old straw. I will not be able to save anyone who is still living in Babylon.

25 If you have faith in me, you will work hard while it is still "today."

26 Newel K. Whitney and Sidney Gilbert should not sell their store until the rest of the members here in Kirtland have moved to Zion.

27 I have said in my laws that you should not get in debt to your enemies.

28 But the laws do not keep the Lord from taking something and then paying it back when he decides the time is right.

29 As agents for the church, you are doing the Lord's business. Whenever you do the Lord's will, you are doing the Lord's business.

30 Your calling is to make sure the members of the church have the things they need to settle in the land of Zion.

31 I promise you that my people will have their home in Zion. This promise cannot be broken.

32 But everything must happen in due time.

33 Do not grow tired of doing good. You are starting an important work. Out of small things grow great ones.

34 I need people's hearts and minds. I need people to keep my commandments. Those who do will enjoy the good things of the land of Zion.

35 Those who will not keep my commandments cannot live in Zion. They will have to be sent away.

36 People who will not keep my commandments cannot be counted among Ephraim's descendents. They cannot live in the promised land.

37 I have made my restored church like a judge sitting on a hill to bring justice to the world.

38 The people who live in Zion will have power to judge everything that has to do with Zion.

39 They will decide which people are only pretending to be righteous. They will decide who is only pretending to be an apostle or prophet.

40 Even the bishop and his counselors will be judged if they do not do what they are supposed to. If that happens, other people will be called to take their place.

41 Zion will grow and become strong. The Lord's glory will be there.

42 Zion will be like a flag raised high to show people the way to go. People will come to Zion from all over the world.

43 Someday, the whole world will shake for fear because of the power of Zion's people. The Lord says this. Amen.

SECTION 65

Joseph moved from Kirtland to a town called Hiram so he could keep working on his new translation of the Bible. To get himself ready to start translating again, he spent a lot of time studying the scriptures and praying. During this time, he received a revelation. It was different from his other revelations, because it was in the form of a prayer. Section 65 is that revelation.

1 Listen! A voice is calling to all people. It is like the voice of an angel, sent down from heaven with a message for the whole world: "Get ready for the Lord's coming."
2 The authority of God's kingdom has been given to people on earth. The restored gospel will go to every part of the world, like the stone in King Nebuchadnezzar's dream. God's kingdom will grow until it fills the earth.
3 The voice shouts: Get ready for the Second Coming! Get ready to meet the Lord when he comes to live with his people forever!
4 Pray to the Lord. Tell people about the amazing things he has done.
5 Pray that the Lord's kingdom will grow on earth. Pray that people will accept the gospel. Pray that they will get ready for the day when Jesus Christ will come down from heaven in a glorious light to meet God's kingdom on earth.
6 O God, make your kingdom grow on earth. Come rule on earth as you do in heaven. May all your enemies be overthrown. All honor, power, and glory are yours forever. Amen.

SECTION 66

Church leaders held a conference in Hiram, Ohio. During the conference, a member named William E. McLellin asked Joseph Smith for a revelation. William wanted to do what was right. But he had many weaknesses. Section 66 is the revelation the Lord gave for William.

1 This is what the Lord says to William E. McLellin: I will bless you, because you turned away from your sins and accepted the truth. I am your Savior. I am the Savior of everyone who has faith in me.
2 I sent my restored gospel into the world so that people could have life. Those who accept the restored gospel will be part of the glorious things that the prophets and apostles said would happen before the end of the world.
3 You are not perfect, William. I will show you your faults. When I do, repent of them.
4 Now I will tell you what I want you to do.
5 I want you to go to the places round about where people have not yet heard my gospel. Teach my gospel in those places.
6 Do not wait longer than a few days before starting your mission. Do not move to Zion yet. Send whatever money you can to Zion. Other than that, do not think about what you own.

7 Travel east. Bear your testimony to everyone, everywhere. Teach people in their churches. Show them how the restored gospel makes sense.

8 Take Samuel H. Smith with you. Stay with him. Show him this revelation, so he knows what I have told you to do. If you are faithful, you will be strong wherever you go. I will go with you.

9 If you bless the sick, they will be healed. Do not come back from your mission until I tell you to. Be patient in suffering. Ask, and I will give. Knock, and I will open the door.

10 Do not take on more than you can handle. Do not sin in any way. Do not commit adultery. That is something you have been tempted to do.

11 Do these things. Trust my directions. If you do, you will do good work. You will send many people on to Zion. They will come singing songs of eternal joy.

12 If you endure to the end, you will receive eternal life. You will sit with me at the Father's right hand.

13 Your Lord and Savior, Jesus Christ, has said this. Amen.

SECTION 67

At the conference in Hiram, the elders decided that some of Joseph Smith's revelations should be published together as the Book of Commandments. The elders wondered how they could show the world that the revelations in the book were true. The Lord told the elders that one of them should try to write a revelation better than the ones Joseph Smith had received. If they could not write a better revelation, that would show that Joseph Smith's revelations were from God. William E. McLellin tried to write a better revelation, but failed. Section 67 is the revelation in which the Lord told the elders to try to write a better revelation.

1 Listen, elders of my church: I have heard your prayers. I know your hearts and desires.

2 I am watching you. I can give you anything on earth or in heaven.

3 You wanted to believe that you would receive the blessing I offered you. But you did not receive it, because you were afraid.

4 I testify that the revelations written there in front you are true.

5 You know that Joseph Smith does not write perfectly. You also know that you have tried to learn to write better than he does.

6 Choose the shortest, simplest revelation in the Book of Commandments. Then choose the wisest one of you.

7 See if that person, or any one of you, can write a revelation like it. If you can, then you have a reason to think that the revelations in the book may not true.

8 But if you cannot write a revelation like one in the book, then you need to bear testimony that the revelations are true.

9 You know that there is nothing in the revelations that is not good. You know that everything good comes from God.

10 I promise all the elders that if you throw off your envy, your fear,

and your pride, I will show myself to you. You will know for yourselves that I exist. But you will not know this with your earthly minds. You will know it with your spiritual minds.

11 No living person has ever seen God without first being changed by God's Spirit.

12 Only someone who has been changed by the Spirit can stand to be with God. That is why you cannot know God with your earthly minds.

13 Right now, you could not stand to be with God. You could not stand to be visited by angels. You must be patient. You must wait until you are made perfect.

14 Do not give up. When you are ready, and the time is right, you will be able to see and know for yourselves what has been revealed to you through Joseph Smith. Amen.

SECTION 68

Orson Hyde, Luke S. Johnson, Lyman E. Johnson, and William E. McLellin were elders in the church. They came to Joseph to learn how the Lord wanted them to serve him. Section 68 is the revelation the Lord gave for them. Section 68 also has directions for all members of the church.

1 Orson Hyde was ordained to travel from place to place, teaching the gospel through the Spirit. He was told to preach in people's churches. He was told to use the scriptures to show how the restored gospel makes sense.

2 This is an example for everyone who is ordained to the priesthood and called to serve a mission.

3 They should say what the Holy Ghost leads them to say.

4 Whatever the Holy Ghost leads them to say will be scripture. That is because they will be speaking the words and thoughts of the Lord. That is how God will use his power to save people.

5 I make this promise to all my servants.

6 Cheer up! Do not be afraid. I will always be with you. You will testify that I am Jesus Christ, God's eternal Son.

7 This is what the Lord says to Orson Hyde, Luke Johnson, Lyman Johnson, and William E. McLellin. These words apply to all the faithful elders of my church.

8 Go preach my gospel to everyone in the world. Use the authority I have given you to baptize people. Baptize them in the name of the Father, and of the Son, and of the Holy Ghost.

9 Those who have faith and are baptized will be saved. Those who refuse to have faith cannot be saved.

10 After people have faith, they will be blessed with signs, just like the scriptures say.

11 I will teach you the signs of the Second Coming.

12 You will have power to promise eternal life to anyone the Father tells you should receive this promise. Amen.

13 Now, here are some directions in addition to the revelations I already gave you.

14 When the Lord decides the time is right, other bishops will be called to serve the church just like Edward Partridge has.

15 They must be worthy high priests. They must be chosen by the First Presidency of the Melchizedek priesthood, unless they are descendants of Aaron.

16 Someone who is a firstborn descendant of Aaron has a right to be bishop.

17 That is because the firstborn holds the authority to be president of the Aaronic priesthood.

18 No one has the right to be president of the Aaronic priesthood except a firstborn descendant of Aaron.

19 But high priests in the Melchizedek priesthood have the authority to serve in all the offices before theirs. So a high priest can be called to serve as bishop if you cannot find a descendant of Aaron. To serve as bishop, a high priest must be ordained by the First Presidency.

20 Even descendants of Aaron must be found worthy and ordained by the First Presidency before they can hold priesthood offices.

21 The Lord promised that the priesthood would be passed down through Aaron's descendants. So anyone who can prove they are a descendant of Aaron can claim the right to be ordained to a priesthood office. Or the Lord might reveal to the First Presidency that someone is a descendant of Aaron.

22 Only the First Presidency can hold a church court for a bishop or high priest.

23 A bishop or high priest who is found guilty by the First Presidency will be punished.

24 But someone who repents must be forgiven, in keeping with the revelations I have given to the church.

25 Parents in the church must teach their children. They must teach them about repentance, faith in Christ, baptism, and the gift of the Holy Ghost. They must teach their children these things by the time the children are eight years old.

26 This is a law for all the members of the church, wherever they live.

27 Children should be baptized when they are eight years old. They should also receive the gift of the Holy Ghost by the laying on of hands.

28 Parents should teach their children to pray and keep the commandments.

29 The people of Zion should remember to keep the Sabbath day holy.

30 They should faithfully do the work they are given. The Lord will judge those who are lazy.

31 I am not very pleased with the people of Zion. Some of them are lazy. They are letting their children grow up to be wicked. They are greedy. They look for earthly treasures instead of working for heavenly treasures.

32 That is wrong. It needs to stop. That is why I am sending Oliver Cowdery to Zion with this revelation.

33 The people of Zion need to remember to say their prayers. People who do not say their prayers should be reported to the bishop.

34 This is a true revelation. Do what

it says. Do not cut anything out of it.

35 I am Jesus Christ. I am the beginning and the end. I am coming soon. Amen.

SECTION 69

When it came time to publish The Book of Commandments (see Section 67), Oliver Cowdery was chosen to take the revelations to Missouri. That is where the church printshop was. Oliver was also given money to pay for the publishing. The trip to Missouri would be long and dangerous. So the Lord gave Joseph directions about how Oliver should travel. Those directions are in Section 69.

1 The Lord says: Listen to me, so I can help my servant Oliver Cowdery. It is not wise for him travel to Zion alone, with all the revelations and the money. Someone you can trust should go with him.
2 I want John Whitmer to be the one who travels with Oliver Cowdery.
3 John Whitmer should also keep writing the history of the church.
4 Oliver Cowdery and others will give him advice.
5 My servants who are in other places should send reports of their work to Zion.
6 Zion will be the headquarters for everything that has to do with my work.
7 John Whitmer should visit the different branches of the church. That will be the easiest way for him to learn the things he needs to know to write the history of the church.
8 He should preach to the branches when he visits them. He should choose and write down everything that will help the church. He should remember that he is writing this history for the people who will live in Zion in the future. Amen.

SECTION 70

The members of the church were excited about publishing Joseph Smith's revelations. They knew that the revelations were Jesus Christ's words to the people of today. They felt that the revelations were more valuable than anything else in the world. In Section 70, the Lord gave more directions about publishing and selling copies of the revelations.

1 Listen, people of Zion. Listen, members of my church who are far away. Listen to what I say to Joseph Smith, Martin Harris, Oliver Cowdery, John Whitmer, Sidney Rigdon, and William W. Phelps.
2 This is the commandment I give them.
3 I have chosen them to take care of the revelations—both the ones I already gave and the ones I will give in the future.
4 At the Last Judgment, they will have to give me a report of how well they took care of the revelations.
5 Their calling is to be in charge of the revelations. They will also be in

charge of the money the church makes from selling copies of the revelations.

6 They should not give away copies of the revelations for free.

7 They can use the money they make from selling copies of the revelations to live off of. But if they make more money than they need, they must give it to the bishop's storehouse.

8 That way the money can be used to help the people of Zion, either now or in the future.

9 This is what everyone who has been made a caretaker needs to do.

10 There is no one in the church who does not need to obey this law.

11 That includes the bishop and the agent who runs the storehouse. It includes anyone else who is made a caretaker of earthly things.

12 Those who are called to take care of spiritual things should be paid for their work, just like those who are called to take care of earthly things.

13 Not only will they be paid, they will also receive gifts of the Spirit.

14 But you should all be equal when it comes to earthly things. You should share with each other freely. If not, you will not receive as many gifts of the Spirit.

15 I have given my servants this commandment for their good. I will bless and reward them for their hard work. I will make sure they always have what they need to live.

16 I will make sure their families have food, clothes, houses, and land. I want to be sure they have these things no matter what else happens to them or where I send them.

17 They have already taken good care of many things. They have sinned in some things. But they have also done well.

18 I will show them mercy. I will bless them with the joy that comes from doing my work. Amen.

SECTION 71

Ezra Booth was one of the elders who had travelled to Missouri. After he returned to Ohio, he became angry and left the church. He wrote things in the newspapers that caused non-members to grow angry with the church. At this time, Joseph Smith and Sidney Rigdon were working on the new translation of the Bible. The Lord gave them a revelation telling them what to do about the trouble Ezra was causing. Section 71 is that revelation.

1 This is what the Lord says to Joseph Smith and Sidney Rigdon: I need you to go preach the gospel. Use the scriptures to teach people about my kingdom. I will give you my Spirit and my power to help you.

2 Preach to the people in the areas round about until I tell you to stop. You need to preach to members and non-members both.

3 That is your mission for a while.

4 Bear your testimonies to the world. Get people ready to receive the revelations I will give in the future.

⁵ This is wise advice. Everyone who reads it should figure out how it relates to them.
⁶ Those who do will be given power.
⁷ Invite your enemies to meet you, both in public and in private. Then prove that the things they have said are wrong. If you are faithful, everyone will see how wrong they are.
⁸ Let them try to argue against the Lord!
⁹ The Lord says—no weapon can destroy you.
¹⁰ If anyone speaks against you, they will be proven wrong in the end.
¹¹ So keep my commandments. I promise they are true. Amen.

SECTION 72

As the Lord has commanded them in Section 71, Joseph Smith and Sidney Rigdon went out preaching. They held a meeting with members of the church in Kirtland. Joseph Smith received two revelations during that meeting. The revelations talked about how to take care of the members' earthly needs. Those revelations are published together as Section 72.

¹ Listen to what the Lord says, high priests of my church: God's kingdom and power are yours.
² You need to choose a bishop for the part of the church here in Ohio.
³ Everyone who becomes a caretaker needs to give a report of what they have done. They will have to do that both in this life and in the next.
⁴ Those who have been wise and faithful caretakers on earth will receive a home in heaven.
⁵ The elders in this area will give their reports to the person I call to be bishop for this area.
⁶ The bishop of this area will make a copy of their reports to send to the bishop in Zion.
⁷ Some of the bishop's duties have already been revealed. The conference will decide what other duties the bishop should have.
⁸ Newel K. Whitney is the one who should be ordained bishop for this area. That is what the Lord wants. Amen.
⁹ These are the duties of the person who serves as bishop for this area. These are in addition to the duties already revealed.
¹⁰ The bishop should run the Lord's storehouse and collect money from the members in this area.
¹¹ The bishop should receive reports from the elders. The bishop should take care of people's needs. If they can, people who get help from the bishop should pay for it.
¹² That way, what they pay back can be used to help other people.
¹³ If someone cannot pay, a record of how much they received should be sent to Zion. The bishop in Zion will pay it back, out of the money all the members have donated.
¹⁴ If people who serve in the church need help, the service they give the church will count as payment for the help they receive.
¹⁵ Remember that my law commands everyone who moves to

Zion to donate all they have to the bishop there.

16 As I said before, every elder in this area should make a report to the bishop of this area.

17 The bishop in this area should send a certificate to the bishop in Zion, saying that the elders are wise caretakers and faithful workers. Then the elders can receive homes in Zion.

18 If the bishop in this part of the church does not send a certificate for a certain elder, that elder cannot be accepted by the bishop in Zion.

19 Whenever an elder gives a report to the bishop, the elder's branch should send along a recommendation. That way the bishop will know that everyone there is pleased with the elder's work.

20 The bishop (or bishops) should give the people who serve as caretakers of church writings the things they need to live.

21 Then they can spend their time publishing the revelations and sending them all over the world. That will be their way of making money to help the church.

22 Then they, too, can be accepted as wise caretakers.

23 What I have said here is an example for all the branches of my church, wherever they are in the world. That is all I have to say for now. Amen.

24 I have a few more words to add to my kingdom's laws. They are about those members of the church who are chosen by the Spirit to move to Zion.

25 The members should take a certificate to the bishop in Zion. The certificate should be written either by three elders or by the bishop of the branch they are moving from.

26 Someone who moves to Zion without a certificate will be judged an unwise caretaker. This, too, is an example for all the branches of the church. Amen.

SECTION 73

Joseph Smith and Sidney Rigdon preached for about a month. They did a lot to solve the problems Ezra Booth had caused (see Section 71). There were only a couple of weeks left before the next general conference. The elders who were preaching in the area wanted to know what they should do until the conference. Section 73 is the Lord's answer.

1 I need the elders to keep working in the areas round about. They should teach the gospel and preach to the members of the church until conference.

2 The conference will decide what they should each do after that.

3 I need Joseph Smith and Sidney Rigdon to translate again.

4 If you can, you should keep preaching in the areas round about until conference. But after that, you need to start working on the translation of the Bible again. Keep working until it is finished.

5 This is what the elders should do until I give them further revelation.

6 That is all I have to say for now. Work hard. Be serious. Amen.

SECTION 74

Joseph Smith and Sidney Rigdon started working on the new translation of the Bible again. When they reached 1 Corinthians 7:14, the Lord gave them a revelation explaining what the verse meant. Section 74 is that revelation.

1 "Those who do not believe are made holy by their spouses who do. If this were not so, your children could not enter my kingdom. But, in fact, your children are holy" [1 Corinthians 7:14].

2 Back in the time of the apostles, the Jews who did not believe in Jesus Christ's gospel circumcised their children.

3 This led people to argue with each other. Husbands who followed the law of Moses wanted their children to be circumcised. They did not understand that the law of Moses did not apply anymore.

4 Children who were circumcised were raised under the law of Moses. They were taught to believe in the old traditions instead of believing in Christ's gospel.

5 That is why the apostle Paul said a church member should not marry a non-member unless the non-member agreed not to follow the law of Moses. (Paul said this on his own. It was not a commandment from the Lord.)

6 That way church members could keep their children from being circumcised. They could put an end to the idea that little children are not holy.

7 The truth is that little children are made holy through Jesus Christ's atonement. That is what this scripture means.

SECTION 75

A general conference was held in Amherst, Ohio. During the conference, Joseph Smith was ordained president of the high priesthood. In other words, he was ordained president of the church. Several elders came to Joseph after the conference to find out what the Lord wanted them to do next. Section 75 is the Lord's answer.

1 I am the Lord Jesus Christ. I am the beginning and the end. I speak to you through the Spirit.

2 Listen, you who have offered to go out teaching my gospel.

3 Do not wait. I want you to set out now. Do not be lazy. Work hard.

4 Preach loudly, for all to hear. Teach the truth as it is found in the revelations I have given you.

5 If you are faithful, you will receive many blessings. I will reward you with honor, glory, and eternal life.

6 I called William E. McLellin to go preach my gospel in the east. But now I take back that calling.

7 I am taking away his calling because he complained in his heart. I will give him a different calling instead.

8 He sinned, but I forgive him. I say to him—go south.

9 My servant Luke Johnson will go with him. Together they will teach what I have commanded them.

10 They will pray for the Spirit. The Spirit will teach them everything they need to know.

11 They should always remember to pray, so they do not become weak. If they do this, I will always be with them.

12 That is what the Lord wants you to do. Amen.

13 Orson Hyde and Samuel H. Smith should travel east to preach the gospel. If they are faithful, I will always be with them.

14 Lyman Johnson and Orson Pratt should also travel east. I will always be with them, too.

15 Asa Dodds and Calves Wilson should travel west. They should teach my gospel, just as I have commanded them.

16 Those who are faithful will overcome all things. They will be with me at the end of the world.

17 Major N. Ashley and Burr Riggs should travel south.

18 All the people I just named should travel where I have told them. They should work their way from house to house, village to village, city to city.

19 When someone accepts you into their house, bless them.

20 When someone rejects you, leave their house quickly. Shake the dirt off your feet. That is a sign that those people will be punished during the Last Judgment.

21 Then cheer up. At the Last Judgment, you yourselves will judge those people.

22 They will be judged harder than people who have never had the chance to learn the gospel. So work hard and faithfully. If you do, nothing will be able to stop you. In the end, I will bring you to heaven. Amen.

23 I speak again to the elders who asked to know what I want them to do.

24 Church members should help take care of missionaries' families.

25 Ask the members of the church to help you find places for your families to live.

26 Those of you who can find places for your families to live must then go wherever I told you, preaching the gospel.

27 If they ask, they will receive what they need. If they knock, doors will be opened for them. The Spirit will tell them where to go.

28 Those who have to stay to take care of their families should do so. If they serve the church at home, they will still be rewarded as if they had served a mission.

29 Everyone needs to work hard. People who are lazy cannot go on being members of my church unless they change their ways.

30 Simeon Carter should serve a mission with Emer Harris.

31 Ezra Thayre should serve with Thomas B. Marsh.

32 Hyrum Smith should serve with Reynolds Cahoon.

33 Daniel Stanton should serve with Seymour Brunson.

34 Sylvester Smith should serve with Gideon Carter.

35 Ruggles Eames should serve with Stephen Burnett.

36 Micah B. Welton should serve with Eden Smith. Amen.

SECTION 76

Joseph Smith and Sidney Rigdon were working on the new translation of the Bible. Some of the verses they read made them start thinking about heaven. Since everyone is not equally righteous, they thought, there must be different rewards in heaven for different groups of people. While they were thinking about this, they had a vision together. Section 76 tells about that vision.

1 Listen and rejoice, people everywhere: The Lord is God. He is the only Savior.

2 His wisdom is great. His works are amazing. He does more than anyone could ever learn about.

3 His plans never fail. When he sets out to do something, no one can stop him.

4 He lives forever. He never changes.

5 The Lord says, "I will show mercy and kindness to those who respect me. I love to reward those who serve me righteously all their lives.

6 "Their reward will be great. Their glory will last forever.

7 "I will teach them everything there is to know about my kingdom—past and future. I will show them the amazing things I am going to do for my kingdom.

8 "They will know the wonders of eternity. I will let them look many years into the future.

9 "They will understand not only earthly things, but also heavenly things. The best education on earth will be like nothing next to what they know.

10 "My Spirit will teach them things no one on earth has ever seen or heard—things no one has even imagined yet."

11 On February 16, 1832, we, Joseph Smith and Sidney Rigdon, felt the Spirit come over us.

12 The Spirit's power made it possible for us to see and understand God's works.

13 We saw the works God did even before the earth was created. All these works were carried out by God's Son. The Son was with the Father from the very beginning.

14 We bear testimony of God's Son. He is Jesus Christ. We saw him and talked with him during our vision.

15 While we were working on the new translation of the Bible, we came to John 5:29.

16 The verse talks about the time when Christ will raise everyone from the dead.

17 The Spirit told us to translate the verse like this: "Those who have done good will be brought back during the raising up of the righteous. Those who have done evil will be brought back during the raising up of the wicked."

18 This translation made us wonder.

19 We were thinking about what it said, when the Lord gave us a vision. We saw the Lord's glory shining around us.

20 We saw the Son sitting at the Father's right hand. His glory filled us.

21 We saw the angels and everyone who has been made holy standing in front of God's throne. They were worshipping God and Christ. They worship Christ forever.

22 Many people have testified

about him. Now, last of all, we add our testimony. He lives!

23 We saw him at God's right hand. We heard a voice testify that he is the Father's only Son.

24 He created—and is still creating—all the planets. The people on those planets are born again through him.

25 We saw that one of God's angels, who was a leader in heaven, refused to follow the Son. That angel was thrown out of heaven, away from God and his Son.

26 That angel was called Perdition. The angels in heaven cried to see him thrown out. His name was Lucifer—the bright morning star.

27 We saw him fall! The bright morning star has fallen!

28 The Lord commanded us to write down what we saw in this vision while we were still overcome by the Spirit. We saw Satan. He was the one who tempted Adam and Eve. He fought against God. He tried to take over God's kingdom.

29 That is why he fights against the members of God's church.

30 Some members are overcome by Satan. We saw a vision of their suffering.

31 We heard the Lord say to us: "Some people are allowed to know the truth perfectly. They are allowed to share my power. But then some of them give in to Satan. They say that the gospel is false, even though they know it is true. They refuse to follow me, even though they know my power first-hand.

32 "These are the children of perdition. These are the people I say would be better off having never been born.

33 "They must suffer forever with the devil and his angels.

34 "These are the people I have said can never be forgiven. They cannot be forgiven in this life or in the next.

35 "That is because they have rejected the testimony that God's Spirit gave them. They have rejected God's Son. It is as if they themselves nailed him to the cross and made fun of him.

36 "These are the people who will be sent away with the devil and his angels.

37 "These are the only people who cannot be with God.

38 "They are the only people who will not be freed in the end from suffering for their sins.

39 "Everyone else will be freed from suffering when they are brought back from the dead. That is what Christ died for. That is his glory."

40 This is the testimony that the voice from heaven gave us.

41 It testified that Jesus came to earth to die on the cross for everyone's sins. He died to make the world holy and to put an end to wickedness.

42 Because of him, everyone the Father has given him can be saved.

43 He will bring the Father glory, by saving everyone he created except the children of perdition. The Son cannot save the children of perdition. That is because they reject him even after the Father has shown him to them.

44 Because the Son cannot save them, they will have to go away to be punished. The only kingdom they will be allowed to rule will be the devil's kingdom. They will suffer with the devil and his angels.

45 No one knows how long they will suffer. No one knows where they will suffer. No one knows how badly they will suffer.

46 The only ones who will ever know it are those who have to suffer it.

47 The Lord says, "I let many people see this suffering in visions. But I only let them see it for a moment.

48 "So no one truly understands what the children of perdition have to suffer, except the children of perdition themselves."

49 Then we heard the voice say, "This is the end of your vision of the suffering of the wicked. Write down what you have seen."

50 Then we had a vision of the people who will come back from the dead during the raising up of the righteous. This is what we learned about them.

51 These are the people who had faith in Jesus. They were baptized in his name under the water, as a symbol of his being buried. That is how Jesus himself commanded they should be baptized.

52 They were baptized this way so they could have all their sins taken away, if they kept the commandments. They could receive the Holy Ghost, by the laying on of hands, from someone who has been ordained to do this.

53 These are the people who overcome through faith. Because they are faithful, the Father sends his Spirit to promise them eternal life.

54 These are the members of Jesus Christ's church.

55 The Father has given these people everything.

56 They have the priesthood. They have the power to rule in heaven. They are filled with the Father's glory.

57 They have the same priesthood Melchizedek and Enoch had. It is the priesthood of God's Son.

58 That is why the scriptures say they are gods—in other words, the children of God.

59 They have power over everything. They have power over life and death, past and future. All these things are theirs. They are Christ's, and Christ is God's.

60 They will overcome all things.

61 But no one should brag about themselves. They should praise God, because it is he who overcomes all enemies.

62 These are the people who will live with God and Christ forever.

63 These are the people Christ will bring with him when he comes down through the clouds to rule on earth.

64 These are the first people who will come back from the dead.

65 They will come back from the dead during the raising up of the righteous.

66 These are the people who come to Mount Zion, and to God's heavenly city, the holiest place of all.

67 These are the people who come to join the angels. They join the people of Enoch and Jesus Christ's church in heaven.

68 These are the people whose names are written down in heaven.

69 They are good people who have been made perfect by Jesus. He makes them perfect through his atonement, by sacrificing his own blood.

70 These people have celestial bod-

ies. They have the brightest glory of all. They have God's glory, which is like the sun.

71 Then we saw the people who live in the terrestrial kingdom. Their glory is different from the glory of people in the celestial kingdom, the same way the moon's light is different from the sun's.

72 These are the people who died without knowing God's law.

73 Also, they are the people Jesus visited in the spirit prison. He taught them the gospel in the spirit prison. That way they could be judged as if they had heard the gospel while they were alive.

74 They did not accept Jesus' teachings while they were alive. But they did accept them after they died.

75 They were good people. But they failed to see the truth, because others tricked them.

76 They can only receive some of God's glory.

77 They can be with the Son, but not with the Father.

78 That is why they have terrestrial, not celestial, bodies. That is why their glory is like the moon, not the sun.

79 These are people who were not true to their testimonies of Jesus. Because of that, they cannot rule in God's kingdom.

80 This is the end of our vision of the terrestrial kingdom. The Lord told us to write down what we saw while were still overcome by the Spirit.

81 Then we saw the telestial kingdom. The people there have less glory than people in the terrestrial kingdom, just like the stars shine less brightly than the moon.

82 These people did not accept Christ's gospel. They did not receive a testimony of Jesus.

83 But they did not reject the Holy Ghost, like the children of perdition did.

84 These are the people who are in hell after they die.

85 They will have to stay in the devil's power until Christ has finished his work. They are the last people who will come back from the dead.

86 People in the telestial kingdom cannot be filled with Christ's glory. But people from the terrestrial kingdom can visit them to give them the Spirit.

87 People who are in the terrestrial kingdom will be visited by people from the celestial kingdom.

88 People in the telestial kingdom will also be visited by angels. The angels will teach them and serve them. That is because even people in the telestial kingdom are saved.

89 In our vision, we saw that the telestial kingdom is more glorious than anyone can understand.

90 The only way someone could understand how glorious it is, is if God revealed it to them.

91 The terrestrial kingdom is even more glorious than the telestial kingdom.

92 The celestial kingdom is the most glorious of all. That is where God the Father rules forever on his throne.

93 All things bow down before him. They praise him forever.

94 The people who live with him make up Jesus Christ's heavenly church. They are filled with God's grace. They see everything that

God sees. They know everything that God knows.

95 God makes them equal in power and authority.

96 The people in the celestial kingdom all have the same glory, just like every part of the sun has the same brightness.

97 The people in the terrestrial kingdom all have the same glory, just like every part of the moon has the same brightness.

98 The people in the telestial kingdom have glory in the same way as the stars. Some stars are brighter than others. In the same way, some people in the telestial kingdom have more glory than others.

99 That is because people in the telestial kingdom followed different leaders. Some followed Paul, some followed Apollos, some followed Cephas.

100 Some said they were followers of Christ. Others said they were followers of John, or Moses, or Elias, or Esaias, or Isaiah, or Enoch.

101 But none of them accepted the restored gospel or the prophets' teachings. They did not accept the full truth about Jesus.

102 These people will not be brought back from the dead at the same time as the righeous. They will not be lifted into the air to meet Jesus Christ in the cloud during the Second Coming.

103 These people loved to lie. They practiced black magic. They committed adultery and sex sin.

104 While they are alive, they suffer because of their sins.

105 After they have died, they suffer in hell.

106 They will have to suffer until the end of time. Then Christ will overthrow the last of his enemies and finish his work.

107 When his kingdom is pure, he will turn it over to the Father. He will say, "I have won. I have overthrown all the enemies of God's people."

108 Then he will be given a glorious crown and a throne. He will rule in heaven forever.

109 In the telestial kingdom, we saw as many people as there are stars in the sky or grains of sand on the beach—too many to count.

110 We heard the Lord's voice say, "All these people will kneel and confess their sins to God.

111 "They will be judged for everything they have done. Everyone will be given a place in one of the kingdoms God has prepared. What place they are given will be based on what they did while they were alive on earth.

112 "These people will be God's servants. But they will never be able to come to the place where God and Christ live."

113 This is the end of our vision. We were commanded to write down the things we saw while we were still overcome by the Spirit.

114 But some of the things the Lord showed us are too glorious to understand.

115 He commanded us not to write those things down, not even while we were overcome by the Spirit. No one is allowed to talk about those things.

116 Even if people were allowed to talk about them, they would be impossible to explain. They can be seen and understood only through

the Spirit's power. God gives his Spirit to everyone who loves him and repents of all their sins.

117 People who do that will be able to see and know these things for themselves.

118 They will receive the Spirit's power while they are alive on earth, so they can stand to live with God after they are raised from the dead.

119 Glory, honor, and power be to God and Christ forever. Amen.

SECTION 77

The Book of Revelation has always been a hard part of the Bible for people to understand. That is because it uses so many symbols. While Joseph Smith and Sidney Rigdon were working on the new translation of the Bible, the Lord gave them answers to some questions about the symbols in Revelation. Those questions and answers are published in Section 77.

1 *What is the glass sea mentioned in Revelation 4:6?* The glass sea is the earth, the way it will look after it has been made holy and eternal.

2 *The same verse mentions four beasts. What do they mean?* They are symbols used by John the Revelator to describe heaven. Heaven is not just for people. Animals will be there, too. That is because animals have spirits, just like people do. An animal's spirit looks like the animal's body, just like a person's spirit looks like the person's body.

3 *Are the beasts John saw real animals? Or were they symbols standing for different kinds of animals?* The animals John saw were real animals. But they were chosen to stand for the glory which different kinds of animals will enjoy in the next life. God will put each animal in a place where it will be happy forever.

4 *John says that the beasts had eyes and wings. What does that mean?* The eyes are symbols to show how much the animals know. The wings are symbols to show that the animals have power to move and act.

5 *John talks about 24 elders. What do they mean?* They were elders who belonged to the seven branches of the church in New Testament times. After serving faithfully in the Lord's work, they died and went to heaven. That is where John saw them.

6 *John talks about a book with seven locks on it. What does that mean?* All of God's plans for the earth are written in that book. Some of those plans he has revealed. Some are still secret. God plans for the earth to last 7000 years.

7 *What do the seven locks on the book mean?* The first lock opens up the part of the book which talks about the first 1000 years of the earth's history. The second lock opens up the part which talks about the second 1000 years, and so on.

8 *What do the four angels in Revelation 7:1 mean?* God gives these angels power to save or destroy life in the four parts of the earth. The angels are in charge of revealing the restored gospel to all the peoples of the world. The angels have the

power to shut heaven. They can promise people eternal life, or they can punish people for their sins.

9 *Revelation 7:2 talks about an angel coming up from the east. What does that mean?* The angel coming up from the east is supposed to mark the twelve tribes of Israel as God's people. That is why he shouts to the four angels: "Do not destroy the earth until we have marked God's servants." The angel from the east is Elias. Elias is the one who will come to gather the tribes together and restore all things.

10 *When will the things talked about in this chapter happen?* They will happen when the sixth lock is opened. In other words, they will happen during the sixth 1000-year period of the earth's history.

11 *What does it mean when the angel marks 144,000 Israelites—12,000 from each tribe?* The people who are marked are high priests. They come from every country, every race, and every language. The angel who has power over all the countries of the world sends the high priests to teach the gospel. That way everyone has the chance to join Jesus Christ's church.

12 *Revelation 8 talks about seven trumpets being blown. What does that mean?* God created the world in six days. On the seventh day, he finished his work, made it holy, and created human beings. In the same way, during the seventh 1000-year period of the earth's history, God will make the earth holy and finish saving people. He will judge and save everything he has power over. The seven angels blow their trumpets to prepare for the Second Coming. That is when God's work will end.

13 *When will the things written in Revelation 9 happen?* They will happen during the seventh 1000-year period of the earth's history, but before the Second Coming.

14 *In Revelation 10, John eats a little book. What does that mean?* It is a symbol to show that John has a special mission. His mission is to gather the tribes of Israel. John is Elias, the one the scriptures say will restore all things.

15 *Revelation 11 tells about two witnesses. Who are they?* They are two prophets who will be sent to the Jews just before the end of the world, when everything is being restored. These prophets will teach the Jews after they have been gathered and rebuilt Jerusalem.

SECTION 78

In Section 42, the Lord commanded the members to donate all their property to the church. He told them to start a storehouse to help the poor. But a year went by, and the members still had not done this. Finally, the Lord gave Joseph Smith a revelation. The revelation told the members in Ohio why it was so important to start the storehouse. Section 78 is that revelation.

¹ These are the words the Lord gave Joseph Smith for the priesthood holders who had met together.

² Listen to the advice of God, the one who ordained you. I will teach you things that will lead to your being saved.

³ The time has come for my people to be organized. You need to start the storehouse for the poor. You need to set up rules to keep the storehouse running smoothly.

⁴ The storehouse is not just something for here and now. It will be part of my church forever. It will help the church carry out its mission. That mission is to help save Heavenly Father's children. You have accepted that mission.

⁵ The storehouse will make you equal in earthly things. Then you can become equal in receiving heavenly things too.

⁶ Unless you are equal in earthly things, you cannot be equal in receiving heavenly things.

⁷ If you want to live in the celestial kingdom, you must prepare yourselves. You must do what I have commanded you.

⁸ It is very important that you who belong to my United Order do only what will lead people to praise me.

⁹ Newel K. Whitney, Joseph Smith, and Sidney Rigdon need to meet with the members of the church in Zion.

¹⁰ Satan is trying to turn the members in Zion against the truth. He is trying to keep them from understanding what is being prepared for them.

¹¹ That is why I command you to organize yourselves. Join together in a holy promise that cannot be broken.

¹² People who break this promise will lose their places in the church. Satan will have power over them until the day they come back from the dead.

¹³ I am telling you to do this so you will be prepared to carry out my work.

¹⁴ This is my plan for keeping the church strong and free, no matter how difficult things get. If you do what I have told you, the church will not have to depend on anyone. It will rise above everything else on earth.

¹⁵ Then you will be able to come up into the celestial kingdom. You will be made rulers over many kingdoms. The Lord promises this. He is the Holy One of Zion. He is the same God who founded Adam-ondi-Ahman.

¹⁶ He made Michael your prince and exalted him. He placed Michael in charge of the plan of salvation. Jesus Christ tells Michael how to carry out the plan.

¹⁷ You are still little children. You have still not understood what great blessings the Father has prepared for you.

¹⁸ There are many things you are still not ready for. But cheer up, because I will lead you. The kingdom and its blessings are yours. The riches of eternity are yours.

¹⁹ Those who give thanks for everything they receive will be filled with glory. They will be given the riches of the earth. They will have much, much more than what they have now.

²⁰ So do what I have commanded

you. The Son Ahman says this—the Savior. When he has gotten everything ready, he will bring you to him.

21 You are Jesus Christ's church. He will lift you up to meet him in a cloud when he comes again to give everyone their reward.

22 Those who are wise and faithful caretakers will be given everything there is. Amen.

SECTION 79

In Section 52, the Lord commanded that Jared Carter be ordained a priest. Several months later, the Lord gave Joseph Smith another revelation. This new revelation called Jared to serve a mission. Section 79 is that revelation.

1 I want Jared Carter to go back east. He should travel from place to place, and from city to city. He should teach the good news of the gospel. His ordination gives him the power to do this.

2 I will send the Spirit to teach him what is true. The Spirit will show him which way he should go.

3 If he is faithful, I will give him many more blessings.

4 Be happy, Jared Carter. Do not be afraid. Your Lord, Jesus Christ, says this. Amen.

SECTION 80

In Section 75, the Lord called Stephen Burnett to serve a mission with Ruggles Eames. Two months later, Stephen was called to serve another mission. Section 80 is a revelation telling Stephen how to get ready for his new mission.

1 This is what the Lord says to Stephen Burnett: Go out into the world. Share the gospel with everyone you meet.

2 Since you want a companion, I will call Eden Smith to go with you.

3 So go preach my gospel. It does not matter where you go—north, south, east, or west. You cannot go wrong.

4 Teach the things you have heard and believed. Teach the things you know are true.

5 This is what your Savior, Jesus Christ, wants you to do. Amen.

SECTION 81

At first, after the church was restored, there was no First Presidency like there is today. Joseph Smith served as church president. But he did not have counselors. Later, the Lord called Sidney Rigdon and Frederick G. Williams to be Joseph's counselors. Section 81 is the revelation in which Frederick was given his calling.

¹ This is what the Lord says to Frederick G. Williams: Listen! I call you to be a high priest in my church. I want you to serve as Joseph Smith's counselor.
² I have made Joseph Smith president of the high priesthood. That means he is in charge of my whole kingdom.
³ I will bless Joseph Smith. I will bless you, too, if you faithfully serve as his counselor. Always remember to pray. Pray in public as well as in private. Your calling includes teaching the gospel to church members and to the world.
⁴ This is the best way you can serve others. You will be helping bring glory to the Lord.
⁵ Faithfully carry out your calling. Help those who are weak. Lift them up. Make them strong again.
⁶ If you endure to the end, you will receive eternal life in the place where my Father lives.
⁷ Jesus Christ says this. He is the beginning and the end. Amen.

SECTION 82

In Section 78, the Lord commanded the members of the church to start a storehouse for the poor. Since the city of Zion was being built in Missouri, Joseph Smith travelled there to start the storehouse. Section 82 is a revelation telling church leaders how to start the storehouse.

¹ This is what the Lord says: Because you have forgiven each other, I have forgiven you.
² You have all sinned, though. Some of you have sinned very much. Be careful from now on. Do not sin anymore, or you will suffer.
³ Those who receive more are expected to do more. Those who have been given greater revelations will be given a greater punishment if they sin.
⁴ When you ask for revelations, I give them to you. If you do not do what the revelations tell you, that is a sin. Then my law says you must be punished.
⁵ What I say to one, I say to all: Watch out! The devil's kingdom is growing. Darkness rules the earth.
⁶ The people of the world will have to be punished. None of them do what is right. They have all wandered away from my teachings.
⁷ But I will treat you as if you had never sinned. Go on with your lives. Do not sin anymore. If someone sins again, the old sins will return.
⁸ I give you a new commandment. I do this so you will understand what I want you to do.
⁹ In other words, I am telling you how I want you to act, so you can be saved.
¹⁰ When you do what I say, I have to bless you. But unless you do what I say, you have no promise.
¹¹ Edward Partridge, Newel K. Whitney, A. Sidney Gilbert, Sidney Rigdon, Joseph Smith, John Whitmer, Oliver Cowdery, W. W. Phelps, and Martin Harris need to be joined together by a holy promise. If they break this promise, they will be

punished. They need to bring together everything they have been made caretakers over.

12 They need to do this so they can take care of the poor and do everything else the bishops are called to do.

13 I am going to make Kirtland a stake of Zion. I am doing it for the good of the members of God's church.

14 Zion needs to become more beautiful and more holy. It needs to spread out and become stronger, like a tent does when stakes are added to it. Zion must stand up and put on her beautiful clothes, like the scriptures say.

15 That is why I command you to join yourselves together with this holy promise. That promise must be made in keeping with the Lord's laws.

16 I give you this advice for your good.

17 Be equal. In other words, you must all have an equal right to use each other's property. That way you can take care of everything you have been put in charge of. Everyone will have the things they need. They will also have the things they want, if those things are fair.

18 This will help God's church, because everyone will be able to improve the things they have been given to take care of. I want them to earn more money—100 times more, if they can. They will donate what they earn to the Lord's storehouse. Then everyone in the church can use it.

19 This way, everyone will work to meet the needs of those around them. God's glory should be their only goal.

20 The United Order you form will last forever, if you do not sin. After you are gone, other people will take your places in the order.

21 If someone refuses to keep this holy promise, do with them what the laws of the church command. Satan will have power over them until they come back from the dead.

22 You would be wise to make friends among the wicked. That way they will not destroy you.

23 Let me be the one to judge them. I will give them whatever they have earned. Be at peace. My blessings are still with you.

24 The kingdom is still yours. If you stay faithful, it will be yours forever. Amen.

SECTION 83

When members started to donate their property to the church, the way the Lord had commanded, only men were made caretakers over church property. This meant that women without husbands had no way of earning the things they needed to live. Neither did children without fathers. Section 83 is a revelation explaining how to deal with this problem.

1 This is what the Lord says about women and children who are members of the church and whose husbands or fathers have died. This

is as an addition to the laws of the church.

2 Women have the right to expect their husbands to take care of them as long as their husbands are alive. If their husbands die, then the church should take care of them, as long as they are faithful members.

3 If a woman is not a faithful member of the church, she cannot expect the church to take care of her. But she can keep the land her husband was given, in keeping with the laws of your country.

4 All children have the right to be taken care of by their parents until they become adults.

5 After that, if their parents do not have land to pass down to them, they can get help from the Lord's storehouse.

6 Church members will donate whatever they do not need to the storehouse. That way it can be used to help the poor, and people who do not have someone to take care of them. Amen.

SECTION 84

Many of the elders who had been sent on missions began to return. They told Joseph Smith about the work they had been done. It was a joyful time. The elders told Joseph they wanted to know more about Zion and the priesthood. Joseph and six elders prayed together for the Lord to teach them. Section 84 is the Lord's answer.

1 This is a revelation which Jesus Christ gave to Joseph Smith and six elders while they were praying together.

2 It contains directions from the Lord for his church. He restored his church so he could bring his people back to their proper place, like he promised he would through the prophets. He wants to gather the members of his church in Zion, the New Jerusalem.

3 The New Jerusalem will be built in Missouri. The Lord himself chose the place where it would be built. That place was dedicated by Joseph Smith and some others who had pleased the Lord.

4 The members of the church will gather together to build the New Jerusalem. They will start gathering at the place where the temple is going to be built. That temple will be built by the people of today.

5 Before all the people of today have died, the Lord's house will be built. A cloud will settle down on the house and fill it. That cloud will be the Lord's glory.

6 Moses' descendants will be filled with the Lord's glory there in the temple. Moses' descendants are those who have received the same priesthood Moses did. Moses received the priesthood from his wife's father, Jethro.

7 Jethro received it from Caleb.

8 Caleb received it from Elihu.

9 Elihu received it from Jeremy.

10 Jeremy received it from Gad.

11 Gad received it from Esaias.

12 Esaias received it from God.

13 Esaias lived at the same time as Abraham. Abraham blessed him.

14 Abraham received the priesthood from Melchizedek. Melchizedek received it as part of a line running through his ancestors, all the way back to Noah.

15 From Noah, the line runs back to Enoch.

16 From Enoch, it runs back to Abel. Abel received the priesthood from his father Adam. Adam was the first man on earth.

17 The priesthood is always found in God's church. The priesthood has always existed and always will exist.

18 The Lord gave another priesthood to Aaron and his descendants. This priesthood also exists forever, alongside the Melchizedek priesthood.

19 The Melchizedek priesthood brings people the gospel. It has the power to teach people about God's kingdom. It helps them come to know God.

20 God shows his power through the ordinances of this priesthood.

21 Without those ordinances, or this priesthood's authority, God's power could not be shown to people living on earth.

22 Without those ordinances, no one can stand to be face-to-face with God the Father.

23 Moses taught all this to the Israelites while they were in the desert. He tried hard to make his people holy, so they could see God face-to-face.

24 But they would not listen. They could not stand to be near God. Because of this, the Lord could not fill them with his glory while they were in the desert.

25 He had to take Moses and the Melchizidek priesthood away from them.

26 They were left with only the Aaronic priesthood. The Aaronic priesthood gives people the power to receive visits from angels. It prepares people to receive the full gospel.

27 The Aaronic priesthood teaches people about repentance, baptism, and the forgiveness of sins. In Bible times, it included the law of Moses. That law stayed with the Israelites until God sent John the Baptist. John the Baptist was given the Holy Ghost even before he was born, while he was still inside his mother.

28 He was baptized while he was still a child. When he was eight days old, an angel ordained him to overthrow the Jews' kingdom and to prepare people for Jesus' coming.

29 The offices of elder and bishop are necessary parts of the Melchizidek priesthood, in addition to the office of high priest.

30 The offices of teacher and deacon are necessary parts of the Aaronic priesthood, in addition to the office of priest.

31 Both Melchizedek and Aaronic priesthood holders will serve in the temple that will be built in Zion.

32 In the temple, they will be filled with the Lord's glory. I have given you these priesthoods. I have given them to many others who have been called to build up my church in all the world.

33 Everyone who receives these two priesthoods, and then faithfully carries out their calling, will be made holy by the Spirit. Their bodies will be made like new.

34 They will become descendants of Moses, Aaron, and Abraham. They will be chosen members of God's church and kingdom.
35 Whoever accepts the priesthood accepts me.
36 Whoever accepts my servants accepts me.
37 Whoever accepts me accepts my Father.
38 Whoever accepts my Father accepts my Father's kingdom. They will be given everything my Father has.
39 That is the holy promise which comes with the priesthood.
40 My Father makes this holy promise with everyone who receives the priesthood. He cannot break or change it.
41 But people who receive the priesthood and then completely reject their side of the promise can never be forgiven of their sins. They cannot be forgiven in this life or in the next.
42 People must accept the priesthood if they want to receive all my blessings. I testify that I have given the priesthood to all of you here today. I have commanded my angels to watch over you.
43 Watch out for yourselves. Pay careful attention to my words. They will bring you eternal life.
44 You should live in keeping with all of God's words.
45 The Lord's words are true. Whatever is true is light. Whatever is light comes from the Spirit of Christ.
46 The Spirit gives light to everyone who is born. It teaches everyone in the world who is willing to listen.
47 Everyone who listens to the Spirit is led to God the Father.
48 When people come to the Father, he teaches them about the same holy promise which he has given to you. He has not given it to you for your own good only. He has given it for the good of everyone in the world.
49 Everyone in the world suffers because they are trapped in sin and darkness.
50 You can tell they are trapped in sin because they do not come to me.
51 Whoever does not come to me is trapped in sin.
52 Someone who does not accept my words does not know my voice. That person is not one of mine.
53 That is how you can tell the righteous from the wicked. It is how you can tell that the whole world is suffering in sin and darkness even now.
54 You, too, used to suffer in darkness. You did not know or understand God's truth, because you did not have faith. You did not take seriously the things you were given.
55 The whole church is guilty of this.
56 Every one of the people of Zion is guilty—all of them.
57 They must all repent. They must remember the new promise I made with the world. That promise is found in the Book of Mormon and the other revelations I gave them. It is not enough to talk about the revelations. They must do what the revelations say.
58 Then they will do works worthy of the Father's kingdom. But if they do not repent, they will suffer a terrible punishment.
59 I will not let the members of my

kingdom make my chosen land unholy.

60 Those of you who have heard these words will be blessed if you do them.

61 I will forgive your sins. But I also command you to stay faithful and serious. Remember to pray always. Testify to the world about the revelations you have been given.

62 Go out to every part of the earth. Wherever you cannot go yourselves, send someone else to go for you. That way your testimony can reach every person on earth.

63 I tell you the same thing I told my apostles, because you are my apostles. You are God's high priests. You are the ones my Father has allowed me to save. You are my friends.

64 So I tell you what I told my apostles: Everyone who believes what you teach them and is baptized in water to have their sins forgiven will receive the Holy Ghost.

65 Those who who have faith will be able to do miracles.

66 They will do many amazing works in my name.

67 They will throw devils out of people in my name.

68 They will heal the sick in my name.

69 They will heal people who cannot see or hear in my name.

70 They will heal people who cannot speak.

71 If someone tries to poison them, the poison will not hurt them.

72 Poisonous snakes will not be able to hurt them.

73 But I command them not to brag because they can do these things. They should not even tell people they can do these things. These miracles are a private gift to you, for your own good.

74 People who reject what you teach them and refuse to be baptized in my name, or to receive the Holy Ghost, will not be able to live in my Father's kingdom.

75 This revelation I have given you holds true for everyone in the world. The gospel must be taught to everyone who has not accepted it.

76 But you must tell the members of my kingdom that they, too, need to repent. They have not had enough faith. Also, the members in Zion need to repent for not doing what you taught them when I sent you to visit them.

77 I am giving you this commandment so you can be like the friends I had when I was on earth. My friends travelled with me preaching the gospel. So from now on, I will call you my friends.

78 When I was on earth, I did not let my friends take money or a wallet. I did not even let them take an extra coat.

79 I am sending you out to put the world to the test. I will reward you for the work you do.

80 No one who faithfully preaches my gospel will become tired in mind or body. I will watch over them always. I will not let them go hungry or thirsty.

81 So do not worry about what you will eat, drink, or wear.

82 Think how flowers grow. They do not work to provide for themselves. Yet they grow to be the most beautiful things in the world.

83 Your Heavenly Father knows what your needs are.

84 So worry about your needs one day at a time.

85 Do not plan what to say ahead of time, either. Keep studying the scriptures. always think about what they mean to you. If you do that, the Spirit will tell you what each person needs to hear the moment you go to speak.

86 From now on, no one who goes out to preach my gospel should take money with them. This commandment is for every member of the church who is called to do God's work.

87 I am sending you to correct the people of the world for their sins. I am sending you to teach them about the Last Judgment.

88 Whoever lets you in to teach them will also be letting me in. That is because I will travel with you. I will be in front of you and on both sides of you. My Spirit will be in your hearts. My angels will be all around you, to lift you up.

89 Whoever accepts you accepts me. They will give you the food, clothes, and money you need.

90 Whoever gives you food, clothes, or money will be rewarded by God.

91 Someone who refuses to give you the things you need is not one of my followers. That is how you can know who my true followers are.

92 When someone rejects you, leave them and go off by yourselves. Wash your feet in clean water. Do this no matter how cold it is. It will show your Heavenly Father that those people did not accept you. Do not visit them again.

93 Do this in every village or city you go to.

94 Do everything you can to find people who will listen to you. But if a family, or a village, or a city rejects you or your message, they will be punished.

95 I repeat—if they reject you, they will be punished.

96 The time has come when the wicked will suffer for the things they have done.

97 The earth will be filled with disease and destruction until I have finished my work. I will finish it quickly, in order to save the righteous.

98 Then the righteous will know me fully—every one of them. They will come together to sing a new song:

99 *The Lord has set his people free,*
And Zion is restored at last,
In keeping with the promises
God made to Israel in the past.

100 *The Lord brought Zion down from heaven,*
And Satan knew the end had come.
The Lord took Zion to himself
And gathered all things into one.

101 *This earth has suffered many things,*
But now it shines with heavenly light,
For God himself has come to earth
To rule the world with truth and right.

102 *Our God is full of truth and peace.*
Our God is just, yet full of love.
All praise and honor be to God
Forever, here and up above. Amen.

103 Missionaries who have families should send any money they are given back home. Or, depending on what the Lord tells them to do, they could use the money for their families' good without sending them the money itself.

104 Missionaries who do not have families should send any money

they are given either to the bishop in Zion or to the bishop in Ohio. That way the money can be used to publish the revelations and to build Zion.

105 If anyone gives you a coat or suit, give your old one to the poor. Then go on your way with joy.

106 Those of you who are strong in the Spirit should be paired up with those who are weaker. Build them up, so they can become strong, too.

107 This means you should take Aaronic priesthood holders with you on your missions. Send them ahead to set up times for meeting with people. Let them take charge of getting everything ready. Let them meet with people you do not have time to see yourselves.

108 That is how my apostles of long ago built up my church.

109 Everyone should serve in their own calling. Do not think that your calling is more important than someone else's. The church is like a body. The head cannot say that it does not need the feet. Without the feet, the body could not stand.

110 The church needs all its members, just like the body needs all its parts. Working together, the members build each other up and keep the church running perfectly.

111 Only high priests, elders, and priests should travel. Deacons and teachers should stay at home to take care of the members of the church.

112 Bishop Newel K. Whitney should visit the different branches of the church, so he can find out what the poor need. He should remind the rich that they need to share what they have with the poor.

113 Bishop Whitney should hire an agent to take charge of his business. Then he will be able to spend all his time doing my work.

114 He should go to New York, Albany, and Boston. He should teach the gospel to the people in those cities. He should warn them that they will be completely destroyed if they reject the gospel.

115 If they reject the gospel, it will not be long before their houses are left empty.

116 If Bishop Whitney trusts me, he will not be put to shame. I will watch over him always.

117 The rest of my servants should go out preaching, if they can. They should go to all the larger cities and towns. Warn the people in those places to repent of their sins. Explain to them clearly that sinners will be destroyed at the end of the world.

118 I am the Lord. I have all power. I tell you that I will tear down the kingdoms of the wicked. I will shake the earth and sky.

119 I am ready to use all the powers of heaven. Soon you will see me coming to rule with my people. Then you will know for certain that I exist.

120 I am Jesus Christ. I am the beginning and the end. Amen.

SECTION 85

Bishop Edward Partridge was supposed to give the members in Zion land to live on. But he was not doing this the way the Lord had commanded him to. William Phelps was one of the members in Zion. He wrote a letter telling Joseph Smith what was happening. Joseph wrote a letter back. Part of that letter was a revelation from the Lord. Section 85 is taken from Joseph's letter.

1 The person serving as church clerk should keep a record of everything that happens in Zion. The clerk should make a list of everyone who donates their property to the church and receives land from the bishop.

2 The record should describe the members' faith and how they live. It should list the names of people who leave the church after the bishop gives them land.

3 God has given a law telling how church members should be given land. God gave that law so he could keep his storehouse full. He gave it so he could prepare church members for the time when the wicked will be destroyed. Those who do not receive their land the way God's law says should not be listed with God's people.

4 Their family history should not be kept anywhere in the records of the church.

5 No one in their family should have their names written in the book of God's law. The Lord himself says this.

6 I feel the still small voice speaking to me. It is only a whisper, but it has the power to pass through anything. Sometimes when it speaks to me, it makes my bones shake. This is what it says to me.

7 "I will send someone mighty and strong to put God's house back in order. He will be filled with God's power. He will be filled with truth, so he can speak the words of God. The Lord will tell him how to give land to church members. He will give land only to those whose names are listed in the book of God's law, along with the names of their families.

8 "Edward Partridge was called by God. But then he tried to do God's work his own way. If he does not repent, he will be like Uzzah, who fell down dead when he tried to hold up the ark of the covenant.

9 "Those whose names are not listed in the book will not be given land to live on with the rest of the members of the church. They will have to live with those who did not accept the gospel. They will be unhappy. They will suffer."

10 I am not saying these things myself. It is the Lord who says this. He will do what he says.

11 People whose names are not written in the book of God's law, or who have left the church, cannot be given a place to live among God's people. It does not matter if that person is a Melchizidek priesthood holder, an Aaronic priesthood holder, or any other member of the church.

12 This is in keeping with what it says in Ezra 2:61-62.

SECTION 86

Joseph Smith was working on the new translation of the Bible. He came to Matthew 13:24-30, which is a story Jesus told. The story talks about a field full of wheat and weeds growing together. Joseph Smith received a revelation explaining what the story means. Section 86 is that revelation.

1 This is what the Lord says about the story of the wheat and the weeds.

2 The field in the story stands for the world. The workers who planted the wheat stand for the apostles.

3 The enemy who plants weeds in the field after the workers fall asleep is Satan. In other words, after the apostles died, Satan and the church's enemies made things so bad that the church was taken off the earth.

4 The time when the wheat is just starting to grow is now. In other words, now is the time when the Lord is restoring the gospel.

5 The workers who want to harvest the field stand for angels. The angels are waiting to come down and put an end to evil. Day and night, they beg the Lord to send them to work.

6 But the Lord tells them, "Do not tear out the weeds while the wheat is still young. If you did, you might kill the wheat, too." (This means that your faith is still weak.)

7 "Let the wheat and the weeds grow together until the wheat is ready to be harvested. Then gather the wheat first. After that, tie the weeds up in bunches and burn the field."

8 This is what the Lord says to you who have the right to hold the priesthood because it was passed down through your ancestors.

9 You are descendants of the families to whom the priesthood was promised long ago. God has hidden you from the world with Christ.

10 That is why there are still people on earth with the right to hold the priesthood. You will keep passing it on to your descendants until everything the prophets wrote about has been restored.

11 If you keep following my good example, you will be blessed. You will use the priesthood to teach everyone on earth. You will use it to save my people. The Lord says this. Amen.

SECTION 87

1832 was a frightening year. Many people all over the world were dying of disease. The people of South Carolina tried to break away from the United States, and the president sent an army to stop them. (About 30 years later, the Civil War started for the same reason.) Many church members felt that these problems meant the world was about to end. Joseph Smith worried about these problems, too. On Christmas Day, 1832, he received the revelation that is now Section 87.

1 This is what the Lord says about the wars which are going to happen soon. They will start when South Carolina breaks away from the United States. They will end only after many people have died and suffered.

2 Someday, war will spread from here to every other country in the world.

3 The South and the North will fight against each other. The South will ask for help from other countries, including Great Britain. Those countries will ask for help from other countries in order to fight yet other countries—and then all the countries on earth will be at war.

4 In time, slaves will turn against their masters. The slaves will be formed into armies and taught how to go to war.

5 The Lamanites who are left will also go to war. They will strike back against the people who took over their land.

6 People will be filled with sorrow because of the wars and killing. Because of their sins, the peoples of the world will suffer famine, disease, earthquakes, thunder, and lightning. In the end, the whole world will be destroyed.

7 That is how those who hurt and killed God's people will finally be punished.

8 Stand in holy places until the Second Coming. The Lord promises that it will be soon. Amen.

SECTION 88

The members of the church in Zion began to have hard feelings for the members in Kirtland. The Lord gave Joseph Smith a revelation for the members in Kirtland. The revelation was to let the members in Kirtland know that the Lord accepted them, even if the members in Zion talked badly about them. Section 88 is that revelation. Joseph sent a copy of the revelation to the members in Zion. He also sent them a letter, warning them to repent.

1 This is what the Lord says to you who have met here in Kirtland. You have come to learn what the Lord wants you to do.

2 The Lord and his angels are very happy that you have done this. The Lord has heard your prayers. He has written your names in the book that lists everyone who can live in the celestial kingdom.

3 You are my friends. I now send you the "other Comforter" I promised my followers in the Gospel of John. That Comforter will live in your hearts. It is the Holy Spirit of promise.

4 It is the promise of eternal life, or the glory of the celestial kingdom.

5 The glory of the celestial kingdom is God's glory. God will give this glory to the members of the church. He will give it to them through his Son, Jesus Christ.

6 Jesus Christ rose above all things and sank below all things. He did this so that he could be everywhere, and so he could make the light of truth shine through everything.

7 Truth shines. It is Christ's light. Christ is in the sun. He is its light and the power that created it.

8 He is also in the moon. He is its light and the power that created it.

9 He is the light of the stars and the power that created them.

10 He is in the earth on which you are standing. He is the power that created it.

11 He is the light that lets you see and the light that makes you understand. They are the same thing.

12 That light shines out from God to fill all space.

13 It is everywhere. It is what brings everything to life. It is the law that controls all things. It is the power of God. He sits on his throne in the middle of the universe.

14 Christ's sacrifice is what makes it possible for you to come back from the dead.

15 The spirit and the body together make up the soul.

16 A person's soul is saved when the person comes back from the dead.

17 Souls are saved through Jesus Christ. He brings everything to life. He has promised that the poor and humble will someday receive the earth as their own.

18 For that to happen, the earth must be made holy. All wickedness must be taken off it, so it can become a celestial kingdom.

19 Once the earth has done everything it was created to do, the Father will cover it with glory. He himself will come to live on the earth.

20 Then those who are brought back from the dead with celestial bodies will own the earth forever. That is why it was created. That is why they were made holy.

21 Those who are not made holy through Christ's law will have to live in either a terrestrial or a telestial kingdom.

22 Someone who cannot obey the law of a celestial kingdom cannot stand a celestial glory.

23 Someone who cannot obey the law of a terrestrial kingdom cannot stand a terrestrial glory.

24 Someone who cannot obey the law of a telestial kingdom cannot stand a telestial glory. Such people cannot live in any kingdom of glory. They will have to live in a kingdom without any glory at all.

25 The earth obeys the law of a celestial kingdom, because it does everything it was created to do. It keeps God's law perfectly.

26 That is why the earth will be made holy. It will have to die first. But then it will be filled with God's power. The righteous will live on it forever.

27 They, too, will die. But then they will be brought back from the dead with heavenly bodies.

28 People whose spirits have become celestial will come back from the dead with the same bodies they had on earth. But when you get your bodies back, they will be filled with the same glory you started to receive on earth.

29 So people who received part of the celestial glory while they are alive, will be filled with that same glory when they come back from the dead.

30 People who received part of the terrestrial glory while they are alive, will be filled with that same

glory when they come back from the dead.

31 People who received part of the telestial glory while they are alive, will be filled with that same glory when they come back from the dead.

32 Those who are left will also come back from the dead. But then they will have to go away to their own place. There they will be given exactly as much glory as they were willing to accept while they were alive—which is none. They were not willing to accept the glory God wanted to give them.

33 What good is it to give a gift to someone who will not accept it? The gift will not make the person happy. And the person who receives the gift will not be happy being with the one who gave them the gift.

34 Whoever lets themselves be ruled by law will be saved and made holy by law.

35 Some people break laws because they want to make up their own laws. All they want to do is sin, and so that is all they do. Such people cannot be made holy by any law—not by mercy, justice, or punishment. They can never come into God's kingdom.

36 All kingdoms have a law.

37 There are many kingdoms, because there is no place in the universe that is not part of some kingdom.

38 Every kingdom has its own law. Every law sets up certain limits and rules.

39 The blessings of a certain kingdom can come only to those who obey that kingdom's law.

40 That is because it is the nature of a thing to draw close to other things that are like it: intelligence to intelligence, wisdom to wisdom, truth to truth, goodness to goodness, light to light. Mercy comes to those who show mercy. Justice comes to those who should receive justice. God is the judge. He rules all things from his throne.

41 God understands all things, because he can see them all. He is at the center of all. He is above all, in all, through all, and around all. He made all things. All things belong to him forever.

42 He has given all things a law. That law is what makes them move where they do, when they do.

43 The paths of the earth and the planets are set by the law God has given them.

44 There are certain times set for each planet to give light to the others. Each planet also has its own set way for measuring time—minutes, hours, days, weeks, months, and years. That is why people measure time differently on different planets. For God, though, it is all the same.

45 The earth rolls through space. The sun shines during the day. The moon shines during the night. The stars shine as they fly through space. All this happens through God's power.

46 How can I explain these kingdoms to you?

47 Anyone who has seen even the smallest of these kingdoms has seen God himself moving in glory and power.

48 I repeat—that person has seen God himself. But God was not un-

derstood when he came to his people.

49 When the light shines, the darkness does not understand it. But someday God will give you new life. Then you will be able to understand him.

50 Then you will know that you have seen me. You will know that I exist. You will know that I am the light inside you. You will know that I am all around you. I make it possible for you to live and grow.

51 These kingdoms are like a man who sent his servants to work in his field.

52 He said to the first servant, "Go work in the field. During the first hour, I will visit you. You will see the joy of my face."

53 He said to the second servant, "Go work in the field as well. During the second hour, I will visit you. You will see the joy of my face."

54 In the same way, he promised to visit the third servant.

55 Then he promised to visit the fourth, and so on up to the twelfth.

56 During the first hour, the master went to visit the first servant. He stayed with him for a whole hour. The light that shone from the master's face made the servant happy.

57 Then he left the first servant so he could visit the second servant, then the third, then the fourth, and so on up to the twelfth.

58 So each servant received the light of his master's face at the time the master had set for him.

59 He went from the first to the last, from the last to the first, and from the first to the last.

60 Each servant was visited in order, until his hour was up, just as the master had said. Each servant brought the master glory, and the master brought each servant glory. So the master and his servants were made glorious together.

61 This story explains what all these kingdoms and the people who live in them are like. The Lord visits each kingdom at the time and in the order God has set.

62 My friends, I leave you to think about all this. I command you to pray to me while I am close to you.

63 If you draw close to me, I will draw close to you. If you look for me faithfully, you will find me. If you ask, I will give. If you knock, I will open the door.

64 Anything you ask the Father for in my name, you will be given, as long as it is truly for your good.

65 If you ask for something that is not for your good, it will only end up hurting you.

66 You are listening to the voice of someone you cannot see. That voice is my Spirit. My Spirit is truth. Truth lasts forever. If truth is in you, it will grow.

67 If my glory is your only goal, your bodies will be completely filled with light. There will be no darkness left in you. When you are filled with light, you will understand everything.

68 Make yourselves holy. Think only of God, and the day will come when you will see him. He will show himself to you. He will do it whenever he decides the time is right and in whatever way he decides is right.

69 Remember this last, great

promise I have made to you. Stop thinking about things that do not matter. Be more serious.

70 Stay in this place. Hold a special meeting with all those who have been called to be the first workers in this last kingdom.

71 As my servants have travelled, they have given a warning to people. Those people should spend some time thinking about that warning.

72 I will take care of the people you have converted. I will have elders ordained and sent to them.

73 I am going to speed up my work.

74 I command you again to meet together. Organize and prepare yourselves. Make yourselves holy. Make your hearts pure. Wash your hands and feet, so that I can make you clean.

75 Then I will be able to testify to God our Father that you are clean of the sins of the people of today. Then, when the time is right, I will be able to keep the last, great promise I made you.

76 I command you to keep praying and fasting.

77 I command you to teach each other about my kingdom.

78 If you work hard at teaching each other, I will help you better understand the doctrines and laws of the gospel. I will help you understand everything you need to know about God's kingdom.

79 You will learn about things in heaven and on earth. You will learn about the past, the present, and the future. You will learn about what is happening here at home and in other places. You will learn about the wars and problems of the world. You will learn about other countries and kingdoms.

80 Learning these things will prepare you to go back into the world to carry out the mission I gave you.

81 I sent you out to bear your testimonies and to warn people to repent. Those who have already been warned should warn those around them.

82 After they have been warned, people have no excuse for their sins.

83 Those who look for me early will find me. I will never leave them.

84 Stay here and work hard. Then, when I call you, you will be completely prepared to go out to teach the world for the last time. You will bear your testimonies of the restored gospel. You will prepare church members for the Second Coming and the Last Judgment.

85 If the members are prepared, they will not suffer with the wicked. But until I call them, all the elders, except the first elders, need to stay here. That is because they are not yet clean of the sins of the people of today.

86 You have been made free. Stay that way. Do not let yourselves be trapped in sin again. Stay clean until the Lord comes.

87 Soon the earth will toss back and forth like someone who is drunk. The sun will refuse to shine. The moon will be covered with blood. The stars will become angry. They will throw themselves out of the sky, like fruit falling off a tree.

88 After you have shared your testimony with the people on the world, they will be punished for their sins.

89 After you have warned people that they need to repent, there will be earthquakes and underground noises to warn them. People will fall onto the ground. They will not be able to stand.

90 There will be thunder and lightning. There will be storms. Giant waves will throw themselves onto the land.

91 There will be trouble everywhere. People will give up hope. Everyone will be afraid.

92 Angels will fly through the sky, blowing trumpets. They will shout, "Get ready, people of earth! The time has come for you to be judged. Jesus Christ is coming to live with his people. Go out to meet him."

93 As soon as the angels have said this, a great sign will appear in the sky for everyone to see.

94 Another angel will blow his trumpet and say, "The devil's kingdom had power over the whole earth. It led people all over the world to sin and to suffer. It hurt and killed God's people. But now it has lost its power. It is waiting to be destroyed." Then he will give a loud, long blast on his trumpet. Everyone on earth will hear it.

95 That is the last sound that will come from the sky for half an hour. As soon as that half hour is up, the curtain of heaven will roll back to reveal the Lord's face.

96 The righteous people who are still alive will be lifted up off the earth. They will meet the Lord in the air.

97 The righteous people who have already died will be brought back from the dead. They will be lifted up out of their graves. They, too, will meet the Lord in the air.

98 Those who come down from heaven with Christ are Christ's people. So are those who are lifted up off the earth to meet him. They will be the first people who are brought back from the dead. All this will happen when the first angel blows his trumpet.

99 Then a second angel will blow his trumpet. This will bring back from the dead all those who become Christ's people after the Second Coming. These are the people who accepted the gospel in the spirit prison.

100 A third angel will blow his trumpet. Then the spirits of all the people who have not yet come back from the dead will be judged. These are people will still have to be punished for their sins.

101 These people cannot come back from the dead for another 1000 years. They cannot come back from the dead until the very end of the world.

102 Then a fourth angel will blow his trumpet and say, "Some of the people who have to wait to come back from the dead are children of perdition. They will have to go on being punished even after they come back from the dead."

103 The angel who blows the fifth trumpet is the one who flies through the sky bringing the gospel to everyone on earth. He offers it to all people, no matter where they are from, what race they belong to, or what language they speak.

104 He will blow his trumpet. All people will hear what he says—

those who are in heaven, those who are on earth, and those who are still dead. He will say, "Respect God, and give glory to Jesus Christ forever! It is time for all people to be judged." When everyone hears this, they will kneel down and confess their sins.

105 The sixth angel will blow his trumpet and say, "The devil's kingdom has finally been destroyed!"

106 Then the seventh angel will blow his trumpet and say, "God's work is done! Jesus Christ has overcome all things. He has overthrown the devil's kingdom. All the wicked have been punished."

107 The angels and the righteous will be filled with God's glory. He will give them homes in heaven. He will make them equal with him.

108 Then the first angel will blow his trumpet again for all who are alive to hear. He will reveal everything that was done during the first 1000 years of the earth's history. He will reveal the evil works that people kept secret. He will also reveal the amazing works of God.

109 After that, the second angel will blow his trumpet. He will reveal everything that was done during the second 1000 years of the earth's history.

110 This will go on until the seventh angel blows his trumpet. He will stand with one foot on the land and one foot on the sea. He will swear in Jesus Christ's name that time will end. Satan will be powerless for 1000 years.

111 After the 1000 years, Satan will be set free for a little while. He will bring his armies together.

112 Michael will bring together the armies of heaven. Michael is the seventh angel, and the chief of all the angels.

113 The devil and his armies will go to battle against Michael and his armies.

114 It will be God's last battle. The devil and his armies will be driven back into their own place. They will never again have any power over God's people.

115 Michael will fight for God's people. He will overcome Satan. Satan wants Jesus Christ's throne for himself.

116 This is the glory of God and of all those he has made holy. They will never die again.

117 So, my friends, hold the special meeting I commanded you to.

118 Since you do not all have faith, work hard to get wisdom. Teach each other from the world's best books. Learn by studying as well as through faith.

119 Organize yourselves. Prepare everything you need to build a house for God. It will be a house for praying and fasting. It will be a house of faith and learning. It will be a house of glory and order.

120 Whenever you go in or out of that house, you will do it in the Lord's name. You will greet each other in the Lord's name, lifting your hands up toward God.

121 Be more serious. Stop talking about things that do not matter. Stop lusting. Stop being proud. Repent of all your sins.

122 You should choose one of you to act as teacher. That way you will not all be talking at once. Speak one at a time. When someone is talking, everyone else should lis-

ten. That way you can all build each other up. Everyone will be treated equally.

123 Be sure to love each other. Stop wanting what belongs to other people. Learn to share with each other the way I have commanded you.

124 Use your time wisely. Be clean. Stop finding fault with each other. Stop sleeping more than you need to. Go to bed early, so you will not be tired when you wake up. Get up early, so your bodies and minds will be strong.

125 Above all, wrap yourselves in love. Love will keep you close together. It will make you perfect. It will bring you peace.

126 Always remember to pray, so you will stay strong until I come. I will come soon to be with you. Amen.

127 This is what you will do in the school of the prophets. This school is being started to teach everyone—from high priests to deacons—what they need to know.

128 The person who is chosen to be the president, or teacher, of the school should be standing in place before anyone else comes in.

129 The teacher will be the first person to go into God's house. Everyone else in the house needs to be able to hear the teacher. The teacher will speak clearly, but not loudly.

130 The teacher goes into the house first—this is beautiful—in order to set an example.

131 The teacher will kneel and pray to God. This is to remind people of God's holy promise.

132 Whenever someone else comes into the house, the teacher will stand. The teacher will lift his hands up toward the sky, and greet whoever came in by saying this:

133 "Are you a brother (or brothers)? I greet you in Jesus Christ's name and in memory of God's holy promise. Because we have both made that promise, I accept you as an equal. I promise to always be your friend and your brother. God's grace unites us in love. Together we will keep all his commandments. We will give thanks to him forever. Amen."

134 If someone is not worthy to be greeted like this, you will not let that person stay in my house and make it unholy.

135 If those who come in are faithful, and are brothers, they will greet the teacher. This means they will raise their hands towards the sky and repeat the words the teacher said. Or they can say "Amen" to mean the same thing.

136 This is how you should greet each other in the school of the prophets which will be held in God's house.

137 Do this with prayer. Give thanks to God. The Spirit will tell you what to say during everything you do in the Lord's house. That way it will be a holy place. God's Spirit will be there, to build you up.

138 A person who is not yet clean of the sins of the people of today should not join the school of the prophets.

139 People become part of the school of the prophets through the ordinance of foot-washing. This is why that ordinance was set up.

140 The foot-washing should be done by the president, or first elder of the church.

141 The ordinance begins with a prayer. You should take the sacrament. Then the president should wrap a towel around himself and do what is described in John, chapter 13. Amen.

SECTION 89

In Section 88, the Lord told Joseph Smith to start a "school of the prophets" for priesthood holders. Like many men of their time, the priesthood holders who attended the school smoked and chewed tobacco. This made the school very dirty. Joseph asked the Lord if it was right for church members to use tobacco. Section 89 is the Lord's answer.

1 This is a Word of Wisdom. It is for the good of the Kirtland high priests council and all other church members.

2 It is not sent as a commandment. It is not something that people will be forced to do. But it is a revelation from God telling church members how they can be saved from earthly troubles.

3 There are promises for those who keep this revelation. It is has been given in such a way that even the weakest church members can keep it.

4 This is what the Lord says: I reveal this Word of Wisdom to you as a warning. I do it because of evil plans that people are making now and will make in the future.

5 Heavenly Father does not find it good for you to drink wine or alcohol, except when you take the sacrament.

6 When you take the sacrament, you should use only pure grape wine. It should be wine which you yourselves have made.

7 Alcohol is for cleaning your bodies. It is not for drinking.

8 Tobacco is not good for people's bodies. It can be used as a medicine, especially for animals, but only by people who know what they are doing.

9 Hot drinks are not good for people's bodies.

10 God has made all healthy plants for people to eat.

11 People should use fruits and vegetables wisely. They should remember to thank God for them.

12 I have also given people the meat of animals and birds to eat. But people should not eat very much meat.

13 It is best that you eat meat only during the winter, when it is cold, or at other times when plants will not grow.

14 Grains should be your main food. They were made to be the main food for animals and birds as well.

15 God wants people to use animals and birds for food only when plants will not grow and people are starving.

16 All grains and fruits are good for people to eat, whether they grow below or above the ground.

17 But wheat is for people. Corn is for oxen. Oats are for horses. Rye is for birds, pigs, and all other farm animals. Barley is for work animals and for making drinks. All other

grains can be used to make drinks, too.

18 All church members who do what I have just said and keep the commandments will have healthy bodies and strong bones.

19 They will become wise. They will learn many wonderful things. They will even learn secret things.

20 When they run, they will not get tired. When they walk, they will not lose strength.

21 I promise that the destroying angel will pass over them, just like he passed over the Israelites, without killing them. Amen.

SECTION 90

Around the time that the First Presidency was first set up in the restored church, Joseph Smith received directions from the Lord for himself, his counselors, and several other church members. Those directions are published as Section 90.

1 This is what the Lord says: My son, I have forgiven your sins, as you asked me to. I have heard your prayers. I have also heard your friends' prayers.

2 You who have been placed in charge of my kingdom will be blessed from now on. I have restored my kingdom for the last time.

3 You will never lose the authority I have given you to lead my kingdom. You will have it as long as you are alive. You will have it even after you have died.

4 It is through you that revelations will be given to all the members of the church.

5 The members need to be careful not to treat the revelations as if they did not matter. If they treat the revelations that way, they will suffer. They will be overcome in times of trouble.

6 I forgive Sidney Rigdon's and Frederick G. Williams' sins. They are your equals in leading the restored church.

7 Give them authority to help lead the school of the prophets.

8 The school of the prophets will completely prepare my servants to carry out their mission. Then Zion and everyone else in the world who accepts the gospel can be saved.

9 Through you, I will teach my word to my servants. They in turn will teach it to people all over the earth. First they will go to the Gentiles. Later they will go to the Jews.

10 Finally the day will come when the Lord will openly show the world his power. Then those who have never heard the gospel will be converted. So will the descendants of Joseph.

11 Someday everyone will be taught the restored gospel in their own language. Jesus Christ will give his ordained servants the power to do this through the Spirit.

12 Keep doing my work. Keep serving in the presidency.

13 When you have finished translating the Old Testament, spend your time taking care of church business and leading the school of the prophets.

14 The Spirit will give you revelations now and then. It will keep teaching you about my kingdom.

15 Make sure the branches of the church are in order. Study and learn. Read good books. Learn about other languages and peoples.
16 Your life-long mission is to lead church councils and to keep church business in order.
17 Never let yourself be put to shame. Let yourself be corrected whenever you become proud, because pride will trap you.
18 Make sure all is well with your families. Do not be lazy. Stay clean.
19 Frederick G. Williams and his family need to be given a place to live as soon as possible.
20 Joseph Smith's father has grown old. He and his family should keep living where they are now. They should not sell their home until the Lord tells them to.
21 Sidney Rigdon should also stay where he is living until I give him other directions.
22 The bishop needs to find an agent. The agent should be someone with plenty of money and with strong faith.
23 The agent needs to be able the pay all the church's debts. That way people will not start to talk badly about the Lord's storehouse.
24 Look hard. Always remember to pray. Have faith, and everything will work out for your good. You must do what is right. Remember the holy promise you have made with each other.
25 Do not bring a lot of people who are not members of your family into your home. I say this especially to Joseph Smith's father.
26 That way you can be sure that the things you are given so you can do my work do not go to unworthy people instead.
27 If that happens, you will not be able to do what I have commanded you.
28 Give my servant Vienna Jaques the money she needs to move to Zion.
29 The rest of her money should be donated to the church. I will reward her when the time is right.
30 I want the bishop in Zion to give Vienna Jaques land to live on. That way she can have a home of her own.
31 If she is faithful, she can settle down in peace. But this does not mean she should spend her days doing nothing.
32 Send a copy of this revelation to the members of the church in Zion. Greet them with love. Tell them that when the time is right, I will send you to Zion to lead them in person.
33 They should stop bothering me about this subject.
34 The angels are happy to see that the members in Zion are starting to repent.
35 But there are still things going on that make me unhappy. I am not very pleased with William E. McLellin, Sidney Gilbert, or Edward Partridge. Others have many things to repent of, too.
36 But I will keep working to save Zion. I will beg Zion's leaders to repent. I will correct the people of Zion until they overcome and become clean.
37 Zion will not be moved out of its place. I, the Lord, have said it. Amen.

SECTION 91

While Joseph Smith was working on the new translation of the Bible, he wondered what to do with the Apocrypha. The Apocrypha is a group of books that appear in some translations of the Bible, but not in others. Some churches accept the Apocrypha as part of the Bible; others do not. (The LDS Church is one that does not. But you can read about the Apocrypha in the LDS Bible Dictionary.) Joseph asked the Lord if he should make a new translation of the Apocrypha. Section 91 is the Lord's answer.

1 This is what the Lord says about the Apocrypha: Much of what is in the Apocrypha is true, and the translation in the King James Version is mostly correct.
2 But there is much in the Apocrypha that is not true—things which people have added.
3 You do not need to include the Apocrypha in your new translation of the Bible.
4 People who read the Apocrypha will be able to understand it if the Spirit shows them which parts are true.
5 If people have the Spirit, reading the Apocrypha will do them good.
6 If they do not have the Spirit, reading the Apocrypha will not do them good. So you do not need to translate it. Amen.

SECTION 92

In Section 82, the Lord commanded several church leaders to form a special group called the United Order. The members of the United Order were supposed to get the church storehouse started. After Frederick G. Williams was ordained to be Joseph Smith's counselor in the First Presidency, the Lord gave the revelation now known as Section 92.

1 This is what the Lord says to the members of the United Order: I command you to accept Frederick G. Williams into the United Order. What I say to one of you, I say to all of you.
2 This is what the Lord says to Frederick G. Williams: Be an active member of the United Order. If you faithfully keep all the commandments you have received, you will be blessed forever. Amen.

SECTION 93

Joseph Smith and the other leaders of the church were very busy doing the Lord's work. They were so busy, in fact, that they did not pay enough attention to their families. Section 93 is a revelation from the Lord reminding the leaders how important it was for them to take care of their families. The revelation also restores some writings from Bible times.

1 This is what the Lord says: Everyone who repents and comes to me, who prays, and who keeps my commandments, will see me face-to-face someday. They will know for themselves that I exist.

2 They will know that I am the true light which shines on everyone who is born.

3 They will know that the Father and I are one—that I am in the Father and the Father in me.

4 I am called the Father because the Father gave me everything he has. I am called the Son because I was born and lived with people on earth.

5 While I lived on earth, I received glory from the Father. I did the Father's works for people to clearly see.

6 John saw that I was filled with my Father's glory. He testified about my glory. Later I will reveal to you the rest of John's record.

7 He testified, "I saw Christ's glory. I saw that he existed even before the world was created.

8 "In the beginning was the Word. That is because Christ was the Word—the messenger who teaches us how to be saved.

9 "He gives light to the world. He is the Savior of the world. He is the Spirit of truth. Because he created the earth, he came to live on it. He gave everyone life and light.

10 "He created all the planets. He created all people. Everything was created by him and through him. Everything belongs to him.

11 "I, John, testify that I saw his glory. It was the glory of the Father's only Son. He was filled with love and truth. He was the Spirit of truth. He took on a body and lived with us.

12 "I saw that he was filled with glory not all at once, but little by little.

13 "He was not given everything from the start. Instead, he grew little by little. He received one thing after another, until finally he received all things.

14 "That is why he was called God's Son—because he was not filled with God's glory from the start.

15 "I saw the Holy Ghost come down from heaven in the shape of a dove and land on him. I heard a voice from heaven say, 'This is my dear Son.'

16 "I testify that he was filled with the Father's glory.

17 "He was given all power in heaven and on earth. All the Father's glory was with him, because he and the Father were one."

18 Someday, if you are faithful, you will be given the rest of John's record.

19 I have given you this part of his record so you will understand how to worship and what you worship. You need to understand this so that through me you can come to the Father. In time, you can receive all that he has.

20 If you keep my commandments, you will be filled with the Father's glory, just like I was. You, too, will grow little by little until you have received everything.

21 I was with the Father in the beginning. I am his first child.

22 Everyone who receives new life through me shares my glory. They become members of my church.

23 In the beginning, you were also with the Father—the Spirit of truth.
24 Truth is an understanding of things as they are now, as they were in the past, and as they will be in the future.
25 Anything else is the spirit of Satan. Satan was a liar from the beginning.
26 The Spirit of truth comes from God. I am the Spirit of truth. John bore this testimony about me: "He was filled with truth—all truth."
27 No one can be filled with truth unless they keep God's commandments.
28 Those who keep the commandments receive truth and light little by little until they are filled with glory and know everything.
29 All people existed with God in the beginning. Intelligence—the light of truth—was not created. It cannot be created.
30 All truth and all intelligence is free to act for itself within the limits God has placed on it. If this were not the case, nothing could exist.
31 That is why people are free to choose. It is also why they are punished. The light of truth, which existed from the beginning, is clearly shown to them. But they do not follow the light.
32 Every person who chooses not to follow the light must be punished.
33 People have spirits. They also have bodies. Their bodies are made of matter. Matter, like spirit, has existed forever. In order for people to know full joy, their spirits must be joined to their bodies forever.
34 When their spirits and bodies are apart, people cannot know full joy.
35 God lives in matter. He lives inside people. Their bodies are his temples. If a temple becomes unholy, it will be destroyed.
36 God's glory is intelligence—in other words, light and truth.
37 Light and truth reject Satan.
38 In the beginning, people's spirits were innocent. Because God saves them from the Fall, people are still innocent when they are born as babies.
39 But then Satan leads people to disobey. He causes them to lose the light and truth they are born with. Satan does this through the false beliefs and customs people learn from their parents.
40 That is why I have commanded you to raise your children in light and truth.
41 But you, Frederick G. Williams, have not kept this commandment.
42 You have not taught your children light and truth. This gives Satan power over you. That is why you suffer.
43 If you want to be freed from suffering, you must correct the problems in your family.
44 Sidney Rigdon has also not done everything I commanded about his children. He, too, needs to correct the problems in his family.
45 As for my servant Joseph Smith—when I say "servant" I mean "friend," because you are my friends and will someday live with me.
46 I call you "servants" because I have chosen you to serve the people of the world for me.
47 Now, I say to Joseph Smith—you have not kept the commandments. You must be corrected.
48 Your family has some things to

repent of. If they do not pay better attention to what you tell them, they will lose the blessings I have given them.

49 These next words are for all of you. Always remember to pray. Then Satan will not have power over you. He will not be able to make you lose your blessings.

50 Bishop Newel K. Whitney also needs to be corrected. He needs to correct the problems in his family. He needs to be sure his family members work harder at home. They must always remember to pray, or they will lose their blessings.

51 Now, my friends, I want Sidney Rigdon to go quickly to preach the gospel. I will tell him what to say. If you pray together for him with faith, I will support him.

52 Joseph Smith and Frederick G. Williams should also act quickly. If they ask with faith, I will give. If you do what I tell you, you will never be put to shame—not in this life or in the next.

53 I want you to hurry and finish translating the Bible. I want you to study history. I want you to learn about other countries and kingdoms. I want you to study laws—both God's laws and people's laws. Learning all this will help you save Zion. Amen.

SECTION 94

At first, the church did not own any buildings in Kirtland. Church members rented someone else's building to hold their meetings in. As the Lord's work grew, the members realized they would need buildings of their own. Section 94 is a revelation telling the members in Kirtland how to start making the buildings they needed.

1 My friends, I command you to start getting ready to build a city here in Kirtland. It will be a stake of Zion. You should start by building the temple.

2 It must be built the way I have shown you.

3 The first piece of land south of the temple should be set aside for a building for the presidency. That is where the presidency will receive revelations. It is where they will carry out church business.

4 Inside, this building should be 55 feet wide and 65 feet long.

5 It will have two floors, as I will show you later.

6 You will dedicate the building to the Lord the priesthood way. I will teach you how to do this later.

7 This building will be used only for the presidency's work.

8 Nothing unholy must be allowed inside it. My glory will be there. Even I myself will be there.

9 But if anything unholy comes into the building, my glory and I will leave it.

10 The second piece of land south of the temple should be set aside for a printshop. There you can publish the new translation of the Bible and whatever else I command you to.

11 It will be the same size as the presidency's building. It will also have two floors.

12 The printshop should be dedicated to the Lord. That means it will be used to publish only what I command. Nothing unholy must be allowed inside it.
13 Hyrum Smith will live on the third piece of land south of the temple.
14 Reynolds Cahoon and Jared Carter will live on first and second pieces of land north of the temple.
15 I have chosen these men to take charge of making these buildings. They must do it the way I have commanded.
16 Do not start work on the presidency's building and the printshop until I tell you to.
17 That is all I have to say for now. Amen.

SECTION 95

In Section 88, the Lord had told the members in Kirtland to start building a temple. Six months later, they had still not started. Section 95 is a revelation from the Lord correcting the members for not starting the Kirtland Temple when they were told to. Hyrum Smith and some other members started work on the temple the very next day.

1 This is what the Lord says: Because I love you, I correct you. I do this so that your sins can be forgiven and so you can escape all temptation.
2 You need to be corrected.
3 You have committed a very serious sin. You have not kept the important commandment I gave you about building the temple.
4 I need you to build the temple so I can prepare my apostles to do my work for the last time. Once you have built the temple, I will be able to do the "strange work" Isaiah wrote about. I will be able to give my Spirit to all people.
5 Many of those who have been ordained to the priesthood are not living worthy of it.
6 They have committed a very serious sin. It is as though they are walking in the dark, even though the sun is shining.
7 This is why I commanded you to hold a special meeting—so you could fast and repent. I am the Lord of Sabaoth, the one who created the first day. I am the beginning and the end.
8 In the temple, I will give heavenly power to those I have chosen.
9 The Father promises this. That is why I told you to stay here in Kirtland. It is just like when I told my apostles long ago to stay in Jerusalem until they had been given heavenly power.
10 But my servants committed a very serious sin. They argued with each other in the school of the prophets. That made me very unhappy. So I sent my servants out to be corrected.
11 I want you to build the temple. You will have power to build it if you keep my commandments.
12 If you do not keep my commandments, the Father will stop blessing you. He will stop teaching you.

13 I do not want the temple to look like the kinds of buildings the world makes. That is because I do not want you to live the way the world lives.

14 I will show three of you how I want the temple to be built. You yourselves will choose those three. You will ordain them to receive this revelation.

15 Inside, the temple will be 55 feet wide and 65 feet long.

16 The first floor will be used for sacrament meetings, preaching, fasting, and praying. There you will tell me your holiest wishes.

17 The second floor will be set aside for the school of my apostles. Son Ahman—the Lord Jesus Christ—says this. Amen.

SECTION 96

In order to get land for the Kirtland Temple, church leaders bought a farm from a man named Peter French. Besides building the temple, the leaders also needed to give some church members land to live on. They were not sure how they could use Peter French's farm to do all this. They asked the Lord what they should do. Section 96 is the Lord's answer.

1 I will teach you what to do, because it is important to me that this stake of Zion be made strong.

2 Newel K. Whitney should take charge of Peter French's farm. That is where I plan to build my temple.

3 Decide together how best to divide the land for the good of those who need places to live.

4 Be sure to set aside those pieces of land which I have said I need for my work. That way I will be able to bring my word to people.

5 It is very important that people be taught my word. Then their hearts will be touched. They will stop trying to hurt you. Amen.

6 I also have something to say about John Johnson. I have accepted his sacrifices. I have heard his prayers. If he keeps my commandments from now on, I promise him eternal life.

7 He is one of Joseph's descendants. He shares the blessings promised to his ancestors.

8 He needs to become a member of the United Order. That way he can help bring my word to people.

9 Once he is a member of the United Order, he will pay off the debt on Peter French's farm. Then he can have a home there. Amen.

SECTION 97

While the members in Ohio were starting to build the Kirtland Temple, the members who were building the city of Zion were having serious problems. There were hard feelings between church members and non-members in Missouri. Non-members finally became so angry that they attacked the members. They made the members promise to leave Zion. Oliver Cowdery was sent at once to tell Joseph Smith what was happening. By the time Oliver arrived, the Lord had already given Joseph the revelation now known as Section 97.

1 My friends, I will tell you what I want the members in Zion to do. Many of them are truly humble. They are trying hard to learn wisdom and to find truth.

2 These people will be blessed. I will teach them what they want to know. I show mercy to those who are humble. I may show mercy to the wicked as well. But if they do not repent when they have the chance, they will be punished in the end.

3 I think it is good to have a school for the elders in Zion. I am very happy with Parley P. Pratt, because he keeps my commandments.

4 He will keep serving as president of the school in Zion as long as he is faithful or until I command him to do something else.

5 He will receive many blessings. He will be able to explain all the scriptures. He will build up the elders and all the other members in Zion.

6 I am willing to show mercy to the other members of the school. But some of them need to be corrected. In time, their sins will be known.

7 Everyone must repent and do good works, or they will be destroyed. The Lord says this.

8 I accept all those who are humble and truly sorry for their sins. My people must be willing to make all the sacrifices necessary to keep the promises they have made with me.

9 If they do this, I will make them like a tree planted in good soil near a clean stream. Such a tree grows much valuable fruit.

10 I want the members in Zion to build a temple. It should be like the one I have shown you how to build in Kirtland.

11 It needs to be built quickly. It will be built with donations from my people.

12 I expect my people to make whatever donations or sacrifices are necessary to build a temple in Zion. Then I will be able to save them.

13 The temple will be a place where church members can meet to give thanks. They can meet there to learn how to carry out their callings.

14 They will come to understand their callings perfectly. They will have a perfect understanding of the doctrines of God's kingdom on earth. You have been placed in charge of that kingdom.

15 If my people build a temple and do not allow anything unholy inside it, my glory will settle down on it.

16 I myself will come into it. Everyone who comes into the temple with a pure heart will see God.

17 But if anything unholy is allowed inside the temple, my glory will not be there. I will not enter unholy temples.

18 If the people in Zion do all this, things will go well for them. Zion will grow so glorious and powerful that the people of the world will become frightened.

19 Every country on earth will respect Zion. They will say, "Truly, Zion is God's city. It cannot be overthrown, because God himself is there.

20 "He has promised to watch over Zion with all his power. He has promised to save Zion."

21 The Lord says: The wicked will suffer. But Zion should rejoice, for the people of Zion are THOSE WHOSE HEARTS ARE PURE.

22 Soon the wicked will be punished for their sins, as if by a whirlwind. No one will be able to escape.

23 They will be punished night and day. Everyone will become afraid when they hear about the things the wicked are suffering. The wicked will keep suffering until the Second Coming.

24 The Lord is angry with all their sins and wickedness.

25 But the people of Zion will escape if they do everything I have commanded them.

26 If they do not keep my commandments, they will suffer, too. They will suffer from disease, war, and fire.

27 This once, tell them that I have accepted their sacrifice. If they stop sinning, they will not have to suffer any of these things.

28 Instead, I will bless the people of Zion and their descendants forever. The Lord says this. Amen.

SECTION 98

After they were attacked by non-members and forced to leave their homes, many of the members in Missouri wanted to fight back. They felt that since their enemies had broken the law by attacking them, they didn't need to keep the law anymore either. Section 98 is a revelation for the members in Missouri. It tells the members how the Lord wanted them to deal with their troubles.

1 My friends, do not be afraid. Be comforted. Always rejoice and give thanks.

2 Be patient. The Lord has heard your prayers. He has promised to give you what you asked for.

3 That promise cannot be broken. Everything you have suffered will turn out for your good and for the good of my work. The Lord says this.

4 As for your country's laws—I want my people to do everything I command them.

5 All laws which are in keeping with your country's constitution, and which protect people's freedoms and rights, are acceptable to me. All people on earth should have such laws.

6 You should support those laws which are in keeping with your country's constitution.

7 A law that is not keeping with

your constitution is evil. (I am talking about earthly laws.)

8 I, the Lord, make you truly free. Your laws also make you free.

9 But people suffer when their rulers are wicked.

10 That is why you should look for people who are honest and wise to be your rulers. Anything less is evil.

11 Reject evil. Hold tightly to good. Keep all of God's commandments.

12 God will teach the faithful little by little. I do this in order to test you.

13 Whoever dies for my work will be rewarded with eternal life.

14 So do not be afraid of your enemies. You are being tested. Are you willing to keep the promise you made with me, even if that means you have to die?

15 If you will not keep the promise, you cannot form part of my people.

16 Do not go to war. Try to make peace. Work hard to bring people together.

17 Keep teaching the gospel, so you can keep everyone on earth from being destroyed.

18 Do not worry. I have prepared a place for you in my Father's house. You will be with us.

19 I am not pleased with many of the members in Kirtland.

20 They have not left behind their wicked ways. They are proud. They want the things other people have. They are not doing what I taught them they need to do in order to receive eternal life.

21 They will suffer if they do not repent and do everything I have told them.

22 If you keep all my commandments, I will protect you. I will not let Satan overpower you.

23 Now I have something to say about your families. The first time people hurt you or your families, be patient. Do not hurt them back, and I will reward you.

24 If you hurt them back, I will excuse them for what they did to you.

25 If your enemies hurt you a second time, and you are still patient, I will give you a greater reward than I did the first time.

26 If your enemies hurt you a third time, and you are still patient, I will give you a even greater reward.

27 If your enemies do not repent, I will always remember the three times they hurt you. They will be judged for hurting you.

28 After your enemies have hurt you three times, warn them never to hurt you or your family again.

29 If your enemies do hurt you or your family again, then you are allowed to fight back.

30 If you choose not to fight back, I will reward you for that righteous choice.

31 But you are allowed to fight back against your enemies for what they have done to you. If they have tried to kill you, you are allowed to do whatever is necessary to protect yourself.

32 This is the law I gave to the prophets and apostles long ago. I gave this law to Nephi, Joseph, Jacob, Isaac, Abraham, and all the others.

33 I commanded them not to go to war against anyone unless I told them to.

34 I commanded them to try to

make peace if someone came to war against them.

35 I told them they should try to make peace three times. If their enemies still wanted to fight, they should testify to the Lord that they did everything they could to make peace.

36 Only then would I allow them to go to war against their enemies.

37 I promised I would fight for them, and for their families, against their enemies.

38 I tell you this to show all people when it is acceptable to go to war.

39 If your enemies repent and ask for your forgiveness after they have hurt you, you must forgive them. You cannot hold it against them.

40 You must forgive them no matter how many times they hurt you, if they repent.

41 The first time they hurt you, you will forgive them even if they do not repent.

42 The second time they hurt you, you will forgive them even if they do not repent.

43 The third time they hurt you, you will forgive them even if they do not repent.

44 But if they do not repent after the fourth time they hurt you, you will not forgive them. Instead, you will ask the Lord to remember what they have done to you. They will be judged for it unless they repent. They must pay you back for the suffering they caused you.

45 If they do this, you will forgive them with all your heart. If they do not do this, they will suffer even more than what they made you suffer.

46 Their descendents will suffer as well.

47 But if their descendents repent with all their hearts, and pay you back for what they or their ancestors did to you, then you will forgive them.

48 Then they and their families will no longer suffer or be judged for your having been hurt. Amen.

SECTION 99

John Murdock and his wife were church members living in Ohio. They had five children. The last two children were twins. Sister Murdock died while giving birth to the twins. John kept raising the three oldest children, but Joseph and Emma Smith took care of the twins. Section 99 is a revelation calling John to serve a mission. The revelation also told him how to make sure his children would be taken care of while he was gone.

1 This is what the Lord says to John Murdock: You are called to go east. Travel from place to place, teaching my gospel. You are traveling to a wicked land. People there may hurt you.

2 Whoever accepts you, accepts me. The Spirit will testify to people that what you teach is true.

3 Whoever accepts you like a little child, accepts my kingdom. I will show them mercy.

4 Whoever rejects you will not be able to be with my Father. Wash

your feet in secret by the road to show that they rejected you.

⁵ I am coming soon to judge people for all their sins, like the scriptures say I will.

⁶ You do not need to leave until your children have been sent to the bishop in Zion. He will see that they are taken care of.

⁷ After a few years, you can go live in Zion, too, if you want.

⁸ If you decide that is not what you want, you must keep preaching my gospel the rest of your life. Amen.

SECTION 100

In the middle of all the work getting started in Kirtland and all the problems going on in Zion, the Lord sent Joseph Smith and Sidney Rigdon on a mission to Canada. Joseph and Sidney obeyed the Lord's call. But they were worried about their families and the members in Zion.. Section 100 is a revelation Joseph and Sidney received while they were out on their mission.

¹ This is what the Lord says to Sidney and Joseph: Your families are well. I will take care of them as I see fit. Remember that I have all power.

² So follow me. Listen to my advice.

³ There are many people here in the east who will accept my gospel. I will open doors for you in the areas round about.

⁴ That is why I needed you to come here—so people could be saved.

⁵ Teach these people. If you tell them what I put into your minds, no one will be able to put you to shame.

⁶ I will tell you what to say the very moment you go to speak.

⁷ But I command you always to speak in my name. You should always be serious and humble.

⁸ If you do this, I promise to send the Holy Ghost. It will testify to people that everything you teach is true.

⁹ Sidney, I need you to speak for Joseph. I will ordain you to that calling.

¹⁰ I will give Joseph the power to bear a strong testimony.

¹¹ I will give you the power to explain the scriptures well. Joseph will teach you what to say for him. That way you can know the truth about everything that has to do with my kingdom on earth.

¹² Go on your way. Rejoice. I will always be with you.

¹³ Now I have something to say about Zion. The people there will be saved from their enemies. But they need to be corrected for a little while first.

¹⁴ I am watching over Orson Hyde and John Gould. If they keep my commandments, they will be saved.

¹⁵ So be comforted. For the righteous, everything will work out for the best. By suffering, the members of my church will become holy.

¹⁶ I need to have a pure people, who will serve me righteously.

¹⁷ Everyone who prays to the Lord and keeps his commandments will be saved. Amen.

SECTION 101

The church members in Missouri were attacked again by their enemies. They were forced to leave Jackson County, where they had been trying to build the city of Zion. Winter was coming. The members had nowhere to stay. Many families had been broken up and were trying to find each other. Joseph Smith was living in Kirtland when all this happened. He was very upset about the suffering of the members in Missouri. Section 101 is a revelation from the Lord explaining why all this had happened. The revelation also explained what the members should do next.

1 This is what the Lord says about the members of the church who have been attacked and thrown off their land.

2 They have suffered this way because of their sins.

3 They are still my people. I will make them glorious when I come again.

4 But first they must be corrected. They must be tested, like Abraham was when he was commanded to sacrifice his only son.

5 If they stop having faith in me because they cannot stand to be corrected, they cannot become holy.

6 They made their land unholy. They did this through their arguing, and fighting, and envy, and lust.

7 They put off doing what the Lord commanded them. That is why the Lord cannot help them as quickly as they want.

8 When everything was going well for them, they did not take my advice seriously. Now that they are in trouble, they start looking for my help.

9 Even though they have sinned, I am full of love for them. I will not give up on them. They are going to have to suffer. But I will show them mercy.

10 I promised in an earlier revelation that their enemies would be punished. That promise will be kept.

11 The time is coming when the wicked will be punished for all their sins. But before that time comes, people will become even more wicked than they are now.

12 When that time comes, my people will be saved.

13 Everyone who has been scattered will be gathered together again.

14 Everyone who has suffered will be comforted.

15 Everyone who has died for following me will be rewarded.

16 So do not worry about Zion. Be calm. Remember that I am in control of everything that happens.

17 The people of Zion have been scattered. But Zion will not be moved out of its place.

18 Those whose hearts are pure will come back to Zion. They will come singing songs of joy. They will return with their children to their homes and land. They will rebuild Zion.

19 Everything the prophets wrote will come true.

20 I have not chosen to gather the members of my church into any other place but Zion. I will never choose any other place but Zion.

21 When the time comes that there is no more room in Zion for anyone else to live, then I will choose other

places for my people to live. Those places will be called "stakes of Zion." They will make Zion stronger the same way that adding stakes makes a tent stronger.

22 I want everyone who prays and worships the way my gospel teaches to come together in holy places.

23 There they will get themselves ready for the time when I will pull aside the curtain between heaven and earth and show myself to all people.

24 Every living thing on earth will be destroyed—people, animals, birds, and fish.

25 The matter that makes up the earth will become so hot it will melt. Everything will be changed, so that I can live on the earth in person. I will fill the earth with my glory.

26 When that happens, everyone on earth will live in peace. People and animals will not be enemies anymore.

27 During that time, people will be given anything they ask for.

28 Satan will no longer be able to tempt people.

29 There will be no more sorrow, because no one will die.

30 Babies will not die anymore. No one will die until they have lived to be as old as a tree.

31 When they do die, their bodies will not be buried in the ground. Instead, they will become brought back from the dead in the blink of an eye. They will be taken up to live in heaven.

32 When the Lord comes, he will reveal everything.

33 He will reveal secrets from the past that no one knew about. He will reveal how the earth was created, and why it was created.

34 He will reveal valuable information about things in heaven and on earth.

35 Everyone who is hurt or killed for living my gospel, without losing their faith, will share all this glory.

36 So do not be afraid to die. You cannot have full joy during this life—only when you come to live with me.

37 Do not worry about earthly things. Worry about spiritual things.

38 Always work toward being able to see the Lord. If you are patient, you will have eternal life. Then you will be your own masters.

39 When people accept the restored gospel and make holy promises with me, they become the salt of the earth.

40 They are called to be the salt of the earth. But if the salt loses its flavor, it is no longer good for anything, except to be thrown out and stepped on.

41 Many of the people of Zion—though not all—have sinned. They need to be corrected.

42 Those who think highly of themselves will be humbled. Those who humble themselves will be lifted up high into God's kingdom.

43 Now I will tell you a story to help you understand how I plan to free Zion.

44 A rich man had a piece of very good land. He told his servants, "Go plant twelve olive trees on my land.

45 "Put guards all around the trees.

Build a tower so a guard can stand on top of it to watch all the land round about. That way, my enemies cannot come break down my olive trees and steal their fruit."

46 The servants did what the rich man told them. They planted the olive trees and built a fence around them. They put guards all around the trees. Then they started to build the tower.

47 But while they were still just starting to build the tower, they began to ask each other, "Why does our master need this tower?"

48 They talked about it for a long time. They said, "Why does our master need us to build a tower during peacetime?

49 "Couldn't this money be better spent on something else? There is no real need for a tower."

50 While they were arguing about this, they became lazy. They did not do what their master had told them.

51 One night their enemies came and tore down the fence. The servants woke up and ran away, frightened. Their enemies destroyed everything they had built. They broke down the olive trees.

52 The rich man ordered his servants to come to him. He said, "How did this terrible thing happen?

53 "You should have done what I told you. You planted the trees. You built the fence. You put guards all around the trees. But you should also have built the tower and put another guard on top of it. Then you should have watched over my trees, instead of falling asleep.

54 "The guard on the tower would have been able to see my enemies coming while they were still far away. Then you could have been ready. You could have kept them from tearing down the fence and destroying the trees."

55 The master said to one of his servants, "Go gather all my servants who are able to go to war, except the ones I have commanded to stay here.

56 "Lead them to my land, and take it back from my enemies. That land is mine. I paid for it.

57 "Go quickly. Tear down the enemy's walls. Pull down their tower. Send their guards running away in every direction.

58 "If they come together to fight, punish them for what they did. Then I will be able to move to that land with the rest of my people."

59 The servant asked, "When will that happen?"

60 The master said, "When I decide the time is right. Now go do everything I have told you.

61 "I promise that if you are a wise and faithful servant, I will make you a ruler in my kingdom."

62 The servant went at once. He did everything his master had commanded. It took a long time. But in the end, everything the master had said came true.

63 Now I will tell you what all the branches of the church should do. If they will let me lead them in the right way, they will be saved.

64 My people will be able to keep gathering together. I will be able to make them strong in holy places. The end is coming. Everything I have said must come true.

65 I must gather my people the way the story of the wheat and the

weeds teaches. The wheat will be gathered into safe places. At the Last Judgment, they will be rewarded with eternal life and celestial glory.

66 The weeds will be tied up tightly, so they can be burned in a fire that never goes out.

67 I command all the branches of the church to keep gathering in the places I have chosen.

68 But remember what I told you earlier. Do not gather quickly, as if you were running away from your enemies. Make sure everything is ready before you go.

69 Everything will be ready for you if you keep the commandment I gave you.

70 In that commandment, I told you to buy all the land you could in the place I chose to be Zion.

71 Buy all the land you can in Jackson County. Buy all the land you can in the other counties round about, too. The rest of the land will be for me to take care of.

72 All the branches of the church should pool their money together. This does not need to be done right away, or in a hurry. But you do need to get everything ready.

73 You should choose people who are honest and wise to go buy the land for you.

74 The branches in the east should also buy land in Missouri, as soon as they are able. That way they, too, can help build Zion.

75 All together, the members of my church already have more than enough money to free Zion. If they do what I have commanded them, they can rebuild Zion. It will never be destroyed again.

76 Those who have been scattered by their enemies should keep asking the government to help them get their land back.

77 Your country's laws and constitution give you this right. I allowed those laws to be set up. They are based on fair and righteous ideas. They should be used to protect the rights of all people.

78 A country's laws should let people take charge of their own futures. The laws should let people make their own choices. That way I can judge everyone based on the choices they themselves have made.

79 It is not right for someone to take away another person's freedom.

80 That is why I prepared wise people to set up this country's constitution. That is why I allowed the people of this country to fight a war to become free.

81 The people of Zion are like the woman in the story of the unfair judge. The story teaches people to never give up praying. This is the story.

82 In a certain city there lived a judge who did not obey God. He did not truly care about helping people.

83 There was a woman in the city whose husband had died. She came to the judge and said, "Punish my enemy."

84 For a long time the judge refused to help her. But finally he thought, "I couldn't care less about God or anyone else. But this woman will never stop bothering me unless I help her."

85 That is what the people of Zion should be like.

86 They should keep asking the judge to help them.
87 If the judge will not listen, they should ask the governor.
88 If the governor will not listen, they should ask the president.
89 If the president will not help them, then the Lord himself will come to punish those who have hurt you.
90 If the rulers of this country do not use their power to correct the wrongs you have suffered, they will be destroyed in time. So will the rest of the wicked.
91 Satan will have power over them in the next life. They will suffer for not having helped you.
92 So pray that they will listen to you. Then I can show them mercy. Then they will not have to suffer.
93 But if they will not help you, then they will suffer as I have said.
94 The rulers of the world, and those who are well-educated, are going to see things they never imagined.
95 I am going to carry out the "strange work" Isaiah wrote about. Then people will be able to see who is righteous and who is wicked.
96 I command Sidney Gilbert not to sell the church storehouse to my enemies.
97 Those who claim to be my people must not allow my enemies to make what is mine unholy.
98 To do so would be a very serious sin against me and my people. Remember all the terrible things I have said are going to happen to the world soon.
99 I want my people to keep their claim to the land I chose for them, even if they are not allowed to live on it.
100 I am not saying they will not be able to live on it. If they act the way members of my kingdom should, they will be able to live on their land again.
101 No one will take away my people's homes again. No one else will eat the fruit from my people's orchards. Amen.

SECTION 102

In Kirtland, Joseph Smith met with the high priests to teach them how to hold a church court. Joseph warned the high priests to be very careful about judging other people. He said it is easy for people to make unfair judgments, because of their own unrighteous feelings. He warned that people who are judged wrongly by a church court may someday judge the ones who judged them. Oliver Cowdery and Orson Hyde took notes of the meeting. Their notes were published as Section 102.

1 Today 24 high priests met at Joseph Smith's home, as the Lord commanded them. There they organized the high council of Christ's church. The high council is made up of twelve high priests. The high council also has one or three presidents, depending on how many are needed.
2 The high council was formed to handle major problems in the church. These would be problems the bishops could not settle in a way that everyone could accept.

3 Joseph Smith, Sidney Rigdon, and Frederick G. Williams were voted presidents of the high council. Joseph Smith Senior, John Smith, Joseph Coe, John Johnson, Martin Harris, John S. Carter, Jared Carter, Oliver Cowdery, Samuel H. Smith, Orson Hyde, Sylvester Smith, and Luke Johnson were chosen to be high councilors.

4 The high councilors were asked if they accepted the calling. They were asked if they would carry out the calling the way God commanded. They all said they accepted the calling. They said they would carry it out with God's help.

5 The people who voted to choose the high councilors were 9 high priests, 17 elders, 4 priests, and 13 other members—43 people in all.

6 It was decided that the high council cannot act unless seven of the high councilors are there at the meeting.

7 The seven who are there can choose other high priests to fill in for the high councilors who are absent.

8 It was also decided that when one of the high councilors dies, the president(s) will choose a new high councilor. They will do the same if a high councilor loses the calling because of sin or leaves the church. A special meeting of high priests has to be held, so they can vote to accept the new high councilor.

9 The president of the church is also president of the high council. The Lord will reveal who that person should be. The members of the church vote to accept that person.

10 The president is the one who leads the council. If necessary, two other presidents can be chosen to help. They too must be chosen by the Lord and accepted by the members.

11 If one or both of the other two presidents are missing, the first president can lead the council alone. If the first president is missing, one or both of the other two presidents can lead the council instead.

12 Whenever a high council meets, the twelve councilors should pick numbers from 1 to 12 to decide who speaks first.

13 Whenever they meet for a church court, the councilors must decide if the case is hard or not. If it is not, only the councilors who pick the numbers 1 and 2 will speak.

14 If the case is harder, then four councilors should speak. If it is even harder, six should speak. But that is the most that can ever speak.

15 Six of the councilors are in charge of making sure that the person who is being judged is treated fairly.

16 After the evidence has been given, the councilors who have been chosen to speak should explain the case to the rest of councilors. They should speak fairly and truly.

17 The councilors who pick the numbers 2, 4, 6, 8, 10, and 12 are the ones who need to make sure that the person being judged is treated fairly.

18 The person being judged and the person who accused them will both have the chance to speak to the council. They can do this after the evidence has been given and the councilors have finished explaining the case.

19 After everyone has spoken, the president will think about everything they said and make a decision about the case. The president will then ask the councilors to approve that decision by vote.

20 If any of the councilors think the president has made a mistake, they can say so. The case will then have to be heard all over again.

21 If the council understands the case differently after hearing it a second time, the president's decision will be changed.

22 But if most of the councilors think the president's decision was right after they have heard the case a second time, the first decision will stand.

23 If a case has to do with church doctrine, and the scriptures do not say enough to make things clear to the councilors, the president can ask the Lord to give more revelation.

24 When the high priests are travelling in other places, they have the authority to form councils like this one whenever someone taking part in a church court asks them to.

25 In a case like that, the high priests can choose one of themselves to lead that council for as long as necessary.

26 The council must send a record at once to the First Presidency. The record should tell what they did and how they made their decision.

27 If either side in the church court feels the council has made the wrong decision, they can ask the First Presidency to hear the case again. The First Presidency will hear the case all over again, as if no decision had been made.

28 The high priests who are travelling should form councils only for the hardest cases. An easy or ordinary case does not need to be decided by a whole council.

29 The high priests in other places have the authority to decide whether or not a council is needed.

30 There is a difference between a council of high priests and the council of the twelve apostles.

31 The decision of a high priests' council can be taken to the First Presidency to be heard again. The decision of an apostles' council is final.

32 Only the general authorities can question the decision of an apostles' council, and then only if one of the apostles has sinned.

33 It was decided that the First Presidency has the authority to decide if a certain case truly needs to be heard a second time, or if the first decision was good enough.

34 The twelve councilors then picked numbers to decide who would speak first. This is the order that came out: (1) Oliver Cowdery, (2) Joseph Coe, (3) Samuel H. Smith, (4) Luke Johnson, (5) John S. Carter, (6) Sylvester Smith, (7) John Johnson, (8) Orson Hyde, (9) Jared Carter, (10) Joseph Smith Senior, (11) John Smith, (12) Martin Harris. The meeting ended with a prayer. Signed: Oliver Cowdery and Orson Hyde, clerks.

SECTION 103

The members in Missouri sent Lyman Wight and Parley P. Pratt to Ohio. There they told Joseph Smith what was happening to the members, now that their enemies had forced them to leave their land. The members had found places to live for the time being. But they wanted to know how they could get their land back. Section 103 is the Lord's answer.

1 My friends, I will tell you what to do to save the members in Zion who have been scattered.

2 The time will come when your enemies will be punished for everything they have done to you.

3 Every time your enemies hurt you, they make the punishment which is coming to them that much greater.

4 Your enemies have had power over you because you did not listen to the commandments I gave you.

5 Still, I have made my people a promise. That promise will come true if they begin, right now, to listen to my advice.

6 Starting right now, they will begin to overcome their enemies.

7 If they do everything I tell them, they will go on overcoming their enemies until the Second Coming. Then I will rule the world. My people will own the whole earth forever.

8 But unless the members do everything I tell them, the world will overcome them.

9 You were supposed to be setting an example for the world. You were supposed to be helping to save them.

10 If you do not carry out that calling, you become like salt that has lost its flavor—it is good for nothing, except to be thrown out and stepped on.

11 But I have promised that the members who have been scattered will get their land back. They will rebuild Zion.

12 As I told you before, you will suffer much. But in the end you will be blessed.

13 After all the trouble the members of my church have suffered, I will bless them. I will free them from their enemies. I will bring them back to Zion. They will never be thrown out again.

14 The only way they could be thrown out again is if they stopped keeping the commandments. If they make the land unholy, they will have to be punished.

15 Zion must be freed by power.

16 I will prepare someone to lead my people, like Moses led the people of Israel.

17 You are part of the people of Israel. You are descendants of Abraham. You must be freed by someone with God's power, just like your ancestors were.

18 That is how Zion will be freed.

19 Do not give up. I promise you something better than what I promised your ancestors. To them I promised, "My angel will lead you, but not I myself."

20 But to you I promise, "Both my angels and I myself will lead you. In time, you will have your land back."

21 In the story I told you about the twelve olive trees, the master's

chosen servant stood for Joseph Smith.

22 So I tell Joseph Smith the same thing I told the servant in the story. Gather all my servants who can go to war and lead them to the land of Zion. It is my land, because I bought it with the money donated by the members of my church.

23 All the branches of the church should send people to Missouri to buy land for them, like I commanded them.

24 If your enemies come together again to throw you off your land, tell them, in my name, that they will be punished.

25 I will punish them as you say. You will fight against them for me.

26 I myself will be with you. I will help you overthrow all your enemies.

27 No one should be afraid to die fighting for me. Those who give up their lives for me will be given eternal life in return.

28 Someone who is not willing to die for me is not truly my follower.

29 I want Sidney Rigdon to preach to the branches of the church back east. He must prepare them to keep the commandments I have given them about helping to free Zion.

30 Parley P. Pratt and Lyman Wight should not go back to Zion until they have gathered an army of 500 to take with them.

31 That is what I want you to do. If you ask, I will give. But people do not always do what I want.

32 So if you cannot gather 500, try to gather 300.

33 If you cannot gather 300, try to gather 100.

34 But do not go back to Zion until you have gathered an army of at least 100 to take with you.

35 As I said, if you ask, I will give. Pray that it will be possible for Joseph Smith to go with you. That way he can lead my people. He can organize my kingdom on the land I have chosen. Then you will be able to rebuild Zion in keeping with the revelations.

36 If you work hard and pray with faith, you will overcome all your enemies. You will receive all glory.

37 Parley P. Pratt should travel with Joseph Smith.

38 Lyman Wight should travel with Sidney Rigdon.

39 Hyrum Smith should travel with Frederick G. Williams.

40 Orson Hyde and Orson Pratt should travel together wherever Joseph Smith tells them. Carry out the commandments I have given you. I will take care of the rest. Amen.

SECTION 104

Because of the problems in Missouri, as well as problems in Kirtland, the church had many debts. Up until this point, the church's money had been handled by an organization called the United Order. The United Order had been handling the church's money both in Missouri and in Ohio. Section 104 is a revelation for the members of the United Order. It tells them how to deal with the church's debts.

1 My friends, I give you advice about the property belonging to the United Order. The United Order was formed to help my church carry out my work until I come again.

2 I promised the members of the United Order that if they were faithful, I would give them many blessings.

3 But if they were not faithful, they would be punished.

4 Some of my servants have not kept my commandments. They have broken the holy promise they made with me. They have been selfish. They have lied. They have brought a terrible punishment on themselves.

5 I have sworn that any member of the United Order who breaks the holy promise which joins members of the order together will be destroyed.

6 I warn you to take these things seriously.

7 Those of you who have kept the holy promise will not be punished with those who haven't. Those of you who have kept the promise will be rulers with me in heaven.

8 But if you break the promise, you will suffer for it as long as you live.

9 You will be thrown out of the United Order. You will be in Satan's power until the day you are brought back from the dead.

10 I give you the authority to throw out any member who breaks the promise and does not repent. You need to do this so that the person who sinned does not cause all of you to be punished.

11 I command you to organize yourselves. Each one of you should be given something to take care of.

12 I will judge each of you based on how well you take care of the things you are given.

13 Everyone needs to help take care of the earthly blessings I have prepared for my creatures.

14 I created heaven and earth with my own hands. Everything in them is mine.

15 I will use everything that is mine to take care of my people.

16 But this must be done in my own way. My way of caring for people is for the rich to share what they have with the poor. That way everyone is equal.

17 I have filled the earth with good things. There is more than enough for everyone. I have given people the power to use these things as they choose. But they will be judged for their choices.

18 So the rich must share the good things of the earth with the poor, the way my gospel commands. If they do not, they will suffer in the next life, like the rich man who refused to help the beggar Lazarus.

19 As for the property which belongs to the United Order—

20 Sidney Rigdon should be made caretaker of the tannery. He should also be made caretaker of the house where he is now living. That is how he will support himself while he serves in the church.

21 All the members of the United Order in Kirtland must agree to any decision about how to use the order's property.

22 I will allow Sidney Rigdon to remain caretaker over these things all his life. After he dies, these things will be passed on to his descendants.

23 If he is humble, I will give him many blessings.
24 Martin Harris should be made caretaker of the piece of land which John Johnson traded his old land for. After Martin dies, the land will be passed on to his descendants.
25 If he is faithful, I will give many blessings both to him and to his descendants.
26 He should donate his money to help spread my word, as Joseph Smith directs.
27 Frederick G. Williams should be given the house where he is now living.
28 Oliver Cowdery should be given the land set aside for the printshop. He should also be given the land where his father lives.
29 Frederick and Oliver will own the printshop together. They will also own everything belonging to the printshop.
30 That is what they will be made caretakers over.
31 If they are faithful, I will give them many blessings.
32 This is just the first thing I will give them to take care of. After they die, their descendants will take care of the same things.
33 If they are faithful, I will give them and their descendants many blessings.
34 John Johnson should be made caretaker over the house he lives in. He should be made caretaker over all his land, except the parts where my houses will be built and the parts Oliver Cowdery has been given to take care of.
35 If he is faithful, I will give him many blessings.
36 I want him to sell the pieces of land which have been set aside for my people to build their city on. The Spirit and the other members of the United Order will help him decide how to do this.
37 This is the first thing I will give him to take care of. It is a blessing both for him and for his descendants.
38 If he is faithful, I will give him many other blessings.
39 Newel K. Whitney should be given the land where he now lives, along with the houses that are on it. He should also be given the store building, the ashery, and the piece of land on the corner south of the store.
40 Those are the things I am making him caretaker over. They are a blessing for him and his descendants. I am doing this for the good of the Kirtland stake's store.
41 Newel, his agent, and his descendants will serve as caretakers over the whole store.
42 If he keeps my commandments, I will give him and his descendants many blessings.
43 Joseph Smith should be given the land which has been set aside for building my house. He should also be given the land his father lives on.
44 These are the first things I will give him to take care of. They are a blessing for him and his father.
45 I have set aside land for his father. He should be counted as part of Joseph's family.
46 If Joseph is faithful, I will give his family many blessings.
47 I now command you to separate from the United Order in Zion.
48 From now on, you will be called The United Order of Kirtland,

Stake of Zion. The group in Zion will be called The United Order of the City of Zion.

⁴⁹ The group in Zion will do their business in that new name. They will also do business in their own names.

⁵⁰ You, too, will do business in your group's new name, as well as in your own names.

⁵¹ I command you to do this because of the members in Zion having been thrown off their land. This way, you and they both can be saved from the terrible things that are coming.

⁵² I also command it because of those members of the order who sinned and broke their holy promise.

⁵³ So from now on, you are a separate group from the United Order in Zion. You can make loans to the Order in Zion, though, if you are able to. But you must all be agreed.

⁵⁴ I now give you a commandment about the things I have made you caretakers over.

⁵⁵ Everything you have been given to take care of really belongs to me. Unless you truly believe that, you are lying when you call yourselves "caretakers," and you are breaking the holy promise you made with me.

⁵⁶ Unless these things truly belong to me, you cannot truly be caretakers.

⁵⁷ But I have chosen you to be true caretakers over my house.

⁵⁸ I have told you to organize yourselves so you can publish the new translation of the Bible. I also want you to publish the revelations I have given you.

⁵⁹ You need to do this if my church—my kingdom on earth—is to become strong. You need to do it to prepare my people to live with me after the Second Coming. It is not far off.

⁶⁰ Build a safe. Dedicate it to me.

⁶¹ One of you should be ordained to take care of the safe.

⁶² Keep all your holy things in the safe. No one person can claim to own anything in the safe. It belongs to all of you together.

⁶³ Use everything you have been given to take care of, except what is holy, to raise money to publish the scriptures. The scriptures are one of the things you should keep in the safe.

⁶⁴ The money you make from selling the scriptures should be kept locked in the safe until I command you to use it.

⁶⁵ That way the money will be saved for holy purposes.

⁶⁶ This safe will be called the Lord's holy treasury. It will be kept locked, so it stays holy.

⁶⁷ You should build another safe. Choose someone to take care of it.

⁶⁸ This second safe is for the money you make from the land I gave you to take care of. This money might come from building houses or keeping cows on your land, for example. You should put all the money you make into the safe.

⁶⁹ It does not matter if you make a little money or a lot. It should all go into the safe.

⁷⁰ No one can call any of the money in the safe their own.

⁷¹ No one can use that money unless the United Order agrees.

⁷² When I say that the United Order

needs to agree, this is what I mean. The person who wants to use the money needs to go the one in charge of the safe and say, "I need so much money to help out with the things I have been given to take care of."

73 The one in charge of the safe can give that person however much money is needed.

74 If the members of the United Order know that someone is not a wise and faithful caretaker, that person should not be given any money.

75 But someone who is an active member of the church, and a wise, faithful caretaker, should be given the money they need.

76 If the person has sinned, then the United Order can tell the one in charge of the safe not to give the person any money.

77 If the one in charge of the safe turns out not to be a wise, faithful caretaker, someone else will be chosen to take charge of the safe.

78 I want you to pay off all your debts.

79 If you are humble, work hard, and pray with faith, I will bless you. I will make you able to pay off the debts.

80 I will touch the hearts of the people you owe money to, so they will give you more time to pay off the debt. Then I will send you the money you need.

81 Write a letter quickly to New York. My Spirit will tell you what to write. I will make the people you owe money to forget about taking action against you.

82 Be humble. Have faith. Pray. Then I will be able to help you win the fight.

83 This once, I promise to free you.

84 If you have the chance to borrow money to free yourselves, you may do so.

85 If you decide it is a good idea, you can sign your property over to the people you owe money to, until you are able to pay off your debts.

86 I will let you to do that only this once, though. Remember that you are my caretakers. I am your master. If you do everything I have told you, the master will not let his house be broken up. Amen.

SECTION 105

In Section 103, the Lord told the members in Ohio to raise an army of 500 to go free Zion. Only 200 men actually joined. They were called Zion's Camp. Joseph Smith led Zion's Camp to Missouri. When they got to Missouri, they tried to make peace with their enemies. But their enemies refused to let the members move back to their homes in Jackson County. Section 105 is a revelation the Lord gave Joseph Smith. The revelation explains why Zion's Camp was not able to free Zion.

1 This is what I have to say to you: You have come to learn how my suffering people can be freed.

2 If it were not for the sins of my people—meaning the church as a whole—they could have been freed by now.

3 But they have not learned to keep my commandments. They are full of evil. They do not share their

goods with the poor and suffering among them, as my people ought to do.

4 They are not united the way the law of the celestial kingdom says they need to be.

5 Unless Zion is built in keeping with the law of the celestial kingdom, I cannot accept it.

6 My people must be corrected until they learn to be obedient, even if that means they have to suffer.

7 I am not talking about those who were chosen to lead my people—the first elders. Not all of them are guilty of these sins.

8 But I have this to say about the branches of the church in other places: Many people will say, "Where is God? If God isn't going to free the people of Zion from their troubles, we're not about to go there or buy land there."

9 Because of my people's sins, my elders need to wait a while before they can free Zion.

10 By waiting, my elders will be able to prepare themselves. My people need to be taught more perfectly. They need to have experience. They need to understand more fully their duty and what I expect of them.

11 But this cannot happen until my elders are given power from heaven.

12 If they stay faithful and humble, I will send them the wonderful gift I have prepared for them.

13 So my elders need to wait a while before they can free Zion.

14 They themselves will not have to fight for Zion. As I promised you earlier, I will fight for you.

15 Your enemies have fallen into Satan's power. He will destroy them. In a few years, none of them will be left on the land I have chosen for gathering my people.

16 I told Joseph Smith to call together all my servants who could go to war. I told them to free my people. I told them to tear down my enemies' towers and scatter their guards.

17 But my servants have not listened to me.

18 There are some who have listened to me. If they stay faithful, I have a gift prepared for them.

19 I have heard their prayers. I will accept their sacrifice. I needed them to come this far so I could test their faith.

20 Those who can stay nearby, should stay.

21 Those who need to go back east to their families should stay just a little longer, until Joseph lets them go home.

22 I will tell Joseph what to do about this. My servants should do everything he tells them.

23 Those of my people who live in the areas round about need to be very faithful. They need to pray very hard. They need to be humble. They must not tell the world about the things I have revealed to them until I tell them to do so.

24 Do not go around talking about the wicked being punished. Do not boast about your faith or about powerful works. Be careful. Gather as many church members into one place as you can without making the non-members angry or afraid.

25 I will touch the non-members' hearts, so they think well of you. Then you will be able to live in

peace and safety. Say to the people, "Give us justice. Right our wrongs."

26 If you do this, the people will stay friendly towards you until Israel's army has become great.

27 I will touch the people's hearts, the way I touched Pharaoh's heart. Then Joseph Smith and the elders I have chosen will have enough time to gather my servants for war.

28 They need time to send people to buy land in Jackson County and the counties round about, as I commanded earlier.

29 I want the members of my church to buy these lands. Then they should settle on them in keeping with the law I gave about making people caretakers of church property.

30 After these lands have been bought, I will let Israel's army take back the lands they bought earlier. I will let them tear down whatever towers my enemies may have built there and scatter their guards. I will let them punish my enemies.

31 But first my army needs to become very great. It needs to become holy. Then it will shine like the sun and moon. The whole world will be afraid of its flags.

32 Every government on earth will be forced to admit that Zion is indeed God and Christ's kingdom. They will say, "We must obey Zion's laws."

33 The first elders of my church need to receive power from heaven. This will happen in the temple I have commanded you to build in Kirtland.

34 After Zion has been freed, you will need to keep all the commandments I have given about Zion. You will need to keep Zion's law.

35 I have been calling many people to do my work. Now it is time to find out which of those people are truly worthy.

36 The Spirit will tell my servant who is worthy. Those who are worthy will be made holy.

37 If they follow the advice they are given, they will have power to do everything I have promised about Zion. But it will be a long time before that happens.

38 Try to make peace, not only with those who have hurt you, but with all people.

39 Cry "Peace!" to everyone on earth.

40 Offer to make peace with your enemies, in keeping with what the Spirit tells you. If you do this, everything will work out for the best.

41 So be faithful. Remember I will always be with you. Amen.

SECTION 106

Oliver Cowdery had an older brother named Warren. Warren lived in a town called Freedom, in the state of New York. After Zion's Camp travelled from Missouri back to Kirtland, the Lord gave Joseph Smith a revelation for Warren. The revelation called Warren to be branch president in Freedom. Section 106 is that revelation.

1 I want Warren A. Cowdery to be ordained branch president for Freedom and the areas round about.
2 He should teach the restored gospel. He should warn people to repent. He should do this both in his own county and in the counties nearby.
3 He should give all his time to this calling. If he works hard to build my kingdom, I will give him everything he needs to live.
4 I repeat what I have said before—the Second Coming is almost here. It will take the world by surprise.
5 Walk in the Father's light. Then you will be ready for the Second Coming.
6 There was joy in heaven when Warren accepted me as his king. He left behind the wicked ways of the people of the world.
7 I will bless Warren. I will show him mercy. There is pride in his heart. But if he becomes humble, I will lift him up.
8 I will give him grace and comfort. I will help him stand strong. If he keeps being a faithful witness and an example for church members, I promise to make him a ruler in my Father's kingdom. Amen.

SECTION 107

Almost five years after the church was restored, the Quorum of the Twelve Apostles was finally formed. The new apostles soon decided to set out on a mission. Before they left, the apostles told Joseph Smith they did not feel worthy of their callings. They asked Joseph for a revelation to help them in times of trouble. Section 107 is the revelation the Lord gave for them.

1 There are two priesthoods in the church—the Melchizedek priesthood and the Aaronic priesthood. The priesthood held by the Levites is part of the Aaronic priesthood.
2 The first priesthood was named after Melchizedek because he was such an important high priest.
3 Before Melchizedek's time, it was called the Holy Priesthood after the Order of God's Son.
4 But church members long ago starting calling it the Melchizedek priesthood. They did this out of respect for God's name, so they would not be repeating it so much.
5 All offices in the church are part of the priesthood.
6 But the priesthood has two main branches—the Melchizedek priesthood and the Aaronic priesthood.
7 The office of elder is part of the Melchizedek priesthood.
8 In every period of history, the Melchizedek priesthood has been the authority which governs all church offices. It is the power which brings spiritual blessings to people.
9 The First Presidency have the authority to carry out any church office.
10 High priests are called to bring spiritual blessings to people. They are led by the First Presidency. A high priest has the authority to carry out the office of an elder, a priest, a teacher, a deacon, or any other member of the church.

11 An elder can carry out a high priest's office if there is no high priest there.

12 High priests and elders bring people spiritual blessings. They do this in keeping with the revelations which have been given to the church. They have the authority to carry out all church offices if there are no higher authorities there.

13 The second priesthood is called the Aaronic priesthood because it was given to Aaron and all his descendants.

14 It is called the "lower priesthood" because it is a branch of the "higher" or Melchizedek priesthood. It gives people the first, more basic, ordinances.

15 The bishop and his counselors have the authority to lead the Aaronic priesthood.

16 The person who serves as bishop and leads the Aaronic priesthood is supposed to be a descendant of Aaron.

17 But high priests in the Melchizidek priesthood have the authority to carry out all offices in the Aaronic priesthood. So a high priest can serve as bishop if there is no descendant of Aaron to do it. In such a case, the high priest must be ordained by the First Presidency.

18 The power of the Melchizedek priesthood makes it possible for church members to receive all spiritual blessings.

19 The Melchizedck priesthood makes it possible for people to receive revelation. It makes it possible for them to become members of Jesus Christ's church. It makes it possible for them to be with God the Father and Jesus.

20 The power of the Aaronic priesthood makes it possible for church members to be baptized and to receive the sacrament. The Aaronic priesthood also makes it possible for people to be visited by angels.

21 In both the Aaronic and Melchizedek priesthoods, there must be quorum leaders. The quorum leaders are chosen from among those who have been ordained.

22 The First Presidency is made up of three high priests who have been chosen by the church and ordained to this office. They depend on the trust, faith, and prayers of church members for support.

23 The Twelve Apostles are called to travel as special witnesses of Christ in all the world. This makes their calling different from that of other church offices.

24 The Quorum of the Twelve Apostles is equal in power and authority to the First Presidency.

25 The Seventy are also called to preach the gospel and be special witnesses in all the world.

26 The Quorum of Seventy is equal in power and authority to the Quorum of the Twelve Apostles.

27 When these quorums make a decision, every member of the quorum must be agreed. If that is not the case, the one quorum's decisions cannot be equal in power to the other's.

28 If not all the members of the quorum are able to meet together, the quorum can still make decisions, as long as most of the quorum members are there.

29 But unless every quorum member there is agreed, the quorums' decisions cannot receive the same

blessing that the decisions of First Presidencies long ago received.

30 When the members of these quorums make decisions, they must be righteous, humble, and patient. They must act the way the Lord himself would act.

31 The scriptures promise that as people become more like the Lord, the Lord will guide and teach them.

32 If one of the quorums makes an unrighteous decision, the other quorums can meet together to overturn it. That is the only way such a decision can be overturned.

33 The Twelve are a travelling high council. They act in the Lord's name, as directed by the First Presidency. Their calling is to build up the church in all the world. They keep the church running the way it should.

34 The Seventy act in the Lord's name, as directed by the Twelve. The Seventy help the Twelve carry out their calling.

35 The Twelve are sent out with Jesus Christ's authority. They have the same authority given to Peter in Bible times. By preaching the gospel of Jesus Christ, they make it possible for all people to come to God.

36 The stake high councils form a quorum equal in authority to the First Presidency or the Twelve, when it comes to making decisions about running the church.

37 The decisions made by the high council in Zion are equal in authority to the decisions made in the stakes by the councils of the Twelve.

38 The Twelve should call on the Seventy whenever they need help bringing people the gospel. They should not call on someone else.

39 In all large branches of the church, the Twelve should ordain patriarchs. I will reveal to the Twelve who the patriarchs should be.

40 The office of patriarch was meant to be handed down from father to son. It rightfully belongs to members of the family I made special promises to.

41 Adam was the first patriarch. This is how the office was passed down after him—

42 Seth was 69 when Adam ordained him. Three years before Adam died, Adam gave Seth a blessing. In the blessing, God promised Seth that his descendants would be the Lord's chosen people. They would never be completely destroyed.

43 God made this promise because Seth was so righteous. Seth was exactly like Adam. People could tell them apart only by their ages.

44 Enos was 134 years and 4 months old when Adam ordained him.

45 When Cainan was 40, God spoke to him in the desert. Cainan met Adam while travelling to Shedolamak. He was 87 years old when he was ordained.

46 Mahalaleel was 496 years and 7 days old when Adam ordained him. Adam also blessed him.

47 Jared was 200 when Adam ordained him. Adam blessed him as well.

48 Enoch was 25 when Adam ordained him. He was 65 when Adam blessed him.

49 Enoch saw the Lord and was always with him. He walked with

God for 365 years after being ordained. That made him 430 when he was taken up off the earth.

50 Methuselah was 100 when Adam ordained him.

51 Lamech was 32 when Seth ordained him.

52 Noah was 10 when Methuselah ordained him.

53 Three years before he died, Adam held a meeting with Seth, Enos, Cainan, Mahalaleel, Jared, Enoch, and Methuselah. These men were all high priests. The rest of Adam's descendants who were still righteous were also at the meeting. The meeting was held in the valley Adam-ondi-Ahman. There Adam gave them his last blessing.

54 The Lord appeared to them. They stood up and blessed Adam. They called him Prince Michael, the chief angel.

55 The Lord comforted Adam. The Lord told him, "I have made you ruler of all. Your descendants will fill the world. You will be their prince forever."

56 Adam stood up in the middle of everyone, even though he was bent over from old age. He was filled with the Holy Ghost. He told about everything that would happen to his descendants until the end of the world.

57 All these things were written in the Book of Enoch. They will be testified of in due time.

58 The Twelve are in charge of ordaining all other church officers. They are in charge of making sure that the officers carry out their callings properly. This is in keeping with the revelation which says—

59 This is a revelation to the branch of Christ's church in Zion. It is an addition to the laws telling how to carry out church business.

60 This is what the Lord says: Certain elders must be chosen to lead the other elders.

61 Certain priests must be chosen to lead the other priests.

62 Certain teachers must be chosen to lead the other teachers. The same with the deacons.

63 So deacons, teachers, priests, and elders will all have their own leaders. Those leaders will be chosen in keeping with the revelations given to the church.

64 The office of high priest is the highest of all.

65 So the high priest who is chosen to lead the other high priests will also serve as President of the Church.

66 In others words, this person will serve as the church's leading high priest.

67 The power to perform ordinances or bless church members by the laying on of hands comes from the Melchizedek priesthood.

68 The office of bishop is not equal to the Melchizedek priesthood. That is because a bishop's calling is to take care of earthly concerns.

69 But bishops must also be high priests, unless they are descendants of Aaron.

70 That is because only a descendant of Aaron can lead the Aaronic priesthood.

71 But high priests in the Melchizidek priesthood can be called to take care of earthly concerns, because they have the Spirit to teach them what to do.

72 High priests can also be called to

carry out church business. They can be called to hold church courts. Their counselors will help them do this. The counselors will be chosen from among the elders.

73 These are the duties of bishops who are high priests in the Melchizedek priesthood, rather than descendants of Aaron.

74 The bishops will serve as judges in the stakes or branches where they are called to work. As Zion grows, more bishops will be called.

75 Any bishops called in the future will carry out these same duties.

76 A descendant of Aaron who serves as bishop does not need to have counselors, except when holding a church court for a member of the First Presidency.

77 In any case, the decision of a church court must be in keeping with the commandment which says—

78 If a church court has to deal with a very hard case, and if the person being judged feels like the court has made the wrong decision, the case can be heard again by the First Presidency.

79 The First Presidency can call twelve other high priests to act as counselors. Together they will decide the case a second time. They will make their decision in keeping with church laws.

80 After they have decided the case a second time, it cannot be heard again. That is because the First Presidency is the highest authority in God's church. Its decisions about spiritual concerns are final.

81 The First Presidency has authority over every church member.

82 When a member of the First Presidency sins, the case should be heard by the common council of the church. Twelve high priests should help out as counselors.

83 Their decision will be final.

84 This way, God's justice and God's laws will apply to everyone. Everything will be done in an organized, serious, and righteous way.

85 A deacons quorum is made up of 12 deacons. The deacons quorum president meets with the deacons to teach them their duties. That way they can build each other up, as I have commanded.

86 A teachers quorum is made up of 24 teachers. The teachers quorum president meets with the teachers to teach them their duties as explained in the revelations.

87 A priests quorum is made up of 48 priests. The priests quorum president meets with the priests to teach them their duties as explained in the revelations.

88 The priests quorum president should be a bishop, because that is one of the bishop's duties.

89 An elders quorum is made up of 96 elders. The elders quorum president meets with the elders to teach them their duties as explained in the revelations.

90 An elders quorum presidency is not the same as a seventies quorum presidency, because elders are not called to travel throughout the world.

91 The duty of the president of the high priests is to lead the whole church, like Moses led the people of Israel.

92 The President of the Church will be a prophet. God will give the

President every gift needed to lead the church.

93 God has revealed that seven members of the Quorum of Seventy should be chosen to serve as presidents of that quorum.

94 Out of those seven presidents, one will be chosen to lead the other six.

95 These seven presidents will choose seventy more people to serve as a Second Quorum of Seventy.

96 The presidents can form up to seven Quorums of Seventy, if that many are needed to carry out the Lord's work.

97 Members of these quorums will travel throughout the world. They will teach my gospel to all people.

98 Only the Twelve and the Seventy are called to travel throughout the world. But this does not mean that other church offices are any less important than those of the Twelve or the Seventy. Other officers can travel, too, if they are able.

99 Let everyone learn their duties and work hard to carry out the callings they have been given.

100 People who do not learn their duties or work hard to carry them out are not worthy to keep their offices. Amen.

SECTION 108

Lyman Sherman was one of the seven presidents of the Quorum of Seventy. He was very worried about whether or not the Lord accepted him. Lyman told Joseph Smith what he was feeling. He asked Joseph for a revelation. Section 108 is the revelation the Lord gave for him. In the revelation, the Lord promised Lyman he would become an apostle. Lyman did receive that calling. But he died before he could be ordained.

1 This is what the Lord says to Lyman: By coming here this morning to receive advice from my prophet, you have obeyed me. So your sins are forgiven.

2 Stop worrying about whether or not I accept you. Stop fighting my voice.

3 Be more careful from now on about keeping the promises you have made, and you will receive very great blessings.

4 Wait patiently until my servants hold their special meeting. Then you will be called to be an apostle.

5 As long as you stay faithful, you have this promise from the Father.

6 Once you are ordained an apostle, you will have the authority to preach my gospel wherever I send you.

7 Every time you talk, or pray, or preach, or act, try to make others stronger.

8 I will always be with you. I will bless you and keep you safe. Amen.

SECTION 109

After three years of hard work, the members in Ohio finally finished building the Kirtland Temple. Many more people came for the temple dedication than there was room for. It was a very spiritual meeting. Some people saw angels. People outside saw a pillar of fire come down on top of the temple. Some people heard angels singing. Others heard a sound like a great wind. To dedicate the temple to God, Joseph Smith read a special prayer that had been revealed to him. Section 109 is that prayer.

1 Lord God, we thank you for keeping your promises. We thank you for showing mercy to your servants, who try with all their hearts to do what is right.

2 You commanded us to build a temple for you here in Kirtland.

3 Lord, you can see that we have kept that commandment.

4 We now ask you, Holy Father, in the name of your dear Son, Jesus Christ, our Savior, to accept this temple.

5 You know that we built it during a time of great trouble. We were poor, but we donated our goods to build a temple. We did it so your Son would have a place where he could show himself to his people.

6 You called us your friends. You gave us a revelation that said, "Hold the special meeting I commanded you to.

7 "Since you do not all have faith, work hard to get wisdom. Teach each other from the world's best books. Learn by studying as well as through faith.

8 "Organize yourselves. Prepare everything you need to build a house for God. It will be a house for praying and fasting. It will be a house of faith and learning. It will be a house of glory and order.

9 "Whenever you go in or out of that house, you will do it in the Lord's name. You will greet each other in the Lord's name, lifting your hands up toward God."

10 Now, Father, we ask you to help us hold a meeting that will be acceptable to you.

11 Help us to be worthy of receiving what you promised, in your revelations, to give us.

12 Send down your glory to your people. Send it down on this temple. We dedicate it to you to be a holy house, where you yourself can always be.

13 Then everyone who comes into the temple will be able to feel your power. They will know that you have made it your holy house.

14 Let everyone who worships here learn wisdom from the world's best books. Let them learn both by studying and through faith, as you said.

15 Help them grow spiritually. Fill them with the Holy Ghost. Organize them in keeping with your laws. Prepare them to receive everything they need.

16 Let this be a house for praying and fasting. Let it be a house of faith and glory. Let it be your house.

17 Whenever your people come into this house, may they do it in your name.

18 Whenever they go out of this

house, may they do it in your name.

19 Whenever they greet each other, may they do it in your name, with holy hands lifted up to God.

20 Let nothing come into your house that will make it unholy.

21 When any of your people sin, may they quickly repent and come back to you. May they again be worthy to receive the blessings you have promised to give those who worship you in the temple.

22 Father, we ask you to give your servants power. Let them leave here with your authority. Let them leave surrounded by your glory and guarded by your angels.

23 Let them take the glorious news from here to every part of the world. Let people know that this is your work. Let them know that you are using your power to make everything the prophets said come true.

24 Father, we ask you to keep those who worship you in this temple safe forever.

25 Do not let them be hurt by any weapon. Let their enemies fall into their own traps.

26 Do not let the wicked have power over your people, who will take on your name in this temple.

27 If anyone comes to fight this people, use your power to help us.

28 If anyone hurts your people, let them be punished. Fight for your people like you did long ago. Save your people from all their enemies.

29 Father, we ask you to bring to shame to everyone who spreads lies about your servants, if they will not repent when they hear the gospel. Let people know that the things they have said about your people are not true.

30 Let all their works come to nothing in the day when the wicked are punished. Put an end to the lies told about your people.

31 Lord, you know that your servants have testified of you, as you commanded. You know that we have suffered for doing it.

32 We beg you to put an end to our suffering.

33 Free us, Lord. Free us from our enemies, so we can do your work among this people.

34 Jehovah, show mercy to this people. Everyone sins. So forgive your people's sins. Let them be forgotten.

35 When your servants are anointed, give them heavenly power.

36 Bless them the way you blessed your followers on the day of Pentecost. Give them the power to speak and understand other languages. Let flames of fire appear over their heads.

37 Send your glory to fill the temple like a mighty, rushing wind.

38 Give your servants powerful testimonies. Then they can go out to teach your word with authority. Help them prepare your people to be strong during the times of trouble that are coming, when the wicked will suffer because of their sins.

39 Give peace and salvation to everyone who accepts your servants. Gather the righteous to Zion, or its stakes. Bring them singing songs of eternal joy on the way.

40 Let nothing happen to a city until the righteous people living there have been able to gather to Zion.

41 But where people reject your servants' testimonies or warnings, we know they must be punished as the prophets have said.
42 Jehovah, we ask you to protect your servants from the wicked. Do not judge your servants for the sins committed by the wicked people of today.
43 Lord, it makes us sad to know that other people may be destroyed. We know how much you care about them.
44 But your words must come true. Help your servants to say, "Your will be done, Lord, not ours."
45 We know the prophets have said that terrible things are going to happen to the wicked before the end of the world. We know the wicked will have to suffer for what they have done.
46 Lord, save your people from the sufferings of the wicked. Help your servants stay true to your law and their testimonies. That way they will be ready for the terrible times that are coming.
47 Father, we ask you to remember the members who have been thrown off their land by the people of Jackson County, Missouri. Free them from their enemies.
48 You know that wicked people have taken away their rights and made them suffer. Our hearts are filled with sorrow because of their suffering.
49 Lord, how long will you let your people suffer? How long must their little children cry before you will show your power? How much blood must be spilled before you will come to their aid?
50 Lord, show mercy to those who have hurt your people. If possible, lead them to repent of their sins. Lead them to stop their attacks.
51 But if they will not repent, show your power. Free the land you gave your people to build Zion on.
52 If there is no other way for your people to do what you have commanded, then let your people's enemies be completely destroyed.
53 But if they repent, you will show them mercy through your Son's atonement.
54 Lord, show mercy to all the peoples of the world. Show mercy to our country's rulers. May the constitution for which our ancestors fought stand forever.
55 Remember the kings, the princes, and all the powerful people of the world. Remember the churches, the poor, the needy, and all who suffer.
56 Touch their hearts when your servants leave this temple to testify about you. Let the truth overcome people's false ideas about us. Let everyone come to respect your people.
57 Then everyone on earth will know that you have spoken to us, your servants. They will know that you have sent us to teach them.
58 Then your servants will be able to gather the righteous from out of the world. They will be able to build a holy city for you, as you commanded.
59 We ask you to choose other stakes for Zion, besides the one here in Kirtland. That way your people can gather together more powerfully. They can carry out your work more quickly.
60 Lord, so far we have been talking

about the commandments you gave to us, who are called Gentiles.
61 But we know that you also dearly love Jacob's descendants. They have been scattered for a long time, waiting for your light.
62 We ask you to show mercy to Jacob's descendants. Start now to set Jerusalem free.
63 Begin to set free the family of David.
64 Begin to gather the Jews back to the land you gave their ancestor, Abraham.
65 Bring an end to the suffering of the Lamanites. Let them be converted to the restored gospel. Let them become a peaceful people.
66 May they put down their weapons. May they make peace.
67 Let the people of Israel scattered all over the world learn the truth. May they accept the Messiah. Free them from suffering. Fill them with joy.
68 Lord, remember everything Joseph Smith has suffered. Remember what he promised you. Remember how hard he has tried to keep your commandments.
69 Show mercy to his wife and children. Protect them. Help them grow. Lift them up to be with you.
70 Show mercy to their family members. Let their family members' false ideas be overcome. That way they, too, can be converted to the restored gospel.
71 Bless all the leaders of your church, along with their families. Lift them up. Let them be remembered forever.
72 Lord, bless all the members of your church, with all their families. Bless all the sick and suffering. Bless the poor and humble. Let your kingdom fill the whole earth, like the stone in Nebuchadnezzar's dream.
73 Then your church can come out of the dark desert. It will shine as brightly as the sun and the moon. It will march forward like an army with flags.
74 It will be like a bride, dressed and waiting for your coming. Then you will show yourself from heaven. The mountains will melt. The valleys will be lifted up. Rough places will be made smooth. The earth will be filled with your glory.
75 When the trumpet blows to bring back the dead, we will be lifted through the air to meet you in the cloud. We will be with you forever.
76 Then we will be given robes of righteousness. We will be given palms and crowns of glory. For everything we have suffered, we will be rewarded with eternal joy.
77 Lord God, answer our prayers. You sit on your throne in heaven. You are filled with glory, praise, power, strength, authority, truth, justice, wisdom, and mercy forever.
78 Hear us, hear us, hear us, Lord! Answer our prayers. Accept this temple which we have built and dedicated to you.
79 Accept also this church. Make it yours. Give us your Spirit's power, so we can sing with the angels, "Hosanna to God and the Lamb!"
80 Save your chosen people. Fill the members of your church with joy forever. Amen.

SECTION 110

On Easter Sunday, 1836, a sacrament meeting was held in the Kirtland Temple. The apostles blessed the sacrament. Joseph Smith helped pass it out to the members. Then Joseph and Oliver Cowdery went behind a curtain to pray. After they prayed, they had a very important vision. Section 110 tells about that vision.

1 We were given a vision.

2 We saw the Lord standing on the pulpit in front of us. His feet were on top of a smooth gold surface colored like amber.

3 His eyes were like fire. His hair was white as snow. His face shone more brightly than the sun. His voice was like a giant stream of water. It was the voice of Jehovah! He said:

4 "I am the beginning and the end. I am the one who was killed and then came back from the dead. I am your defender when the Father judges you.

5 "Rejoice! I have forgiven your sins. I have made you pure.

6 "My people have worked hard to build this temple. Tell them all to rejoice.

7 "I accept this temple. I will make it my house. Here I will show myself to my people in mercy.

8 "If my people keep my commandments and do not make my temple unholy, I will appear to my servants. I will talk with them in person.

9 "The blessings and heavenly power which I give my servants in this temple will bring joy to tens of thousands of people.

10 "People in faraway countries will hear about this temple. Yet even this is just the beginning of the blessing which I will give my people. Amen."

11 After this vision, we saw another. Moses appeared to us. He gave us the power to gather Israel from every part of the world. He gave us the power to lead the ten tribes out of the north.

12 Then Elias appeared. He gave us the same power God gave to Abraham. He told us that everyone in the future would be blessed through us and our descendants.

13 After this vision, we saw another. We saw Elijah the prophet, who was taken to heaven without dying. He said:

14 "Now is the time that Malachi prophesied about, when he said that Elijah would be sent before the Second Coming.

15 "He said that people would be united with their ancestors, to keep the whole world from being cursed.

16 "That is why you have been given these powers. That is how you can know that the Second Coming is almost here."

SECTION 111

The church had gotten into debt building the Kirtland Temple. A church member named Jonathan Burgess said he knew where there was a treasure hidden in Salem, Massachusetts. Joseph Smith and some other church leaders travelled to Salem with Jonathan Burgess. They wanted to get the treasure to pay the church's debts. But once they arrived, Jonathan said the town had changed so much that he couldn't find the treasure. Then he left them. Section 111 is a revelation Joseph received while he was in Salem.

1 You have done some foolish things. But I am not unhappy with you for making this journey.
2 I have many treasures for you in this city, for the good of Zion. There are many people in this city who will be gathered to Zion through you.
3 You need to get to know people in this city. I will help you do this.
4 Someday you will have power over this city. Then no one here will be able to shame you. All its gold and silver will be yours.
5 Do not worry about your debts. I will make sure you are able to pay them.
6 Do not worry about Zion. I will treat the people there with mercy.
7 Stay a while here and in other places nearby.
8 For the most part, my Spirit will tell you where I want you to stay. It will do this by making you feel peaceful.
9 You will be able to rent the place the Spirit leads you to. Work hard to learn about the city's first settlers.
10 There is more than one treasure for you here.
11 Be clever, like snakes, but without sinning. I will make everything work out for your good. I will do it as quickly as you are ready to receive what I have for you. Amen.

SECTION 112

To try to help pay the church's debts, Joseph Smith and other church leaders started their own bank in Kirtland. But things went wrong, and the Kirtland bank failed. Many church members lost their money. They also lost their faith in Joseph. Hundreds of people left the church. Even some of the apostles turned against Joseph. Section 112 is a revelation for Thomas B. Marsh, president of the Quorum of the Twelve. The revelation was to tell him how to lead the apostles during this difficult time.

1 This is what the Lord says to Thomas: I have heard your prayers. I have seen the sacrifices you made to help the other apostles. The apostles were ordained to testify about me among all the peoples of the world.
2 There have been a few things in your heart that made me unhappy.
3 But because you have humbled yourself, I will lift you up. Your sins are forgiven.
4 Cheer up! You will testify about me to all the peoples of the world.

You will send my word to the farthest parts of the earth.

5 Day by day, warn people to repent. Night by night, keep them awake with your preaching.

6 I do not want you to move your family. That is because I have an important work for you to do. It will help spread my word among the people of the world.

7 So get ready to work and to travel. I have chosen you to travel across mountains and in many countries.

8 Through your teaching, many proud people will be humbled. Many humble people will be lifted up.

9 You will tell sinners to repent. You will tell people who spread lies to be quiet.

10 If you are humble, the Lord will lead you by the hand. He will answer your prayers.

11 I know your heart. I have heard you pray for your friends. Love them as you love yourself. But do not love them more than you love other people. Let your love spread to all people, not just those who love me.

12 Be faithful. Pray for the other members of the Quorum of the Twelve. Correct them for all their sins. Be harsh with them.

13 When they are tempted and in trouble, I will reach out to them. If they will open their hearts and be humble, I will convert and heal them.

14 What I say to you now is for all the Twelve: Get ready to face great hardship. Follow my example. Take care of my people.

15 Be humble. Do not turn against Joseph Smith. I am watching over him. The powers I have given him will not be taken away from him until the Second Coming. You share those powers.

16 Thomas, I have chosen you to lead the Twelve in carrying out their share of the work of building my kingdom in all the world.

17 Your calling is to start my kingdom everywhere my servants Joseph, Sidney, and Hyrum cannot go.

18 For a while, I have placed them in charge of the branches of the church that have already been formed.

19 So go wherever they send you. I will go with you. Wherever you teach about me, you will find people who will accept my word.

20 Whoever accepts my word accepts me. Whoever accepts me accepts the First Presidency. The First Presidency are my messengers. Listen to their advice.

21 You and the Twelve can give other people the authority to start my kingdom in any country you send them to.

22 They will have that power as long as they are humble, obey my words, and listen to my Spirit.

23 The earth is covered with darkness, because people do not know the truth. The whole world has become wicked.

24 Very soon, the people of the world will suffer for their sins. It will be a time of fire and destruction. It will be a time of crying and sorrow. It will move across the earth like a whirlwind.

25 It will start in my church. Then it will spread to the rest of the world.

26 It will start among those who say they are my followers but who do not truly know me. These people come into my temple. But they do not respect me.
27 Do not worry about church business here.
28 Instead, work to make your hearts holy. Then go all over the world. Preach my gospel to everyone who has not accepted it.
29 Everyone who believes and is baptized will be saved. Someone who refuses to believe or get baptized cannot be saved.
30 I have given the Twelve and the First Presidency the power to lead my work for the last time before the end of the world. History is coming to its close.
31 The power you hold is the same that has been held by everyone who received power from me since the time the world began.
32 That power was passed down through history. It has been sent for the last time from heaven to you.
33 Do you see now how important your calling is? Make yourselves clean. Then you will not be judged for the sins of the people of today.
34 Be faithful until the Second Coming. It will be soon. When I come, I will give everyone what they have earned for their works. I am Jesus Christ. Amen.

SECTION 113

The problems at Kirtland became very serious. Many church leaders, including Oliver Cowdery, Martin Harris, and Frederick G. Williams, turned against Joseph Smith and left the church. People were so angry with Joseph that, finally, he had to run away from Kirtland. He went to live in Far West, Missouri. Some other church members had already settled there. While Joseph was in Far West, some of the members asked him questions about the Book of Isaiah. Those questions, along with the Lord's answers, are published in Section 113.

1 *Isaiah 11:1-5 talks about the "Stem of Jesse." Who is that?*
2 The Lord says: It is Christ.
3 *Isaiah 11:1 mentions a "rod" coming out of the Stem of Jesse. What is that?*
4 The Lord says: It is a servant of Christ, who is given much power. That servant is a descendant both of Jesse and of Ephraim.
5 *Isaiah 11:10 talks about the "root of Jesse." What is that?*
6 The Lord says: It is a descendant of Jesse and Joseph who holds the priesthood and the power to lead God's kingdom. My people will gather around this person before the end of the world.
7 *Elias Higbee asked: What does Isaiah 52: 1 mean when it commands, "Put on your strength, O Zion"? Which people is Isaiah talking about?*
8 Isaiah is talking about the priesthood holders God would call before the end of the world to restore Zion and save Israel. Zion "puts on her strength" by receiving the priesthood. The people of Zion have a right to receive the priesthood because of who they are descended from. It also means that

Zion should become powerful again.

⁹ *Isaiah 52:2 talks about Zion taking the chains off her neck. What does that mean?*

¹⁰ It means that the scattered people of Israel are being invited to come back to the Lord. If they come back, he promises to speak to them. In other words, he will give them revelation. See Isaiah 52: 6-8. The chains on Zion's neck are the punishments God sent the people of Israel when they were scattered among the Gentiles.

SECTION 114

David W. Patten was one of the first apostles in the restored church. He stayed faithful to Joseph Smith during the problems in Kirtland. Section 114 is a revelation commanding David to get ready to serve a mission. Before David could leave for his mission, though, church members in Missouri got into a battle with their enemies. David was killed during that battle.

¹ The Lord says: David W. Patten should settle his business as soon as possible. He should turn his goods over to someone else. That way he will be able to serve a mission for me next spring. He will travel with eleven others. They will testify about me. They will bring good news to the whole world.

² There are some among you who have not been true to my name. New people will be called to take over their callings. Amen.

SECTION 115

Because of all the trouble in Kirtland, Joseph Smith and the members who still followed him moved to Far West, Missouri. On April 26, 1838, the Lord gave a revelation commanding the members in Far West to build a temple there. Section 115 is that revelation. In the same revelation, the Lord told the members what to call the church. Before this revelation was received, the church was called "The Church of Christ" or "The Church of the Latter Day Saints."

¹ This is what the Lord says to Joseph Smith, Sidney Rigdon, and Hyrum Smith, and your counselors. (I mean the counselors you have now and those who will be called in the future.)

² This revelation is also for Edward Partridge and his counselors.

³ It is for the members of the high council in Zion. It is for all the elders. It is for all the members of my Church of Jesus Christ of Latter-day Saints throughout the world.

⁴ That is what my restored church will be called—The Church of Jesus Christ of Latter-day Saints.

⁵ I say to you all: Stand up and shine. Let the whole world see your good example.

⁶ People from all over the world will gather in the land of Zion and in its stakes. They will gather for

protection from the terrible things that are coming.

7 Dedicate the city of Far West to me. It will be called a most holy land. That is because the place you are standing on is holy.

8 Here you will build me a temple. The members of my church can meet there to worship me.

9 Get everything ready and start working on the temple this summer.

10 Begin work on July 4. Work hard from that time on to build my temple.

11 One year from today, my people should start to work on the temple again.

12 Then they should keep working until the temple is completely finished.

13 Joseph Smith, Sidney Rigdon, and Hyrum Smith should not go into debt again to build a temple.

14 I will show them how I want the temple to be built.

15 If my people build the temple in a way other than the one I show their leaders, I will not accept it.

16 But if they build it the way I show Joseph and his counselors, then I will accept it.

17 I want the members of my church to gather quickly to Far West.

18 Now and then I will tell Joseph to start other stakes in the areas round about.

19 I have placed him in charge of my work. So I will be with him. I will make him holy. Amen.

SECTION 116

Close to Far West was a place called Spring Hill. Joseph Smith taught that Spring Hill is an important place in God's plan. It was where Adam and Eve moved to after they left the Garden of Eden. It was where Adam met with his descendants for the last time before he died. And it is where Adam will come back to earth just before Jesus' Second Coming. Section 116 is part of what Joseph Smith taught about Spring Hill.

1 The Lord calls Spring Hill "Adam-ondi-Ahman," because that is where Adam will come to visit his people. This is what the prophet Daniel meant when he wrote about the Ancient of Days sitting on a throne.

SECTION 117

In Section 115, the Lord told the faithful members still living in Kirtland to move quickly to Far West. But William Marks and Newel K. Whitney stayed behind. They did not want to give up the property they had in Kirtland. Section 117 is a revelation for William and Newel. After Joseph Smith sent them a copy of the revelation, they obeyed and moved to Far West.

1 This is what the Lord says about William Marks and Newel K. Whitney: They should settle their business quickly. They should move out of Kirtland before the snow comes.
2 They need to hurry and get going. The Lord commands this.
3 If they stay in Kirtland, things will go badly for them.
4 They must repent of all their sins and their selfish desires. The Lord asks—what do I care about property?
5 Turn the property in Kirtland over to those you owe money to. If you can keep some of it, fine. But let it go.
6 Do I not own all the birds in the sky, the fish in the sea, and the animals in the mountains? Did I not create the earth? Do I not control what happens to all the armies of the world?
7 Can I not turn deserts into gardens?
8 There is plenty of room in the mountains of Adam-ondi-Ahman and the plains of Olaha Shinehah, the land where Adam lived. You do not need to hang on to things that do not really matter. You should pay more attention to what is truly important.
9 Come join my people in Zion.
10 If William Marks proves faithful over a few things, he will be made a ruler over many things. He will serve as a leader of my people in Far West. He will share their blessings.
11 Newel K. Whitney should be ashamed of my people's enemies and their secret sins. He should be ashamed of the way he has been acting. He should come to Adam-ondi-Ahman. He should start acting like a bishop, not just calling himself one.
12 I have not forgotten Oliver Granger. I tell him that his name will be remembered forever.
13 He should work hard to free the First Presidency from debt. If he fails at first, he should try again. The sacrifice he makes will be holy to me.
14 He should come quickly to Zion. In time, he will be called to run a store to help my people.
15 No one should think badly of Oliver Granger. He will share my people's blessings forever.
16 All my servants in Kirtland should remember the Lord. They should keep my temple holy. Those who have done unholy things in my temple will be overthrown in time. Amen.

SECTION 118

The problems in Kirtland were so bad that four apostles left the church. In the revelation we call Section 118, the Lord called four new apostles to take their places. Section 118 also commanded the twelve apostles to set out for a mission on April 26, 1839, from the spot where the Far West Temple was being built. Before April 26 arrived, though, the members were thrown out of Far West by their enemies. They were told that they would be killed if they ever returned. Still, the apostles wanted to keep the commandment they had been given. So late at night on April 25, they snuck back into Far West. They left for their mission the next morning.

1 This is what the Lord says: A conference should be held at once. The Twelve need to be organized. New apostles need to be called to take the places of those who have become unworthy.
2 Thomas B. Marsh should stay in Zion for a while, to publish my word.
3 The others should keep preaching. If they do this humbly and patiently, I promise to take care of their families. A way will open for them to do my work.
4 Next spring they will cross the ocean. There they will preach my restored gospel and testify about me.
5 They should start out next April 26 from the place where the temple in Far West is being built.
6 John Taylor, John E. Page, Wilford Woodruff, and Willard Richards should be called to be the new apostles.

SECTION 119

In Section 42, the Lord gave church members a law. The law said they should donate everything they had to the church. Then the church would be give them back what they needed to live. But the members were never able to keep the law very well. So the Lord gave them a new law about how much they should donate to the church. Section 119 is that law.

1 This is what the Lord says: My people need to give all their extra property to the bishop in Zion.
2 It will be used to build the temple. It will be used to build up Zion and the priesthood. It will be used to pay the First Presidency's debts.
3 This is how my people will start paying tithing.
4 After they have donated their extra property this way, they will pay one-tenth of everything they make each year. This is what they should do from now on and forever.
5 Everyone who moves to Zion must donate their extra property. They must keep this law, or they cannot live with you.
6 If my people do not keep this law, they will make Zion unholy. This land can be holy only if the people who live on it keep my laws. So if you do not keep this law, you cannot build Zion here.
7 This law is for all of Zion's stakes, too. Amen.

SECTION 120

After Joseph Smith received the new law of tithing (Section 119), he wondered who should decide how to use the members' donations. Section 120 is the Lord's answer to that question.

1 This is what the Lord says: Form a council to decide how to use the tithing the church receives. That council will be made up of the First Presidency, the bishop and his counselors, and the high council. I myself will tell them what to do. Amen.

SECTION 121

Church members in Missouri kept having problems with their enemies. Finally the governor of Missouri passed a law saying that if the members didn't leave Missouri, they would be killed. The members had to run away to Illinois and other places. Joseph Smith and some other church leaders were put in jail. The jail was very small and cold. Sometimes the food was poisoned. Once the guards tried to make them eat human meat. While he was in jail, Joseph wrote a long letter to the members. Section 121 is part of that letter. It begins with a prayer and the Lord's answer.

1 O God, where are you? Where are you hiding?
2 How long will you wait before helping your servants? How long will you sit in heaven, watching your people suffer? How long do they have to cry for help before you will hear?
3 How many crimes do they have to suffer before you will have mercy on them?
4 Lord God, you made the sky, the earth, the sea, and everything in them. You have power over the devil himself. Help us! Stop hiding! See our sufferings! Hear our cries! Have mercy on us!
5 Punish our enemies for what they have done. Use your power to make right our wrongs.
6 Help the suffering members of your church, O God. Then your servants will rejoice in your name forever.
7 Peace, my son. Your sufferings will last only a little while.
8 If you are patient and stay faithful, God will lift you up. You will overcome all your enemies.
9 Your friends still support you. You will be with them again. How happy they will be to see you!
10 You have not suffered as much as Job did. Your friends have not turned against you. They have not charged you with wrongdoing, like Job's friends did.
11 The people who have charged you with wrongdoing will fail. Their plans to destroy you will melt away like frost melting under the sun.
12 God has an amazing plan which will change history. Your enemies cannot understand God's plan. They will be caught in their own traps.
13 They have become so wicked

that they love to hurt others. But everything they wanted to make other people suffer, they will have to suffer themselves.

14 They will not be able to do the things they wanted. They will lose all hope.

15 In a few more years, they and their descendants will be completely destroyed.

16 The Lord says: Everyone who turns against my chosen servants, and charges them with wrongdoing, will be punished. My servants have not done wrong. They have done what I told them to.

17 The people who say my servants have sinned are the real sinners. It is because they are sinners that they say these untrue things.

18 Some people have lied about my servants in court, to get them arrested and killed.

19 Those people will be punished. Because they tried to hurt my children, they will not be able to receive temple ordinances.

20 They will lose the things they own. Their houses and barns will be destroyed. They will be hated by the very same people they were trying to please.

21 They will not be able to hold the priesthood. Neither will their descendants.

22 They would be better off tying a giant stone around their necks and drowning themselves in the sea.

23 Everyone who hurts my people will be punished for what they have done. They will be punished for their lies, and attacks, and murders. In the next life, Satan will have power over them.

24 I have seen everything they have done. When the time is right, I will see that they are punished.

25 I have set a time for everyone to receive what they have earned for their works.

26 Through the gift of the Holy Ghost, God will teach you things that have never before been revealed on earth.

27 Our ancestors looked forward to the time when these things would be revealed. Angels taught them that it would come just before the end of the world. These things will come forth in all their glory.

28 Everything will be revealed. People will know if there is one God, or many gods—they will all be made known.

29 Every power in heaven and on earth will be given to those who have been faithful to Jesus Christ's gospel.

30 People will learn about the farthest reaches of space, the deepest parts of the ocean, and the most faraway parts of the earth. They will learn all about the sun, moon, and stars.

31 They will learn how long the days, months, and years are on all the planets. They will learn which worlds are celestial, terrestrial, or telestial. They will learn all about these worlds' laws and histories. All this will be revealed during the time just before the end of the world.

32 Heavenly Father held a meeting with all the other gods before the Creation. There it was decided that all these things would be revealed only when the world was coming to its end, when everyone came back to live with God forever.

33 How long can rushing waters stay dirty? What power can stop God from carrying out his plan? People might as well try to turn back the Missouri River with their bare hands, as try to stop God from sending revelation to the Latter-day Saints.

34 Many people are called to share God's power. But few prove worthy of it in the end. Why do the others prove unworthy?

35 Because they love the world too much. They want other people to praise them, and so they do not learn this one lesson—

36 Priesthood authority is tied to power from heaven. And power from heaven can only be used in righteous ways.

37 We may be ordained to the priesthood. But as soon as we become proud, or try to hide our sins, or try to get others to praise us, or try to control people in a way that is the tiniest bit wrong—we can no longer receive power from heaven. The Spirit leaves us. Our priesthood authority goes with it.

38 Before they even know what has happened, people like this are left to themselves. They end up getting angry. They try to fight against God and the members of God's church.

39 We have seen for ourselves that almost all people start trying to control others in a sinful way as soon as they receive a little of what they think is authority.

40 That is why so many of the people who are called to share God's power prove unworthy of it in the end.

41 Priesthood authority cannot be used to try to force people to do things. Priesthood leaders must be patient, gentle, and humble. They must truly love the people they are working with. They cannot just pretend to love them.

42 Priesthood leaders must be kind. They should teach people things that will help them grow spiritually. Priesthood leaders should never lie to people or trick them.

43 You should be harsh only when the Holy Ghost tells you to. Then you need to do even more to show those people that you love them. That way they will know you truly want to help them.

44 They need to know that your love for them is stronger even than death.

45 You should be filled with love for all people, as well as for members of the church. Your thoughts should always be holy. Then you will have nothing to worry about when you go to be judged by God. Then the Spirit will be able to teach you about the priesthood.

46 The Holy Ghost will always be with you. You will be a righteous leader and a ruler in God's kingdom forever. All this will happen naturally. It will not happen because you have forced others to obey you.

SECTION 122

While he was in jail (see Section 121), Joseph Smith wrote a long letter to the members of the church. Section 122 is part of that letter. It repeats a promise the Lord revealed to Joseph to help him in his suffering.

1 People in every part of the world will ask about you. Fools will make fun of you. Satan and his angels will hate you.

2 But people with good hearts will come to you for advice. People who are wise and who want to do what is right will come to be blessed by you.

3 Traitors will never be able to turn your people completely against you.

4 They may be able to get you into trouble or put in prison. But people will still see you are a good man. Because you have been righteous, very soon you will be free. You will be like a roaring lion among your enemies. God will be with you forever.

5 You might have troubles. Traitors or robbers might put you in danger. You might be in danger while travelling on land or by sea.

6 People might say you have committed all sorts of crimes. Your enemies might arrest you. They might drag you away from your family. They might push your wife and children away from you with swords. Your oldest son, who is only 6 years old, might grab onto your clothes and say, "Daddy, Daddy, why can't you stay with us? What are the men going to do with you, Daddy?" He might then be pushed away from you with a sword so you can be dragged off to prison. Your enemies might surround you like wolves hungry for blood.

7 You might be thrown into a pit, or turned over to killers. You might be sentenced to die. You might be tossed into the ocean. The waves and winds might try to destroy you. The sky might turn black. Everything on earth might block your way. Hell itself might try to open up and swallow you. But know this, my son—no matter what you might have to suffer, you will learn from it all. It will all be for your good.

8 The Savior suffered more than this. Are you better than he is?

9 Push on, and power from heaven will always be with you. You cannot be killed before the time that I have set for you to die. So do not be afraid of anything people might do to you. God will be with you forever.

SECTION 123

While he was in jail (see Section 121), Joseph Smith wrote a long letter to the members of the church. Section 123 is part of that letter. It tells the members what to do to try to get help from the government. Even though the members had suffered unfairly, the United States government refused to help them. The members finally had to give up hope of going back to their homes in Missouri.

1 It would be a good idea for the members to collect all the facts about what the people of Missouri have made them suffer.

2 They should keep a record of all the damage that was done to them. They should keep a record of everything they suffered and everything they lost.

3 They should make a list of the names of everyone who has hurt them.

4 Maybe a group could be formed to find out all this. They could record people's testimonies about what they have suffered. They could also collect all the lies that have been published about us.

5 They could collect all the lies that have been published in books and magazines, along with the names of the people who wrote them. Then the group could write its own history of all the devilish tricks and murders we have suffered.

6 This history could be published for the whole world to read. Copies could be sent to government leaders. Then they can see how truly terrible our sufferings have been. This is the last thing Heavenly Father expects us to try before we can ask him to use his power to punish our enemies. The whole country needs to learn what we have suffered. That way they will have no excuse for not having helped us.

7 We need to do this for God and the angels. We need to do it for ourselves. We need to do it for our families, who have been hurt and killed by wicked people. Satan led those people to do what they did. He has tricked people into holding on to false beliefs and passing them on to their children. The world is filled with confusion because of what he has done. He has been growing stronger and stronger. He is the cause of all wickedness. He makes the whole earth suffer because of sin.

8 Satan's power makes people suffer. It is like wearing chains. It is like being in prison.

9 We have a duty not only to our own families, but also to those whose husbands and fathers have been killed.

10 What our enemies have done is wicked enough to shock even Satan himself.

11 We also have a duty to the young people who are now growing up. We have a duty to everyone whose hearts are pure.

12 There are many people in other churches and groups who do not accept the truth only because they do not know where to find it. They have been tricked by wicked people.

13 So we should spend our lives making the truth known. We should tell people about all the wickedness which we know has been done in secret. God will help us find out about it all.

14 The members of the church should work hard to do all this.

15 No one should think that these things are not important. Many things in the future of the church depend on them.

16 Remember that in a storm it takes only a little rudder to save a large ship.

17 So, my dear brothers and sisters, let us cheerfully do all that

we can. When we have done everything we can, we may be certain God will show his power to save us.

SECTION 124

Joseph Smith and the other church leaders in jail were allowed to escape. They went to live with the members in Illinois. The members there were living in a swamp. By working hard, they turned the swamp into a beautiful city they named Nauvoo. Members of the church moved to Nauvoo from other parts of the country and even other parts of the world. The church became strong. Section 124 is a revelation Joseph Smith received while he was living in Nauvoo.

1 This is what the Lord says to Joseph Smith: I am pleased with the work you have done. You are weak. But that is why I called you—to use things the world thinks of as weak to make known my wisdom.

2 I accept your prayers. I will now tell you my answer. I call you to write a proclamation of my gospel. In it, you will tell about this beautiful stake of Zion.

3 Make this proclamation to every king on earth. Make it to the new president, and to the governors of your country. Send it to every country in the world.

4 You should write it humbly. You should write it through the Holy Ghost's power. I will give you the Holy Ghost when you sit down to write it.

5 The Holy Ghost will tell you what is going to happen to the rulers of the world in the future.

6 Very soon, I am going to call on the world's rulers to pay attention to Zion's light. It is time for Zion to be praised.

7 So write a powerful proclamation. Bear your testimony to the world. Do not be afraid of anyone. All their glory is like grass or flowers—it quickly fades. Write this proclamation so they will have no excuse when it is time for them to be judged.

8 If they reject my servants, and my servants' testimony, they will be judged for it when I come again. Rulers who have used their power to hurt others will be punished.

9 But many rulers will be touched by your testimony. They will accept what you teach them. You will win their favor. The peoples of the world will help to build up Zion.

10 Terrible things are coming. They will come when you are not expecting them. If Zion has not been built up by then, where will my people be safe?

11 Wake up, you kings of the earth! Come to Zion with your gold and silver. Come help my people.

12 Robert B. Thompson should help you write this proclamation. I am very happy with him. It would be good for him to work with you.

13 If he follows your advice, I will give him many blessings. If he is completely faithful from now on, I will make him great.

14 But he needs to remember that he will be judged for how well he

takes care of the things I have trusted him with.

15 I will bless Hyrum Smith. I love him because his heart is true. He loves what is right.

16 John C. Bennet should help you send my word to the kings and peoples of the world. He should support you when you are in trouble. I will reward him if he listens to your advice.

17 His love will make him great. If he does what I have said, he will be one of my own. If he stays faithful, I will accept the work he has done. I will reward him with blessings and glory.

18 I want Lyman Wight to keep preaching for Zion. If he humbly testifies to the world about me, I will support him with my power. He will be like an eagle high up in the sky. He will earn glory and praise both for me and for himself.

19 When his work is done, I will bring him to live with me, just like I brought David Patten, Edward Partridge, and Joseph Smith's father to live with me. They sit on thrones at Abraham's right hand. He is holy, for he is one of my own.

20 George Miller is an honest man. He can be trusted. His heart is true. I love him because he loves my testimony.

21 I call him to serve as a bishop, like Edward Partridge. He will collect my people's tithing. He will use it to bless the poorer members of the church. No one should think badly of him. He will serve me well.

22 George and Lyman, along with John Snider and some others, should build a house for me. Joseph will show them how and where to do this.

23 It will be a hotel for travelers to stay in. It needs to be an excellent hotel. It will be a place where travelers can rest in health and safety. At the same time, they can learn about the Lord's word and this stake of Zion.

24 The hotel will be a healthy place to stay if it is built the way I tell you, and if the person placed in charge of it keeps it pure. It will be a holy house, or the Lord will not live in it.

25 All the members of my church need to gather from far away.

26 Send messengers quickly. Have them tell the members to bring their gold, silver, jewels, and old valuables. Everyone who knows about old valuables can come help. Bring all kinds of valuable wood.

27 Bring different kinds of metal. Bring all kinds of valuable things. Use them to build a temple where God can live.

28 There is not yet a place on earth where God can come restore the priesthood ordinances which were taken away.

29 There is not yet a baptismal font on earth where the members of my church can do baptisms for the dead.

30 Baptism for the dead is a temple ordinance. I allow you to do baptisms for the dead outside the temple only when you are too poor to build me a temple.

31 But now I command you—all the members of my church—to build a temple. I will give you a certain amount of time in which to do this. During that time, I will accept bap-

tisms for the dead done outside the temple.

32 But once that time is up, I will accept baptisms for the dead only if they are done inside the temple. If you have not built the temple by then, no one in the church will be able to come be with me. You will not be able to save your family members who have died.

33 Baptism for the dead was set up as a temple ordinance even before the world was created. This is why I cannot accept baptisms for the dead done outside the temple once you have had enough time to build me a temple.

34 In the temple, you will be given the power of the holy priesthood. Then you can receive honor and glory.

35 Once the time is up, I will no longer accept baptisms for the dead done by church members living in other places.

36 Baptisms for the dead must be done in the places I have chosen for you to gather. Those places are Zion, Zion's stakes, and Jerusalem.

37 How can I accept your washings unless you do them in a temple?

38 That is why I told Moses to build a tent for the Israelites to carry through the desert. That is why I told them to build a temple in the promised land—so I could reveal those ordinances which had been kept secret since before the Creation.

39 In all periods of history, I command my people to build temples. There they anoint each other with oil. They wash each other. They do baptisms for the dead. They hold special meetings. In the temple, I will reveal the laws you need to start building Zion. There all my people can receive the glory, honor, and endowment I promised them.

40 Build this temple, so I can reveal my ordinances to my people.

41 I am going to reveal to the members of my church things which have been kept secret since before the Creation. These things have to do with the time just before the end of the world.

42 I will show Joseph Smith everything having to do with this temple and its priesthood. I will show him the place where it should be built.

43 Build it in the place where you were already thinking about building it. That is the place I have chosen.

44 If you work as hard as you can, I will make that place holy.

45 My people need to obey me and the servants I have chosen to lead them. If they do, they will never be chased off their land again.

46 But if they do not obey me or their leaders, they will not be blessed. That is because they turn what is holy—my land, my ordinances, my laws, and my words—into something filthy.

47 Unless you do everything I tell you, I will not be able to keep the promises I have made to you, even if you build the temple.

48 Your own works will bring you punishments instead of blessings. You will suffer because of your own foolishness and wickedness.

49 Sometimes, when I command someone to do something, they work as hard and as long as they can to do it. But their enemies keep them from finishing. If that hap-

pens, it is enough for me that they have tried. I will not judge them for not finishing the work.

50 Instead, I will judge their enemies for the fact that my commandments were not kept. Unless they repent, they will cause themselves and their families to suffer.

51 I commanded you to build a city in Jackson County, Missouri. I commanded you to build a temple there. You tried to do what I commanded. But your enemies kept you from finishing. So I accept the work you did.

52 Your enemies in Missouri will be punished for what they did to you. As long as they refuse to repent, they and their families will suffer.

53 What I have said here holds true for everyone who is commanded to do a work for the Lord but then is kept from doing it by their enemies.

54 The righteous members who were killed in Missouri will be saved.

55 Again, I command you to build a temple here. That is how you can show that you are willing to do what I command you. Then I can reward you with glory and eternal life.

56 The hotel I commanded you to build should be dedicated to me. Joseph and his family should live there. They should pass it on to their descendants.

57 That is because I have promised Joseph that his blessings will be passed down to his descendants.

58 I say to Joseph what I said to Abraham—everyone on earth will be blessed through you and your descendants.

59 So let Joseph and his descendants live in that house forever.

60 The hotel will be called the Nauvoo House. It should be a nice place for travelers to rest. That way they can see how glorious Zion and this stake are.

61 They can also get advice from those I have chosen to lead my people.

62 George Miller, Lyman Wight, John Snider, and Peter Haws should form themselves into a quorum for building the Nauvoo House. One of them should be chosen to serve as quorum president.

63 They should set rules about selling shares to raise money for the Nauvoo House.

64 No share should cost less than $50. The quorum can sell up to $15,000 worth of shares to any one person.

65 But no one may buy more than $15,000 worth of shares.

66 No one may buy less than $50 worth of shares.

67 People can become stockholders in the Nauvoo House only if they pay for their shares up front.

68 People will hold as much stock in the Nauvoo House as they buy shares. But no one can become a stockholder who does not pay for the shares up front.

69 Stockholders can pass their shares down to their descendants. But they can do that only as long as they or their descendants do not sell or give up their stock.

70 The money which George, Lyman, John and Peter receive in exchange for shares should be used only to build the Nauvoo House.

71 If they use it for something else without the stockholder's permis-

sion, they must repay the stockholder four times the amount they used. If they do not do this, they will lose their place in the quorum. I am God. My directions must be followed.

72 Joseph can buy as many shares in the Nauvoo House as he sees fit, up to $15,000.

73 Some other people have asked me to tell them what to do.

74 This is what I have to say about Vinson Knight: I want him to buy shares in the Nauvoo House.

75 I want him to preach loud and long. I want him to get people to help the poor and needy. As long as he does not give up, I will accept his sacrifice, like I accepted Abel's sacrifice. I will save him.

76 His family should rejoice and be happy. I have chosen Vinson to be anointed in my temple. I will forgive all his sins. Amen.

77 Hyrum Smith should buy as many shares as he sees fit.

78 Isaac Galland should also buy shares. I love him for the work he has done. I forgive all his sins. He should be allowed to become a stockholder in the Nauvoo House.

79 William Marks should ordain Isaac Galland to be Hyrum's companion. Together they will go do the work Joseph gives them. They will receive great blessings.

80 William Marks should buy as many shares as he sees fit.

81 So should Henry G. Sherwood.

82 So should William Law.

83 I do not want William Law to move his family back east to Kirtland. I will rebuild Kirtland. But something terrible is going to happen to the people there first.

84 I am not very happy with Almon Babbitt. He is trying to get people to follow him instead of the First Presidency. He is like Aaron, building a golden calf for my people to worship.

85 No one who wants to keep my commandments should move away from this place.

86 It is here I want them to live and die. It is here where they will rest and work.

87 William needs to trust me. He needs to stop worrying about his family becoming sick. If you love me, keep my commandments. It is true that many people in this place are getting sick. But in the end, that will work out for your good.

88 William should go preach my gospel in Warsaw, Carthage, Burlington, and Madison. He should follow the Spirit. He should be patient and work hard until the next general conference. Then I will tell him what to do next.

89 I want him to listen to Joseph's advice from now on. He should use his money to help the poor. He should help publish the new translation of the Bible.

90 If he does this, I will give him many blessings. I will never leave him. His family will have everything they need.

91 William should be ordained to serve as Joseph's counselor instead of Hyrum. That way Hyrum can serve as patriarch. His father blessed him to receive that office. It is his by right.

92 From now on Hyrum will have the power to give patriarchal blessings to all my people.

93 Whoever he says will be blessed,

God will bless. Whoever he says will be punished, God will punish. Whatever he does on earth will hold true in heaven.

94 I now give him the power to serve as a prophet for the church, the same as Joseph.

95 He will work with Joseph. Joseph will show him what to do. Joseph will teach him how to call down blessings from heaven. He will have the same priesthood authority which Oliver Cowdery had while he was still my servant.

96 Hyrum will testify about the things I will show him. People will remember him with honor forever.

97 William Law will also be given the power to call down blessings from heaven. If he is humble and honest, he will receive my Spirit. It will show him everything that is true. It will tell him what to say the moment he goes to speak.

98 He will be able to heal the sick and throw out devils. People will not be able to poison him.

99 He will be kept safe from poisonous snakes when he travels. His imagination will soar like an eagle.

100 If I want, he will even be able to bring the dead back to life.

101 So William should be bold about preaching my gospel. He should shout "Hosanna!" to God, who rules in heaven forever.

102 Later I will send William and Hyrum on their own special mission. Joseph will stay at home, because he is needed here. I will explain everything else later. Amen.

103 If Sidney Rigdon will accept the calling, he can serve as Joseph's counselor. But he needs to be humble.

104 If he does what is right and stays with my people, I will heal him. He will again preach in the mountains. He will serve as my messenger.

105 He should move his family to the neighborhood where Joseph lives.

106 Wherever he travels, he should preach boldly. He should warn the people of the world to escape the terrible things that are coming.

107 He and William Law should help Joseph write the proclamation to the world's rulers I told you about earlier.

108 I do not want Sidney to move his family back east. Instead, they should move where I have commanded them.

109 I do not want him to look for safety anywhere else but Nauvoo. Nauvoo is my chosen city.

110 I promise that things will go well for him if he does what I have said. Amen.

111 Amos Davies should buy shares in the Nauvoo House.

112 That is how he can become a stockholder. He should listen to Joseph's advice. He should work to support himself if he wants people to trust him.

113 Once he shows that he can take care of a few things, he will be placed in charge of many things.

114 He needs to be humble. Then he can be lifted up. Amen.

115 I want Robert D. Foster to use every chance he has to keep working on the house he promised to build for Joseph.

116 He needs to repent of his mis-

takes. He needs to show charity. He needs to stop sinning. He needs to stop speaking so harshly.

117 He should also buy shares in the Nauvoo House.

118 He should listen to the advice of Joseph, Hyrum, William Law, and the other leaders I have chosen to build up Zion. If he does, things will go well with him forever. Amen.

119 No one can become a stockholder in the Nauvoo House who does not believe in the Book of Mormon and the revelations I have given you.

120 Anything more or less than that comes from Satan. It will bring punishments instead of blessings. Amen.

121 The members of the quorum for building the Nauvoo House should be paid fairly for their work. They can decide how high their pay should be.

122 If they need to, they can get their pay from the stockholders. Or they can receive shares in exchange for their work. Amen.

123 I now give you the different leaders in the Melchizedek priesthood. Those who have been called will receive the authority that goes with their offices.

124 First, I give you Hyrum Smith to be your patriarch. He will have the power to bless you with the promise that you will be saved. This will make it possible for you to come through times of temptation.

125 I give you Joseph to serve as a president and prophet over all the church.

126 I give him Sidney Rigdon and William Law as counselors. Together, these three form the First Presidency. Their calling is to receive revelation for the whole church.

127 I give you Brigham Young as president of the Quorum of the Twelve.

128 The Twelve have the authority to start my kingdom anywhere in the world. They can send my word to everyone on earth.

129 They are Heber C. Kimball, Parley P. Pratt, Orson Pratt, Orson Hyde, William Smith, John Taylor, John E. Page, Wilford Woodruff, Willard Richards, and George A. Smith.

130 David Patten lives with me now. He will always hold the office of apostle. But someone else can be called to take his place in the quorum.

131 I give you the following people to serve as the high council in Nauvoo.

132 They are Samuel Bent, Henry G. Sherwood, George W. Harris, Charles C. Rich, Thomas Grover, Newel Knight, David Dort, Dunbar Wilson, David Fullmer, Alpheus Cutler, and William Huntington. Seymour Brunson lives with me now. He will always hold his office. But Aaron Johnson should be ordained to take his place.

133 I give you Don C. Smith as president of a high priests quorum.

134 The purpose of this calling is to train leaders in stakes scattered in other places.

135 Such leaders may travel if they want. But they are ordained to serve in one place. That is their calling.

136 I give you Amasa Lyman and

Noah Packard as Don Smith's counselors. Together they will lead the high priests in my church.

¹³⁷ I give you John A. Hicks, Samuel Williams, and Jesse Baker to lead the elders quorum. The members of this quorum may travel. But they are ordained to serve in the branch where they are at.

¹³⁸ I give you Joseph Young, Josiah Butterfield, Daniel Miles, Henry Herriman, Zera Pulsipher, Levi Hancock, and James Foster as presidents of the Quorum of Seventy.

¹³⁹ The members of this quorum are to travel throughout the world testifying about me. They go wherever my apostles send them. They prepare people to accept me.

¹⁴⁰ The Seventy should always be travelling. But the elders should serve as leaders in the branches of the church. This means an elder may be called on to lead a branch of the church. But a Seventy never will.

¹⁴¹ I give you Vinson Knight, Samuel H. Smith, and Shadrach Roundy (if he accepts the calling) to serve as the bishopric. Doctrine and Covenants teaches what the bishopric is for.

¹⁴² Samuel Rolfe and his counselors will lead the priests. There will also be a teachers quorum presidency, a deacons quorum presidency, and a stake presidency.

¹⁴³ I have given you these offices to help you and to lead you. They are to help carry out my work. They are to help the members of the church become perfect.

¹⁴⁴ I command you to fill all these offices. At the next general conference, you can vote for or against the names I have given.

¹⁴⁵ When you build my temple, it should have rooms for all these offices. These are the Lord's words. Amen.

SECTION 125

In Section 124, the Lord told all the members of the church to come to Nauvoo to help build the temple. Some members had already build homes for themselves in Iowa, across the river from Nauvoo. They wondered if the Lord wanted them to move, or if they were close enough to Nauvoo where they were. Section 125 is the Lord's answer.

¹ What does the Lord want the members in Iowa to do?

² This is what the Lord says: If those who call themselves my followers want to keep my commandments, they should gather in the places Joseph will show them. There they should build cities for me. That way they can be ready for the future.

³ They should build a city called Zarahemla across the river from Nauvoo.

⁴ Members gathering in from different places may settle there, if they choose. They may also live in Nashville, Nauvoo, or any of the stakes I have formed. These are the Lord's words.

SECTION 126

Brigham Young joined the church two years after it was restored. Even before he was baptized, he was sent on a mission to Canada. He went out preaching every summer after that. Later, Brigham was called to be an apostle. He went on a mission to England. After two years of hard work there, he returned home to his family in Nauvoo. The Lord then gave Joseph Smith the revelation that is now Section 126.

1 My very dear brother, Brigham Young, this is what the Lord says to you: My servant Brigham, you no longer have to leave your family, like you have in the past. I accept your sacrifice.

2 I have seen how hard you have worked, travelling to preach my gospel.

3 From now on, I command you to send my word throughout the world rather than taking it there yourself. Take special care of your family, from now on and forever. Amen.

SECTION 127

Someone tried to murder the governor of Missouri—the same one who had said that church members would be killed if they didn't leave the state. Joseph Smith's enemies said that he was behind the plan to murder the governor. Joseph had to go into hiding to keep his enemies from arresting him. He knew that if they arrested him and took him back to Missouri, he would probably be killed. While he was hiding, Joseph wrote a letter to the members. Section 127 is that letter.

1 The Lord has revealed to me that my enemies, both here in Illinois and in Missouri, are chasing me again. They have no reason to do this. Their charges against me are wicked lies. But I thought it wise to leave for a little while, so I and this people would be safe. I have left people in charge of carrying out my business while I am gone. They will do whatever is needed to make sure that all my debts are paid. I will come back when I learn that it is safe.

2 The dangers I have to go through seem small to me. That is because I have been dealing all my life with people who are angry with me. I do not know why that should be, unless I was ordained before the Creation for some purpose. Whether that purpose is good or bad, you decide. God knows whether it is good or bad. In any case, I've gotten used to having troubles. In fact, I glory in them, like Paul. God has saved me from all my troubles so far. He will go on doing so. The Lord has promised that I will overcome all my enemies.

3 The members of the church should rejoice, because Israel's God is their God. He will see to it that those who make his people suffer are punished.

4 This is what the Lord says: Do not stop working on the temple or anything else I have commanded you to do. Work twice as hard and twice as patiently. You will be re-

warded for it. If people hurt you, remember that the prophets and the righteous people who lived before you were hurt as well. Remember that God rewards those who suffer for doing his work.

5 Now, I have something to say about baptism for the dead.

6 This is what the Lord says: Whenever someone is baptized for the dead, a recorder needs to watch. That way there is a witness to the baptism.

7 Whatever you record or do on earth will be recorded or done in heaven as well.

8 I, the Lord, am about to restore many things to the earth having to do with the priesthood.

9 All the records you make of baptisms for the dead should be filed in the temple. They will be kept forever. These are the Lord's words.

10 Now I have something to say to all the members of the church. I wanted very much to preach to you about baptism for the dead next Sunday. Since I cannot do that, I will write down what the Lord tells me about that subject from time to time. Then I will send it to you in a letter.

11 That is all I have time to write for now. My enemies are looking for me. Like the Savior said, the prince of this world is coming, but he has no rights over me.

12 I pray to God that you will all be saved. I am the Lord's servant for you, the prophet of The Church of Jesus Christ of Latter-day Saints.

Signed: Joseph Smith

SECTION 128

In the letter that is now Section 127, Joseph Smith promised to teach the church members more about baptism for the dead as soon as he had a chance. Since he was hiding from his enemies at the time, it was hard for Joseph to teach the members. Finally he was able to write another letter about baptism for the dead. Section 128 is that letter.

1 As I promised in the letter I sent you before I left home, I will now teach you more about baptism for the dead. I have been thinking mostly about that subject while my enemies have been chasing me.

2 I sent you a revelation about a recorder. Since then, I have received more revelation about that. In my last letter, I told you that a recorder needs to watch all baptisms for the dead. That way there will be a witness to the baptism.

3 It would be very hard for one recorder to attend all baptisms for the dead. So a different recorder should be called for every part of the city. These recorders must be good, careful note-takers. They must be exact in recording each baptism they attend. They must write down the date, the names, and everything that happens. They should also write down the names of about three other people there, if they can. That way, everything can be proven by two or three witnesses, like the scriptures say.

4 The recorders will sign their records. Then they will turn the

records over to a general recorder. The general recorder will file all the records in a book. There must also be a signed statement in the book, saying that the general recorder believes that what the other recorders have written is true. That will be just as good as if the general recorder had attended all the baptisms.

5 You may find this a picky way of doing things. But it is exactly how God wants this ordinance done. This ordinance was prepared before the Creation. It was prepared to save those who die without learning the gospel.

6 John the Revelator was thinking about this subject when he wrote Revelation 20:12. "I saw that every single person who had died was brought to be judged by God. They were judged for their works. Their works were written in books. One of those was the Book of Life."

7 We learn from this scripture that the dead were judged for their works, which were recorded in the Book of Life and other books. The Book of Life is a record that is kept in heaven. The other books are records that are kept on earth. This is in keeping with what I taught you in my last letter—that whatever you recorded on earth would be recorded in heaven as well.

8 Baptism for the dead is done through the power of the priesthood. Jesus Christ gives you this power. That way, as Matthew 16:19 says, whatever you do on earth will be done in heaven as well. In other words, whatever you record on earth will be recorded in heaven as well. Whatever you do not record on earth will not be recorded in heaven either. The dead will then be judged from those records. It does not matter whether they did the ordinances themselves, or whether someone else did the ordinances for them. All that matters is that the records say the ordinances were done.

9 Some might think us rather bold to say that what we record on earth will be recorded in heaven as well. But throughout history, whenever the Lord has given the priesthood to anyone, he has given them this power. Whenever those people did something with the Lord's authority, and kept a proper record of it, it became law both on earth and in heaven. Jehovah himself promised them this. This is true. Who can accept it?

10 We see this truth taught in Matthew 16:18-19. "From now on I will call you Peter. You will lead my church. The devil's power will not overcome it. I will place you in charge of God's kingdom. Whatever you do on earth will be done in heaven as well."

11 The secret to understanding this is to receive the power of the priesthood. Those who hold this authority will have no problem understanding how both those who are alive and those who are dead can be saved.

12 People receive eternal life through the ordinance of baptism. They need to be baptized completely underwater as a symbol of being buried. When they are brought back up out of the water, that is a symbol of coming up out of the grave. These same symbols are used in baptism for the dead.

13 The baptismal font is placed underground as a symbol of the grave. So living people who do baptisms for the dead are "buried" underground, like the dead. The living become like the dead. Earthly things become like heavenly things. Paul taught this in 1 Corinthians 15:46-48.

14 "Earthly things come first. Then come heavenly things. First came Adam, who was made out of the earth. Then came Jesus Christ, the Lord from heaven. Earthly people are like Adam. Heavenly people are like Jesus Christ." And, I would add, the records you make properly on earth are like the records which are made in heaven. That is what is called the sealing power. It is part of the authority that comes with God's kingdom.

15 My dear brothers and sisters, these are very important doctrines. We cannot be saved unless the dead are saved. As Paul says, our dead ancestors cannot be made perfect without us, and we cannot be made perfect without them.

16 Here is something else Paul said about baptism for the dead, in 1 Corinthians 15:29. "If it isn't true that people who have died will someday come back from the dead, why do people bother to be baptized for the dead?"

17 I will tie this scripture to something said by one of the prophets. He saw the restoration of the priesthood. He saw the glorious revelations which would be given before the end of the world, including baptism for the dead. In Malachi 4:5-6, he said, "I will send you Elijah the prophet before the Second Coming. He will unite people with their ancestors. He will do this to keep the whole world from suffering."

18 I could have made a clearer translation. But this one will work. This scripture tells us that the whole world will suffer unless people become one with their ancestors. How does that happen? Through baptism for the dead. Those who are alive, those who have died knowing the gospel, and those who have died without knowing it, all need each other in order to become perfect. All the gifts that God has ever given anyone, from Adam's time up to now, need to be brought together before the end of the world. Things will be revealed now that have never been revealed since the world began. The wisest people on earth have not been able to learn those things. But now they will be taught even to children.

19 What does the restored gospel teach us? Good news! It teaches us that God will show mercy. It teaches us truths which were buried underground. It brings good news to both the dead and the living. How wonderful it is to see the messengers who bring good news to Zion—the messengers who say, "Your God rules!" God will rain down truth like dew on the mountains.

20 We hear good news from Cumorah. We hear the angel Moroni teaching about the golden plates. We hear the Lord commanding the three witnesses to testify about the Book of Mormon. We hear Michael by the Susquehanna River, warning

us when the devil tried to trick us by appearing as an angel. We hear Peter, James, and John telling us that they have come to give us the power to restore God's kingdom, now that history is coming to its close.

21 We hear God speaking in the Whitmer home. We hear him speaking in other places during all the travels and troubles of The Church of Jesus Christ of Latter-day Saints. We hear the angels Michael, Gabriel, Raphael, and others. We hear them telling us what gifts and authority they received from God during their time on earth. Little by little, they teach us what is going to happen in the future. It will all turn out as we have hoped!

22 Brothers and sisters, how can we not push on in such a glorious cause? Do not turn back. Be brave. March on to victory! We should be very, very happy. Everyone on earth should sing for joy. Everyone who has died should sing praises forever to our Savior. Through him, we have the power to free the dead from spirit prison. They will be set free.

23 Mountains and valleys, shout for joy! Sea and land, tell how wonderful God is! Rivers and streams, be happy as you flow! Forests and fields, praise the Lord! Rocks, cry for joy! Sun, moon, and stars, sing together! Children of God, shout for joy! All creation, make known God's name forever! How wonderful it is to hear God speaking from heaven! He promises us glory, salvation, honor, and eternal life! He promises us kingdoms, thrones, and powers!

24 The Second Coming is almost here. Who will be able to stand it? The Lord is like fire. He will make Levi's descendants holy, so they can offer him a righteous gift. We, the Latter-day Saints, should also offer a righteous gift to the Lord. That gift will be the the records of the ordinances we have done for the dead. We will put those records in a book in the temple.

25 I have much more to tell you about this. But I will have do it later. I am, as always, your humble servant and faithful friend.

Signed: Joseph Smith

SECTION 129

During the church's early years, many members received what they thought were revelations from God or visits from angels. Some of these were really from devils appearing as angels in order to trick the members. Section 129 is something Joseph Smith taught the members so they could know if they were being visited by a real angel.

1 There are two kinds of people in heaven. First, there are angels. By this I mean people who have come back from the dead. These people have bodies.

2 We know this, because Jesus said, "Touch me and see for yourselves that I am not a spirit. A spirit does not have skin and bones, as you can see I have."

3 Second, there are the spirits of righteous people. These people have not come back from the dead yet. But they have the same glory as those who have.

4 If someone appears to you claiming to have a message from God, ask to shake hands.

5 An angel will shake hands with you. You will be able to feel the angel's hand.

6 The spirits of righteous people can only appear to you in their glory.

7 If you ask to shake hands with them, they will not move. That is because it is against heaven's laws for them to trick you. But they will still give you the message they came to bring.

8 A devil appearing as an angel will shake hands with you. But you will not feel anything. That is how you can know if an angel is really a devil.

9 These are three important truths to help you know if a messenger is really from God.

SECTION 130

Orson Hyde was one of the apostles. One day he gave a talk to the members in Nauvoo. After the talk, he had dinner with Joseph Smith and Joseph's sister, Sophronia. Joseph told Orson that some things he had said in his talk were wrong. Joseph then taught Orson several things that Orson, and most other church members, had not known before. Section 130 is a collection of the things Joseph taught.

1 When the Savior appears, we will see him just as he is. We will see that he is a human being just like us.

2 The relationships we have in the next life will be the same as the ones we have in this life. The only difference is that then we will also enjoy eternal glory, which now we do not.

3 When John 14:23 talks about the Father and the Son appearing to people, it means that they will appear in person. Some churches teach that the Father and the Son can live in a person's heart. But that is not true.

4 Someone asked—don't God, angels, prophets, and people measure time differently, based on which planet they live on?

5 My answer is yes. But all the angels who visit the earth either belong or have belonged to it.

6 The planet where angels live is not like the earth.

7 They live with God on a planet like a giant ball of glass and fire. In that ball, they and the Lord can see everything they need to know. They can see the past, the present, or the future.

8 God's home is a giant Urim and Thummim.

9 After the earth has been made holy, it will be like a giant glass Urim and Thummim for everyone who lives on it. They will be able to see everything that goes on in lower kingdoms. The earth will then belong to Christ.

10 Everyone living on the earth will be given a white stone, as Revelation 2:17 says. The stone will act as a Urim and Thummim. Through it

they can see what goes on in higher kingdoms.

11 Everyone who enters the celestial kingdom will be given a white stone with a new name written on it. Only those who receive the stone know what that name is. It is a holy password.

12 As the Lord's prophet, I say that the wars which lead up to the Second Coming will start in South Carolina.

13 The war will probably start over slavery. A voice told me this while I was praying very hard about this subject, on December 25, 1832.

14 Once, when I was praying very hard to know when the Second Coming would be, I heard a voice say—

15 "Joseph, my son, if you live to be 85 years old, you will see the Son face-to-face. That is all you need to know. Stop bothering me about this."

16 I do not know what that meant. It might have been talking about the Second Coming, It might have meant that the Son would appear to me at some time before the Second Coming. Or it might have meant my dying and seeing the Son that way.

17 I believe, though, that the Second Coming will not happen before then.

18 However intelligent we become in this life, that is how intelligent we will be when we come back from the dead.

19 Someone who gets more intelligence during this life, by working hard and being obedient, will be farther along in the next life than someone who does not work as hard.

20 Even before the Creation, God gave an law to control how blessings are received. That law cannot be broken.

21 Whenever we receive a blessing from God, it is because we have obeyed the law that the blessing is based on.

22 Both the Father and the Son have bodies with skin and bones. Those bodies can be touched and felt, just like the bodies people have now. But the Holy Ghost does not have a body. It is just a spirit. That is why the Holy Ghost is able to be inside us.

23 Just because someone received the Holy Ghost does not mean that the Holy Ghost will always stay with that person.

SECTION 131

Section 131 is a collection of several things Joseph Smith taught. Verses 1-4 are something he taught to a husband and wife living in a town near Nauvoo. Verses 5-6 come from a talk Joseph gave about 2 Peter, chapter 1. Verses 7-8 are something Joseph said after a talk by a preacher of another church.

1 There are three "heavens" or levels in the celestial kingdom.

2 In order to enter the highest level, people must receive this priesthood ordinance [temple marriage].

3 If they do not receive it, they cannot enter the highest level.

4 They can enter a lower level in the

celestial kingdom. But that is as far as they can go. They cannot receive any more blessings.

⁵ (May 17, 1843.) The "more certain prophecy" mentioned in the scriptures is the revelation that someone has been promised eternal life through the power of the priesthood.

⁶ No one can be saved without knowledge.

⁷ People who say that spirit is the opposite of matter are wrong. All spirit is matter. But it is a finer or purer kind of matter. Only pure people can see it.

⁸ We cannot see it now. But after our bodies have been made pure, then we will see that everything is matter.

SECTION 132

Soon after the church was restored, Joseph Smith began to wonder why the Lord allowed some men in Bible times to have more than one wife at the same time. The Lord gave Joseph a revelation explaining why. He also commanded Joseph and other church leaders to start marrying other wives. At first they did this in secret, because they were afraid of their enemies. Finally Joseph wrote down the revelation so other people could read it. One of those people was his first wife, Emma. She believed that it was wrong for Joseph to marry other women. Section 132 is the revelation Joseph wrote down.

¹ This is what the Lord says to Joseph Smith: You have asked me to explain why I allowed Abraham, Issac, Jacob, Moses, David, and Solomon to have many wives.

² I will answer your question.

³ But you must be ready to follow the directions I am about to give you. That is because everyone I reveal this law to must obey it.

⁴ I am about to make a new, eternal promise with you. If you do not keep the promise, you cannot be exalted. No one who rejects this promise can enter my glory.

⁵ Everyone who wants a blessing from me must be willing to keep the law that comes with that blessing. Those laws were set up before the Creation.

⁶ This new, eternal promise was set up so that people could enter the highest level of the celestial kingdom. To receive that blessing, you must keep the law I am about to reveal. If you do not, you cannot be exalted.

⁷ This is the law. While they are alive, people form many ties, promises, relationships, and hopes. Unless these are sealed by the Holy Spirit of promise, they will not last into the next life. They will end when the people who formed them die. This sealing is a very holy ordinance. It must be performed by the person I have ordained to do so. I give this power to only one person on earth at a time. Joseph Smith is the one who holds that power now.

⁸ The Lord says—my house must be kept in order.

⁹ I will not accept works that have not been done with my authority.

¹⁰ I will not accept anything from

you that has not been done the way I commanded.

11 The laws I give you are the same ones my Father and I set up before the Creation.

12 The only way people can come to the Father is through me or my law.

13 Everything in the world which has not been set up by me will be torn down. It does not matter how powerful the earthly authority is that sets these things up. They will not last after people die. They will not last into the next life.

14 Only those things which I have set up will last. Everything else will be destroyed.

15 So if a husband and wife make promises to each other for as long as they are alive, those promises will end when they die. Their marriage will not last into the next life. That is because they were not married the way my law commands.

16 Since they cannot get married in the next life, they must become angels. They will live in heaven. But they will be servants of those who are worthy of a much higher glory.

17 Because these angels did not obey my law, they cannot receive greater blessings. They will have to live as single people forever. They will be saved, but not exalted. They will be angels, but not gods.

18 If a husband and wife promise to stay married forever, but the marriage is not sealed by the person I have ordained, their marriage will not last into the next life. They will not be able to enter the highest level of the celestial kingdom. The angels and gods who stand guard will not let them by. Again, the Lord says—my house must be kept in order.

19 But if a husband and wife are sealed in keeping with the new, eternal promise, the sealer will tell them, "You will be among the first people who come back from the dead." Then their names will be written in the Book of Life. As long as neither of them breaks the promise they made with me and murders an innocent person, they will receive all the blessings the sealer promised them, both in this life and the next. Their marriage will last into the next life. They will pass the angels and gods who stand guard. They will be exalted. They will receive all the glory and blessings they were promised. They will have the power to have children forever.

20 Then they will be gods, because they will be neverending. They will be neverending, because they can have children forever. They will have all power, because they will rule over everything, including the angels. That is why they are called gods.

21 Unless you keep this law, you cannot receive this glory.

22 The road to exaltation is narrow. Very few people are able to be exalted. The others cannot be exalted, because they did not accept me while they were alive.

23 If you accept me while you are alive, then you will know me. You will be exalted. You will live with me.

24 "Eternal lives" means knowing the one true God and his messenger Jesus Christ. I am Jesus Christ. Accept my law.

25 The way to "eternal deaths" is very easy. There are many people who go that way. They go there because they do not accept me or keep my law.

26 If someone who has been sealed commits any sin, no matter how terrible, they will still be exalted, as long as they do not murder an innocent person. But they will be destroyed in this life. They will be in Satan's power until they come back from the dead.

27 The only thing that can never be forgiven, either in this life or the next, is sinning against the Holy Ghost. Sinning against the Holy Ghost means murdering an innocent person—which is the same as agreeing to murder me—after having made the new, eternal promise. No one who breaks this law can be exalted.

28 I will give you the law of the priesthood. My Father and I set up this law before the Creation.

29 Everything Abraham did was in keeping with the revelations and commandments I gave him. He has been exalted. He is now a ruler in heaven.

30 I made promises to Abraham about his descendants. Joseph, you are one of those descendants. I promised that in this life and in the next, Abraham would have more descendants than there are stars in the sky or grains of sand on the beach—too many to count.

31 Because you are one of Abraham's descendants, you have the same promise. It is through this law that my Father's works keep growing. That is how he becomes more glorious.

32 Follow Abraham's example. Keep my law, and you will be saved.

33 If you do not keep my law, you cannot receive the promise my Father made to Abraham.

34 God commanded Abraham to take Sarah's maid, Hagar, as his wife. Why did Sarah let Abraham marry Hagar? Because it was the law. It was also a way I could keep my promises, because Abraham and Hagar had many descendants.

35 Was Abraham wrong to marry Hagar? No, because I commanded him to do it.

36 In the same way, it was not wrong when Abraham chose to sacrifice his son Isaac, even though the scriptures said, "Do not kill." It was not wrong, because I commanded Abraham to do it.

37 Abraham lived with other women besides his wife. He and those women had children. None of this was wrong, because those women were given to him in keeping with my law. The same is true of Isaac and Jacob. They did only what they were commanded to. They have been exalted, as they were promised. They are now rulers in heaven. They are gods, not angels.

38 David, Solomon, and Moses had many wives. So did many of my other servants, throughout history. This was not a sin, except when they lived with women I did not give them.

39 I gave David his wives through my servant Nathan and other prophets who held this power. The only case in which David sinned was when he took Uriah's wife,

Bath-sheba. Because he did that, he cannot be exalted. He will not have his wives in the next life. I have given them to someone else.

40 Joseph, I have chosen you so I can restore all things. I promise to give you whatever you ask for.

41 You have asked about adultery. If a woman is sealed to a man when she is already married to another man, she is guilty of adultery, unless I myself commanded her to enter the second marriage. If she is guilty of adultery, she must be punished.

42 If a woman lives with another man without having first been sealed to him, she is guilty of adultery.

43 If her husband lives with another woman, he is guilty of adultery.

44 If, in that case, the wife has been faithful, then you, Joseph, have the power to marry her to a faithful man who has not committed adultery, if I tell you to do so. In that way, the man who has been faithful will receive a larger kingdom.

45 I have given you the power you need to restore all things. I can reveal everything to you when the time is right.

46 Whatever you seal on earth will be sealed in heaven. Whatever you do on earth in my name, and in keeping with my word, will be done in heaven as well. If you forgive someone's sins on earth, they will be forgiven in heaven. If you do not forgive someone's sins on earth, they will not be forgiven in heaven either.

47 Whoever you bless, will be blessed. Whoever you say will be punished, will be punished. That is because I am your God.

48 Whatever you give someone on earth, in keeping with my law, will be blessed by my power. I will support what you do, both on earth and in heaven.

49 I will be with you until the end of the world and forever after. I promise that you will be exalted. I have a throne waiting for you in my Father's kingdom. You will rule with your ancestor Abraham.

50 I will forgive all your sins, because I have seen how much you have sacrificed. I have seen how well you have obeyed my commandments. I will accept you even though it might seem that you are breaking my laws, just like I accepted Abraham when he chose to sacrifice his son Isaac.

51 I gave you Emma Smith to be your wife. I command Emma not to accept the offer I told you to make her. I told you to promise to make that sacrifice only so I could test you all, like I tested Abraham.

52 Emma should accept all the other women who have been given to Joseph, as long as they are righteous and holy. Those who have only pretended to be holy will be destroyed.

53 I am the Lord. Obey me. Joseph has been faithful in taking care of just a few things. So I will make him a ruler over many things. I will make him stronger from now on.

54 I command Emma to stay with Joseph. She must not go after anyone else. If she does not keep this commandment, she will suffer terribly. I repeat—she will suffer terribly if she does not obey my law.

55 If she does not keep this commandment, Joseph will do every-

thing for her he promised. Then I will give him many more blessings. In the next life, I will give him a hundred times more fathers, mothers, brothers, sisters, houses, lands, wives, and children than he had in this life. He will rule in heaven. He will recieve "eternal lives."

56 Emma should forgive Joseph's sins. Then I will forgive her sins. I will give her many more blessings. I will give her joy.

57 Joseph must not give up his property. That way his enemies will not be able to destroy him. Satan wants to destroy him because he is my servant. But I am with him, like I was with Abraham. I will exalt him. I will make him glorious.

58 There is much to be said about the law of the priesthood.

59 Anyone who is called by me and my Father to hold this power cannot sin, as long as that person acts in my name and in keeping with my law. I will support whatever that person does.

60 So no one should turn against Joseph. I will support his actions. He will make whatever sacrifice I require him to because of his sins.

61 I have more to say about the law of the priesthood. If a man marries a woman and then wants to marry another, he may do so if the first woman agrees and if neither woman is promised to someone else. He is not committing adultery in this case, because they are both his wives, and no one else's.

62 He could marry ten women this way, and he still would not have committed adultery, because they are all his wives.

63 But if any of his wives lives with someone else after she is married, she has committed adultery. Men are allowed to marry more than one woman so they can have children and so my Father can keep the promise he made before the Creation. It is also so they can be exalted and have children in heaven. That is how my Father's work keeps growing. That is how he becomes more glorious.

64 If a man holding this power teaches his wife my law about taking other wives, she must accept what he teaches her. If she does not, she will be punished. But I will bless those who obey my law.

65 If she will not accept my law, I will still allow her husband to marry other women. Because his first wife did not accept my law, she becomes the sinner. He does not have to wait for her to agree before he can marry other women, the way Sarah had to agree before Abraham could marry Hagar.

66 I will reveal more about this law later. This is enough for now. I am Jesus Christ. Amen.

SECTION 133

While the members of the church were living in Kirtland, they decided to publish some of Joseph Smith's revelations in a book (see Section 67). The Lord gave Joseph Smith two new revelations. One was to put at the beginning of the book. The other was to put at the end. The revelation for the beginning of the book is what we call Section 1. The revelation for the end of the book is what we call Section 133.

1 These are the Lord's words. Listen, people of my church. Listen to what the Lord has to say about you.

2 The Lord will come suddenly to his temple. He will come down to earth to judge all people. The wicked among you will be punished. The wicked are everyone who does not pay attention to God.

3 The Lord will show his saving power to everyone in the world.

4 So prepare yourselves, my people. Make yourselves holy. All the members of my church should move to Zion, unless they have been commanded not to.

5 Leave Babylon. My servants must keep themselves clean.

6 Meet together and talk with each other often. Everyone should pray to the Lord.

7 I repeat—it is time for you to leave Babylon. Gather together from every country. Gather from every part of the world.

8 Send the elders of my church to faraway countries and islands. They must teach all the peoples of the world.

9 This is what they will say. It is the Lord's message for all people—move to Zion. Then my people's cities can grow. Their stakes can become strong. Zion can spread to the areas round about.

10 Tell all people—get up and go out to meet the Savior. Prepare yourselves for the Second Coming.

11 Always be ready, because you do not know when it will come.

12 Those who are living among the Gentiles should escape to Zion.

13 The Jews should escape to Jerusalem, where Solomon's temple was built.

14 Leave behind the world's wickedness. That is what is called Babylon.

15 But do not go too quickly. Make sure everything is ready for you first. When you leave, do not look back. If you look back, you may be suddenly destroyed.

16 Listen, people on earth. Listen, elders of my church. The Lord commands everyone, everywhere, to repent.

17 He has sent the angel flying through the sky. The angel shouts, "Get ready for the Second Coming! It is very close!

18 "Soon the Savior will stand on Mount Zion. He will have 144,000 of his Father's servants with him.

19 "Get ready for his coming! Go out to meet him!"

20 The Lord will stand on the Mount of Olives. He will stand on the ocean and on the islands. He will stand on the land of Zion.

21 His voice will go out from Zion and Jerusalem. Everyone will hear his voice.

22 His voice will be like the roar of the ocean, or like thunder. It will make the mountains crumble. The valleys will disappear.
23 He will command the ocean to flow back north. All the islands will be joined together.
24 Jerusalem and Zion will return to their proper places. The earth will be like it was before it was divided.
25 The Lord will stand in the middle of his people. He will rule over everyone on earth.
26 The prophets of the people who live in the north will hear his voice. They will hit the rocks and make the ice flow down in front of them.
27 A highway will be thrown up in the middle of the ocean.
28 They will overcome their enemies.
29 Pools of water will appear in the deserts. Lands that have dried up from heat will have all the water they need.
30 They will bring their treasures to Ephraim's descendants, my servants.
31 The eternal hills will shake before them.
32 They will bow down in Zion. Ephraim's descendants will give them crowns of glory.
33 They will sing with joy forever.
34 This is God's blessing for the tribes of Israel. The best blessing goes to Ephraim's descendants.
35 After the Jews have suffered, they too will be made holy. Then they can live with the Lord forever.
36 I have sent my angel to teach you these things. Some people have already seen that angel. He has revealed the restored gospel to them. Many other people will see that angel in the future.
37 The restored gospel will be taught to all people, no matter what country they are from, what race they belong to, or what language they speak.
38 God's servants will go out, shouting, "Respect God! Give him glory, because it is time for him to judge the world!
39 "Worship the Creator of heaven, earth, and sea."
40 Day and night, they will pray to the Lord. They will say, "Tear open the sky and come down. Make the mountains melt before you."
41 That is exactly what will happen. The Lord's coming will be like a fire. It will melt, and burn, and boil.
42 Lord, you will come down to make your name known to your enemies. The whole world will shake for fear when they see you.
43 You will do terrible things, things they were not expecting.
44 The mountains will melt as you come down. You will come to meet those who are righteous. They are the ones who remember your commandments. They are the ones who will rejoice to see you.
45 No one but you, God, knows what wonderful things you have prepared for those who wait for you.
46 People will ask, "Who is this man, coming down from God in heaven? Who is this man in glorious colored clothes? Who is this man with such power?"
47 He will answer, "I am the one who spoke righteously. I am the Savior."
48 The Lord's clothes will be red,

like the clothes of someone who smashes grapes into wine.

49 His glory will be so bright that the sun will stop shining for shame. The moon will turn dark. The stars will be thrown out of their places.

50 He will say, "I alone have smashed the grapes. I alone have judged all people.

51 "The stains you see on my clothes are the stains of their blood. They have been punished for their wickedness.

52 "Now it is time for my people to be free. They will talk forever about how loving and kind the Lord is. They will talk about how good he is, and how much he has blessed them."

53 Everything they suffered, the Lord suffered with them. He sent his angel to save them. Out of love and pity, he set them free. He carried them all through the past.

54 He was with Enoch and all his people. He was with all the prophets, from Adam to Enoch, from Enoch to Noah, and from Noah to Moses.

55 He was with the prophets from Moses to Elijah, and from Elijah to John the Bapist. These all came back from the dead with Christ. They will live with the Savior. So will Abraham, Isaac, Jacob, and the apostles.

56 When the Savior comes, the righteous members of the church will be brought back from the dead. They will stand with him on Mount Zion and the New Jerusalem. They will sing his praises forever.

57 That is why the Lord sent the restored gospel out into the world— so that people can share the glory he is going to reveal. He teaches people clearly and simply.

58 He does this to prepare the weak for everything that is going to happen on earth. He prepares them to do his work. Someday those who are weak will amaze those who are wise. Those who are small now will become a powerful people.

59 The Lord will use the weak to carry out his work in the world. They will have his Spirit's power.

60 That is why these commandments were given. At first the Lord wanted them kept quiet. But now he wants them to go out to all people.

61 That is what the Lord wants. He rules over every living thing.

62 He will give eternal life to those who repent and work to become holy.

63 Those who refuse to listen to the Lord will not be able to live with his people, just like the prophet Moses wrote.

64 What Malachi wrote will also come true. "Soon all the proud and the wicked will be burned up like dry grass. There will be nothing left of them at all."

65 This is what the Lord will tell them—

66 "The first time I came to my people, none of you accepted me. That is why you were thrown out of your homeland.

67 "Later I called you again. I could have helped you. I could have set you free. But no one answered.

68 "Now the seas and rivers are drying up. The fish are dying and rotting.

69 "The sky is turning black.

70 "You are bringing nothing but sorrow on yourselves.

71 "There is no one to save you now. That is because you did not obey me when I called you from heaven. You did not accept my servants when I sent them to you.
72 "Finally they stopped trying to teach you. You were left in darkness, in keeping with the law."
73 Then the people I say this to will be sent to outer darkness. They will suffer because they did not repent.
74 These are the Lord's words. Amen.

SECTION 134

Church leaders first tried to publish Joseph Smith's revelations in a book called "The Book of Commandments." But the church's enemies destroyed the book before it could be printed. Church leaders then decided to publish the first Doctrine and Covenants. They voted to include in the book something Oliver Cowdery had written, explaining the church's beliefs about governments and laws. Section 134 is what Oliver wrote.

1 We believe that governments were set up by God to help people. We believe God judges people based on whether or not they make good laws that will protect all people.
2 We believe that to have peace, governments must make laws allowing everyone to do what they believe is right. Laws must give people the right to control their own property. Laws must help people live safely.
3 We believe that every government needs to have officers and judges to make sure its laws are kept. Officers and judges need to be just and fair. They should be chosen by vote or by the country's ruler, depending on how the country's laws are set up.
4 We believe that religion was started by God. No one should have to answer to anyone but God for their religion, unless their beliefs lead them to take away other people's rights and freedoms. We do not believe that people have the right to make laws telling others what to believe or how to worship. Judges should keep people from committing crimes. But they should never control what people believe. They should punish people who break the law. But they should never limit people's spiritual freedom.
5 We believe that people should support the government of the place where they live, as long as that government protects human rights. When that is the case, people should not disobey or fight against the government. People who do should be punished. All governments have the right to make the laws they think will be best for people. But no government has the right to keep people from living in keeping with their beliefs.
6 We believe that rulers and judges should be respected. They are there to protect the innocent and to punish the guilty. Everyone should respect the law. Without the law there would be no order or peace. Every-

one would live in fear. Earthly laws are made to keep people and countries safe. They are made to see that everyone's earthly needs are met. God also gives spiritual laws to teach people what is true and how they should worship. He expects people to obey those laws.

7 We believe that governments should make laws which will protect people's right to believe and worship the way they choose. As long as people's religious beliefs do not lead them to fight against the government, it is wrong for the government to take away this right. It is wrong for the government to tell people what to believe.

8 We believe that the punishment should match the crime. Murderers, traitors, robbers, and troublemakers should be punished, in keeping with the laws of the place where they commit their crimes. People should do what they can to help the law catch and punish those who commit crimes. That way there will be peace for all.

9 We believe it is wrong to mix church and state. We believe it is wrong for the government to support one church and take away the rights of people who belong to another church.

10 We believe that all religious groups have a right to punish members who break the religion's rules. But no religious group has the right to take away someone's property, or to kill them, or to hurt their bodies in any way. They can only take away the person's right to take part in the group.

11 We believe that people should go to the law for help when their rights are taken away, as long as there is a law which will protect them. But we also believe that if people cannot get help from the law, they have the right to protect themselves. They also have the right to protect their friends, their property, and their government from someone who attacks them.

12 We believe the gospel needs to be taught to the whole world. That way the righteous can save themselves from the world's wickedness. But we do not believe it is right to teach the gospel to slaves or to baptize slaves without their masters' permission. We do not believe it is right to do anything which would make slaves unhappy with their place in life. To do so would put other people in danger in places where slavery is allowed.

SECTION 135

Some members in Nauvoo turned against the church. They started a newspaper of their own. In their newspaper, they said Joseph Smith had committed terrible crimes. As mayor of Nauvoo, Joseph had the newspaper destroyed. His enemies then arrested him. They put him in jail, along with some other church leaders. A large mob attacked the jail. They killed Joseph and his brother Hyrum. John Taylor was one of the apostles. He was in jail with Joseph when the mob attacked. He was hurt, but not killed. He wrote about Joseph's death for the Doctrine and Covenants. Section 135 is what John Taylor wrote.

¹ To seal the testimony of this book and the Book of Mormon, we announce the deaths of the Prophet Joseph Smith and the Patriarch Hyrum Smith. They were shot in Carthage Jail on June 27, 1844, around 5:00 PM. They were shot by a mob of 150-200 people who had painted their faces black. Hyrum was shot first. He shouted, "I'm a dead man!" Then he died quietly. Joseph was shot when he tried to jump out the window. He shouted, "O Lord my God!" Both men were shot even after they were dead. Each body had four bullets in it.

² The only other people in the room were two apostles, John Taylor and Willard Richards. John was shot four times. But he was not killed. God protected Willard so that not even his clothes were hit.

³ The Prophet Joseph Smith has done more to help save people than anyone else who has ever lived, except Jesus. In just 20 years, he did all these things: Through God's power, he translated the Book of Mormon. He had it published in both America and Europe. He sent the restored gospel out to every part of the world. He wrote down the revelations which make up Doctrine and Covenants. He wrote many other important things to help people. He gathered thousands of Latter-day Saints. He started a large city. He made himself famous forever. He lived and died with the respect of God and his people. Like most of the Lord's servants long ago, he and his brother Hyrum finished their mission by giving up their lives. They lived and died together!

⁴ Two or three days before his death, Joseph went to Carthage. He was going to give himself up, to show that he respected the law. On the way, he said, "I am like a lamb going to be killed. But I feel peaceful. I know I have done nothing against God or anyone else. I will die an innocent man. People will know that I was murdered in cold blood." That same morning, he read these verses near the end of Ether 12. Then he folded down the page. He did this after Hyrum was ready to leave for what turned out to be their murder.

⁵ *Then I prayed to the Lord to help the Gentiles have charity. The Lord said to me, "It will not matter to you if they do not have charity, because you have been faithful. Your sins will be forgiven. Because you have seen your weakness, you will be made strong. You will sit down on the throne I have prepared for you in my Father's kingdom." Now I . . . say goodbye to the Gentiles, and to my dear brothers and sisters, until we meet to be judged by Christ. Then everyone will know that I am not guilty of your sins.* Joseph and Hyrum have died, but their testimony is still alive.

⁶ Hyrum was 44 when he died. Joseph was 38. They will be remembered as people who died for their religion. Everyone who reads this will know that the best men of the 1800's died so that the Book of Mormon and Doctrine and Covenants could be published to help save people. If God allows the righteous to die like this, imagine what the wicked will suffer! Joseph and Hyrum lived and died to bring God glory. God will give them

glory as their reward. The righteous will honor them forever.

7 It had already been proven many times that they had not committed any crime. They were put in jail only because wicked people made plans to destroy them. The floor of Carthage Jail is stained with their innocent blood. It stains the state seal of Illinois, because the governor of Illinois broke his promise to help them. It stains the United States flag, and the United States Constitution. It is a testimony of "Mormonism" which no court on earth can reject. It is a testimony of the gospel which not even the whole world could call into question. It is a witness of Jesus Christ's gospel that will touch the heart of every honest person on earth. Their blood is mixed with the blood of all who have died for the gospel. It will shout to the Lord for justice until the wicked have been punished. Amen.

SECTION 136

After Joseph Smith was killed, most church members accepted Brigham Young and the other apostles as their new leaders. Their enemies were attacking them. They wanted to force the members to move out of Nauvoo. In the end, the members were forced to move away. But they fininshed building the Nauvoo Temple first. They started getting ready for the long trip to Utah. The Lord gave Brigham Young a revelation. The revelation told how the members should travel. Section 136 is that revelation.

1 This is how the Lord says he wants the Camp of Israel to travel west:

2 All the members of The Church of Jesus Christ of Latter-day Saints should be organized into companies. So should everyone else who wants to travel with them. They must promise to keep all of God's commandments.

3 Every company of 10, 50, and 100 families will be led by a captain. The captains will be led by a president with two counselors. The president and the counselors will be led by the twelve apostles.

4 We will promise to act in keeping with all the Lord's ordinances.

5 Each company should get as many of the things they will need for the journey as they can. They should get work animals, wagons, food, and clothes.

6 Once the companies are ready to go, they should do everything they can to get things ready for those who are staying.

7 Each company should decide how many people can start travelling next spring. Then they should choose strong men who know what they are doing to go on ahead and plant crops.

8 Each company should pay an equal share for taking care of the poor. They should take care of the families of the men who have died or gone into the army. If those families suffer, the Lord will judge us for it.

9 Each company should build houses and plant crops for those

who are staying behind until next year. This is what the Lord wants his people to do.

10 Everyone should do everything they can to help this people move to their new home. There the Lord will set up a new stake of Zion.

11 If you do this faithfully, with pure hearts, you will be blessed. Your flocks, herds, fields, houses, and families will all be blessed.

12 Ezra T. Benson and Erastus Snow should organize a company.

13 So should Orson Pratt and Wilford Woodruff.

14 So should Amasa Lyman and George A. Smith.

15 Choose the people who are going to serve as presidents and captains.

16 Those of my servants who have been chosen should go teach the other members what I want them to do. That way the members can be ready to travel to a peaceful land.

17 Go do what I have told you. Do not be afraid of your enemies. I will not let them stop my work.

18 Zion will be freed when I decide the time is right.

19 People who try to make themselves important without asking for my advice will be powerless. Everyone else will see how foolish they are.

20 Ask for my advice. Keep all the promises you make each other. Do not waste your time wishing you owned things other people have.

21 Do not use the Lord's name wrongly. Remember that it is the name of your ancestors' God—the God of Abraham, Issac, and Jacob.

22 Long ago I led my people out of Egypt. Now, in the time just before the end of the world, I will again save my people.

23 Stop fighting with each other. Stop talking badly about each other.

24 Stop getting drunk. Say things that will build up other people.

25 If you borrow something from your neighbor, return it or repay it. If you can't, tell your neighbor at once. That way you do not get into trouble.

26 If you find something someone has lost, look hard until you find its owner. That way you can give it back.

27 Take good care of what you have. Remember that it really belongs to God. He gave it to you freely. But he expects you to take care of it.

28 If you feel happy, praise the Lord. Sing, make music, and dance. Thank God in your prayers.

29 If you feel sad, pray to the Lord. Then he will be able to give you joy.

30 Do not be afraid of your enemies. I am in control.

31 My people must be tested. Then they will be ready to receive the glory I have waiting for them. It is the glory of Zion. Those who cannot stand to be corrected will not be able to live in my kingdom.

32 Those who want to become wise should be humble. They should pray to God. God will help them understand things they never did before.

33 I have sent my Spirit into the world. It will teach those who are humble and who repent. The wicked will not enjoy this blessing.

34 The people of your country have thrown you out. They have rejected you and your testimony.

35 The time is coming when they will suffer. They will suffer terribly unless they repent very, very soon.
36 They killed the prophets and the messengers I sent them. The blood of the people they killed cries out against them.
37 Do not be surprised by these things. You are not ready to receive my glory yet. But you will be if you keep all the commandments I have given you. I have given you commandments throughout history—from Adam to Abraham, from Abraham to Moses, from Moses to Jesus and his apostles, and now to Joseph Smith. I sent angels to visit him. I also spoke to him myself. I taught him how to carry out my work.
38 He was faithful. After he started my work, I took him to live with me.
39 Many people have been surprised that he died. But he needed to give up his life in order to seal his testimony. That way he could be honored. But the wicked will be found guilty.
40 It is by leaving a witness of my name that I have been able to save you from your enemies.
41 Listen, people of my church. Listen, elders. I have given you my kingdom.
42 Work hard at keeping all my commandments. If you do not, you will suffer. Your faith will fail you. Your enemies will overpower you. That is all I have to say for now. Amen and amen.

SECTION 137

Joseph Smith had an older brother named Alvin. Alvin died before Joseph started translating the Book of Mormon. So Alvin never had the chance to join the restored church. Years after Alvin's death, Joseph and some other church leaders held a meeting in the Kirtland Temple. During the meeting, they had a vision of the celestial kingdom. Section 137 is what Joseph wrote about that vision.

1 We were given a vision of the celestial kingdom and its glory. I do not know if we saw this with our own eyes, or if our spirits travelled there.
2 I saw the gate which lets people into the celestial kingdom. It was more beautiful than anyone could imagine. It was like rings of fire.
3 I saw the Father and the Son sitting on God's shining throne.
4 The streets of that kingdom were beautiful. They looked like they were covered with gold.
5 I saw Adam and Abraham. I saw my parents. I saw my brother Alvin, who died many years ago.
6 Alvin had died before the Lord restored his church. He had not been baptized to have his sins forgiven. So I wondered how he had been able to enter the celestial kingdom.
7 The Lord said to me, "Everyone who died without learning the gospel, but who would have accepted it if they had had the chance, will enter the celestial kingdom.
8 "The same is true for everyone who dies from now on without

learning the gospel, but who would have accepted it with all their hearts if they had had the chance.

9 "This is because I judge people not just for their works, but also for their desires."

10 I saw that all children who die before they are old enough to know right from wrong enter the celestial kingdom.

SECTION 138

Joseph F. Smith was Hyrum Smith's son. He became the sixth president of the church. On the day before general conference, he was studying the scriptures. While he was studying, he had a vision of the spirit world. He told the members of the church about his vision at general conference the next day. After the conference, he wrote down what he had seen in his vision. Section 138 is what President Smith wrote down.

1 On October 3, 1918, I was sitting in my room studying the scriptures.

2 I was thinking about the atonement God's Son made to save the world.

3 I was thinking about the wonderful love the Father and the Son showed when the Savior came to earth.

4 He came so that all people could be saved. People are saved through his atonement and by obeying gospel principles.

5 Then I remembered Peter's letters to church members living long ago. These members had lived in Pontus, Galatia, Cappadocia, and other parts of Asia. The gospel had been preached in those places after Jesus died.

6 I opened the Bible and read 1 Peter 3-4. I was touched more than ever before by these verses—

7 "Christ was righteous. But he suffered for the sins of the wicked so that he could bring us to God. His body was killed. But the Spirit brought him back to life.

8 "While he was a spirit, he went to teach the people in spirit prison.

9 "These were the people who disobeyed God back during the time when Noah was building the ark. In that ark, eight people were saved from the Flood." (1 Peter 3:18-20.)

10 "The gospel was preached to the dead. That way they could live with God after they died, even though they did things that were wrong while they were alive." (1 Peter 4:6.)

11 While I was thinking about these scriptures, the Spirit gave me a vision of everyone who had died.

12 A huge group of righteous spirits were meeting in one place. These were people who had been faithful witnesses of Jesus while they were alive.

13 These were people who had sacrificed animals as a symbol of the sacrifice of God's Son. They had suffered for worshipping the Savior.

14 They had died knowing that they would come back from the dead through the power of God the Father and his only Son, Jesus Christ.

15 I saw that they were filled with

joy, because it was almost time for them to be freed.

16 They were waiting for God's Son to enter the spirit world. They were waiting for him to come tell them they were free from death.

17 Their bodies would come back together. Their spirits would return to their bodies. Never again would their spirits leave their bodies. Then they could know full joy.

18 The people in this huge crowd were talking to each other while they waited. They were rejoicing, because they knew that soon they would be freed from death. While they were talking, God's Son appeared. He told these faithful spirits that they were free.

19 He taught them the gospel. He taught them about how they would come back from the dead. He taught them that they would be saved from the Fall. He taught them that they could be saved from their personal sins if they repented.

20 He did not go to the wicked. The people who had been wicked while they were alive did not get to hear him.

21 The people who had rejected the prophets' testimonies and warnings did not get to see him.

22 It was dark where those people were. But it was peaceful where the righteous were.

23 The righteous rejoiced in being saved. They knelt down before God's Son. They knew he was their Savior. He had saved them from death and hell.

24 The Lord's glory made their faces shine. They sang praise to him.

25 I was surprised by all this. I knew that the Savior had tried for three years to teach the people of Israel to repent.

26 He did many amazing works and miracles. He taught the truth with power and authority. Even so, only a few people listened to him. Only a few people rejoiced to see him. Only a few people allowed him to save them.

27 But he was able to teach the dead during just the short time between dying on the cross and coming back from the dead.

28 I wondered how Jesus was able to teach all the people in spirit prison in such a short time.

29 While I was wondering this, the Spirit helped me understand. I understood that the Lord did not go in person to teach the wicked. He did not go in person to those who had rejected the truth.

30 Instead he chose messengers from among the righteous. He gave his messengers power to go teach the gospel to all the other spirits. That is how the gospel was taught to the dead.

31 The messengers went out to teach the spirits in prison that the Lord had freed them. They taught the gospel to everyone who would repent.

32 That is how the gospel was taught to those who had died without learning the truth or repenting of their sins. That is how the gospel was taught to those who had rejected the prophets.

33 They were taught to have faith in God. They were taught to repent of their sins. They were taught to accept the baptisms and confirma-

tions for the dead done for them by living people.

34 They were taught all other gospel principles they needed to know to be able to live with God, even though they had not obeyed him while they were alive.

35 That is how all the dead learned that God's Son died on the cross so they could be saved. The wicked learned this as well as the faithful.

36 They learned that our Savior spent his time in the spirit world teaching the spirits of the prophets. These were the same prophets who had testified about him while they were alive.

37 He prepared them to preach the gospel to all the rest of the dead. He could not visit them personally, because of their sins. So he sent his servants to teach them his words.

38 There were many important people in this large meeting of the righteous. I saw Adam, the father of all people.

39 I saw Eve, our glorious mother. With her were many other faithful women from throughout history. These were women who had worshipped the true God.

40 Abel was there. He was the first person to die for the gospel. His brother Seth was there, too. He was an important leader. He looked exactly like his father Adam.

41 I saw Noah, who warned people about the Flood. I saw Shem, the great high priest. I saw Abraham, the ancestor of God's people. I saw Isaac and Jacob. I saw Moses, who gave God's law to the Israelites.

42 I saw Isaiah. He was the prophet who said that the Savior would heal the broken-hearted, free the slaves, and let the prisoners go.

43 I saw Ezekiel. He was the one who had a vision of old bones being covered again with skin and coming back to life.

44 I saw Daniel. He was the prophet who said that God would set up his kingdom in the time just before the end of the world. He said that kingdom would never again be destroyed or given to someone else.

45 I saw Elias. He was the one who appeared with Moses on the mountain when Jesus was transformed.

46 I saw Malachi. He testified that Elijah would come before the Second Coming. Moroni told Joseph Smith the same thing.

47 Elijah was going to come to remind people of the promises made to their ancestors.

48 This would prepare the way for temple work. Then the dead could be saved. Then children could be sealed to their parents. If this did not happen, the whole earth would be destroyed during the Second Coming.

49 I saw all these people and many others. I saw the Nephite prophets who testified about the coming of God's Son. They were waiting with that huge crowd to be freed.

50 I say "freed," because the dead felt that being apart from their bodies for so long was like being in prison.

51 The Lord taught these people. He gave them the power to enter his Father's kingdom after they came back from the dead. There they would receive eternal life.

52 There they would keep doing the work the Lord promised them.

They would share all the blessings God has waiting for those who love him.

53 I saw Joseph Smith, Hyrum Smith, Brigham Young, John Taylor, and Wilford Woodruff in the spirit world, too. They and other spirits were chosen to live on earth in the time just before the end of the world. They were sent to help start the Lord's work for the last time.

54 That work includes building temples and performing ordinances in them to save the dead.

55 These people were among the great ones God chose before the Creation to lead his church.

56 Even before they were born, while they were still living in the spirit world, they and many others were given lessons. They were prepared to be born on earth when the Lord needed them. On earth, they would work to help save people.

57 I saw that faithful elders keep teaching the gospel after they die. They teach people in spirit prison about repentance and the atonement.

58 The dead who repent will be saved if they obey temple ordinances.

59 After they have paid the price for their sins, they will be rewarded for their works. They will be saved.

60 This is the vision I had of the salvation of the dead. I testify that what I have written here is true. This vision is a blessing from our Savior Jesus Christ. Amen.

OFFICIAL DECLARATION 1

After the church members moved to Utah, they stopped keeping plural marriage a secret (see Section 132). The United States government said it was against the law to have more than one wife. Many church leaders and members were put in jail. Others had to go into hiding. The government took away the church's property. They took away the temples. Finally the Lord gave President Wilford Woodruff a revelation. It said that the members needed to stop having more than one wife. Official Declaration 1 tells about that revelation. It is also called "the Manifesto."

There has been a lot of talk in the news lately about a report the Utah Commission made to the United States government a little while ago. The report said that plural marriage is still being practiced. The report says that at least 40 plural marriages were performed in Utah last year. It says that Church leaders are still teaching men to marry more than one wife.

As President of The Church of Jesus Christ of Latter-day Saints, I say that this report is false. We are not teaching plural marriage. We are not allowing anyone to practice it. No plural marriages were performed last year in our temples or anywhere else in Utah.

I have been told that one plural marriage was performed in the Endowment House, in Salt Lake City, in the spring of 1889. But I have not been able to find out who performed the marriage. Whoever it was did this without my knowing about it. As soon as I heard about this, I had the Endowment House torn down.

Congress has made it against the law to have more than wife. The Supreme Court has said that the Constitution allows Congress to do this. I am going to obey those laws. I am going to teach members of the church to obey those laws.

I have not taught anything in the last year that could be understood to support plural marriage. Neither have any other leaders of the church. Any elders who have said something that seemed to support plural marriage have been quickly corrected. My advice to the members of the church is that they not enter marriages which are against the law.

      Signed: Wilford Woodruff,
      President of The Church of Jesus Christ of Latter-day Saints

Wilford Woodruff wrote Official Declaration 1 on September 24, 1890. The members voted to accept Official Declaration 1 as a law for the church. They did this during General Conference on October 6, 1890.

Parts of three talks Wilford Woodruff gave about the Manifesto:

The Lord will never let the church be lost because of its president. That is not part of God's plan. If I tried to turn you against what is right, the Lord would reject me as his prophet. He would do the same thing to anyone who tried to tell people not to follow God's messengers or do their duty.

Whoever is leading the church must do it the way God tells them to, or they will not be able to lead the church at all.

I have had some very important revelations lately. I will tell you what the Lord has said to me. Let's start with the Manifesto.

The Lord has told me to ask the Latter-day Saints a question. He says that if they listen to what I say and answer the question through the Spirit, they will all give the same answer.

The question is—what is best for the Latter-day Saints to do? Should we try to keep practicing plural marriage, even though it is against the law? That would mean having the temples taken away by the government. We would not be able to perform any ordinances in them anymore. It would mean that the First Presidency, the Twelve Apostles, and many fathers would be arrested and lose their property. That would basically stop plural marriage anyway. Or should we obey the law and stop plural marriage? That would let the prophets, apostles, and fathers stay at home. They would be able to teach the people and lead the church. We would be able to keep the temples and do temple ordinances.

The Lord showed me in a vision what would happen if we did not stop plural marriage. All temple ordinances would have stopped. Many men would have been put in prison. The whole church would have suffered. In the end, we would have been forced to stop plural marriage anyway. Now, should we have let it be stopped this way? Or should we have stopped it the way the Lord told us to? The Lord's way left the leaders of the church, and the fathers, free. It allowed us to keep doing temple work for the dead. Many people have been freed from spirit prison by the temple work we have done. Should we have stopped that work? Or should we have allowed it to keep going? That is my question. Give whatever answer you decide. But everything I have told you would have happened if we had not done what we did.

The Spirit told me long ago what would happen if something was not done. But I want you to know that I would have given up the temples. I would have gone to prison. I would have allowed everyone else to go there, too, if God had not commanded me to do what I did. Once he gave the command, everything became clear. I prayed to the Lord and wrote what he told me to.

I leave you to think about this. The Lord is working with us.

Now I will explain what was revealed to me. I will explain what God's Son did. All this would have happened if the Manifesto had not been given. So God's Son gave this revelation to carry out his plan. The Lord had promised to set up Zion. He had promised that we would be able to finish building the Salt Lake Temple. He had promised that we would be able to do ordinances to save the living and the dead. And he had promised that Satan would not be able to stop this. That is the secret to understanding the Manifesto.

OFFICIAL DECLARATION 2

For a long time after the church was restored, people with black skin were not allowed to hold the priesthood or go to the temple. Even someone with white skin who had an ancestor with black skin was not allowed to hold the priesthood. As time went on, many people began to wonder if this was really what God wanted. President Spencer W. Kimball spent many days praying to know what to do. At last God revealed to him that the color of someone's skin should have nothing to do with whether or not they could hold the priesthood. Official Declaration 2 tells about that revelation.

Official Declaration 2 was a letter written by the First Presidency to priesthood leaders all over the world. It was sent on June 8, 1978.

In the letter, the First Presidency said they were thankful that the Lord's work had spread across the earth. They were thankful that people from many countries had accepted the restored gospel and joined the church. They said they wanted to give every worthy member of the church all the blessings that come from the gospel.

The First Presidency knew that the prophets and church presidents before them had promised that in the end, God's plan would let everyone who was worthy hold the priesthood. They saw how faithful the members who were not allowed to hold the priesthood had been. They prayed long and hard in the Upper Room of the Temple, asking the Lord what to do.

At last the Lord answered their prayers. He revealed to them that it was time to give the priesthood to all worthy male members of the church. That way they could hold God's authority. They and their families could enjoy all priesthood blessings. They could receive temple ordinances. The First Presidency said it did not matter what race the members belonged to or what color their skin was. As long as they were worthy, they could receive the priesthood.

The First Presidency bore their testimony that this is what the Lord wanted. They knew that this change would make it possible for the Lord to bless all his children, all over the world.

The letter was signed by the First Presidency: Spencer W. Kimball, N. Eldon Tanner, & Marion G. Romney.

The members of the church voted to accept Official Declaration 2 as a true revelation. They did this during General Conference on September 30, 1978.

What the Twelve Apostles said about Doctrine and Covenants:

This is our testimony about the book of the Lord's commandments. The Lord gave these commandments to his church through Joseph Smith. Joseph Smith was chosen by the members of the church to serve as their prophet.

We want to tell everyone in the world what the Lord has told us through the Holy Ghost. The Holy Ghost has told us that these commandments are revelations from God. They are true. They will be useful for everyone.

We give this testimony to the world. The Lord is our helper. The power of God the Father and his Son Jesus Christ makes it possible for us to bear this testimony. We are very happy that we can do so. We pray to the Lord that our testimony will help people.

Thomas B. Marsh	Orson Hyde	William Smith
David W. Patten	William E. McLellin	Orson Pratt
Brigham Young	Parley P. Pratt	John F. Boynton
Heber C. Kimball	Luke S. Johnson	Lyman E. Johnson

Pearl of Great Price

TO THE READER

The Pearl of Great Price is a collection of things written by the prophet Joseph Smith. Some parts Joseph Smith himself wrote. Other parts are things written by prophets in Bible times. Joseph Smith translated the prophets' writings so that church members could read them. These writings were first published in newspapers run by the church. After Joseph Smith died, the writings were brought together into a little book. The book was called the Pearl of Great Price. It got that name because it is like a pearl—very small, but very valuable. Church members voted to accept the Pearl of Great Price as scripture in 1880, at General Conference.

Some of Joseph Smith's most amazing revelations are found in the Pearl of Great Price. The Pearl of Great Price teaches us about how God made the world. It teaches us where Satan came from. It teaches us that we have always existed in some form. It teaches us that our lives on earth are part of a plan from God. It teaches us about faraway stars and planets. It teaches us that there are people on other planets. It teaches us that those people play a part in God's plan, just as we do. It teaches us what the end of the world will be like, and how we can prepare for it. It teaches us how we need to live with each other before Jesus can come live with us.

I think it is sad that Joseph Smith was killed before he could add more to the writings in the Pearl of Great Price. When I served as a missionary, I loved being able to read from the Pearl of Great Price with people. I loved being able to share its teachings with them. I hope the *Easy-to-Read Pearl of Great Price* will help you begin to understand this little book's amazing teachings.

ABOUT THE BOOK OF MOSES

Almost as soon as Joseph Smith finished translating the Book of Mormon, the Lord told him to start working on a new translation of the Bible. This translation would be very different from any other Bible translation. Normally, a translation means changing the words of the Bible from one language to another. But Joseph's translation would be putting back into the Bible truths which had been revealed long ago and then lost. Only a prophet, not just someone who studied other languages, could make this kind of translation.

Joseph bought a large copy of the King James Version. At that time, the King James Version was the Bible translation used by most people who spoke English. Joseph started marking in the Bible the verses the Lord told him to change. Sometimes the Lord revealed whole new verses or chapters for Joseph to add. The translation took three years to finish. Joseph spent the rest of his life trying to publish the translation. But because of the church's debts and troubles, he was able to publish only small parts of it.

The Book of Moses is the beginning of Joseph Smith's translation of the Bible. It starts with some visions Moses had. The Bible does not tell about these revelations. Then the Book of Moses gives Joseph's translation of the first few chapters of Genesis.

THE BOOK OF MOSES
CHAPTER 1

1 This is what God said to Moses when Moses was lifted up into a very high mountain.
2 Moses saw God face-to-face. He talked with God. God's glory covered Moses, so Moses could stand to be with him.
3 God said to Moses, "I am the Lord. I have all power. My name is Endless, because I have always existed and always will exist.
4 "You are my son. Look, and I will show you my creations. I cannot show you all of them, though. That is because my works never end. Neither do my words.
5 "No one can see all my works without also seeing all my glory. And no one can see all my glory and stay alive.
6 "I have a work for you, my son Moses. You are like my only Son. He will be the Savior. He is full of love and truth. But I am still the only God. For me, there is no such thing as past or future. That is because I know everything now.
7 "Now, Moses, I will show you the earth you are living on."
8 Then Moses saw the earth he was born on. He saw every part of it. He saw all the people who live on it. This amazed him. It put many questions in his mind.
9 God left Moses. When God left, he took his glory with him. As soon as God's glory stopped covering Moses, Moses fell down on the ground.
10 It took Moses many hours to get his strength back. He thought, "Now I know how truly small and powerless people are. I never understood that before.

11 "I have seen God. But I saw him with my spiritual eyes, not my earthly eyes. I could not have seen God with my earthly eyes. I would have shrivelled up and died. But God's glory covered me. It changed my body. Then I was able to look at him."
12 After Moses said this, Satan came to tempt him. He said, "Moses, human child—worship me."
13 Moses looked at Satan and said, "Who are you? I am God's child. I am like his only Son. Why should I worship you? Where is your glory?
14 "I could not look at God unless his glory covered me and changed my body. But I can look at you with my earthly eyes. Isn't that right?
15 "I praise God, because his Spirit has not completely left me. Where is your glory? All I see around you is darkness. I can tell you apart from God. God told me to worship only him.
16 "Go away, Satan. You cannot trick me, because God said I was like his only Son.
17 "When he called to me from the burning bush, he commanded me to pray to God in the name of his only Son. He commanded me to worship him."
18 Moses said, "I will not stop praying to God. I have other things to ask him. I can tell you apart from him, because his glory has covered me. Go away, Satan."
19 After Moses said this, Satan screamed and acted as if he were crazy. He shouted, "I am God's only Son! Worship me!"
20 This made Moses very fright-

Moses

ened. He began to see how terrible hell is. But he prayed to God for strength. He said, "Go away, Satan. I will worship only one God, the God of glory."

21 Now Satan began to shake. The whole earth shook with him. But Moses became strong. He prayed to God and said, "In the name of God's only Son—go away, Satan!"

22 Satan screamed again. Then he left, crying, and howling, and grinding his teeth. Moses could not see him anymore.

23 Moses wrote about this. But because of wicked people, the people of today do not have his record.

24 After Satan left, Moses looked up at the sky. He was filled with the Holy Ghost. The Holy Ghost testifies about the Father and the Son.

25 Moses prayed. God's glory covered him again. He heard a voice say, "You are blessed, Moses. I have chosen you. I will make you stronger than the sea. It will obey you as if you were God.

26 "I will be with you all your life. You will free my people, Israel, from slavery."

27 While the voice was still talking, Moses saw the whole earth. He saw every speck of it through God's Spirit.

28 Through the Spirit, Moses saw every single person living on the earth. He saw as many people as there are grains of sand on the beach—too many to count.

29 He saw many lands. They were all called "earth." They all had people living on them.

30 Moses asked God, "Please tell me why these things are like this. How did you make them?"

31 The Lord's glory covered Moses, so Moses could stand in front of God. He could talk with God face-to-face. The Lord said to Moses, "I have my own reason for making these things. It is a wise reason. But for now it will remain my secret.

32 "I created them through the word of my power. In other words, I created them through my only Son. He is full of love and truth.

33 "I have created an endless number of worlds. They were all created for my wise purpose. They were all created through my only Son.

34 "The very first man on earth I call Adam. There are many Adams, because there are many earths.

35 "But I will tell you only about this earth and its people. Through my Son, many earths have already ended. Many others still exist. There are too many earths for people to count. But I have counted them, because they are mine. I know them all."

36 Moses said to the Lord, "Have mercy on me, God. Tell me about this earth and its people. Tell me about the heavens. That is all I want to know."

37 The Lord said to Moses. "There are many heavens—so many that only I can count them all.

38 "When one earth and its heavens pass away, new ones come. My works, like my words, never end.

39 "This is my work and my glory—to make it possible for people to live forever and to have eternal life.

40 "Moses, my son, I will now tell you about your earth. Write down what I say.

41 "Someday, people will stop caring about my words. They will take many words away from the book you write. When that happens, I will call another prophet like you. I will use him to bring back the words that are taken away. Everyone who believes will have those words."
42 (God said this to Moses on a mountain. The name of that mountain will not be revealed. Now you, too, have heard what God said. Show these words only to those who believe. Amen.)

CHAPTER 2

1 *The Lord said to Moses:* I will teach you about this heaven and this earth. Write down what I say. I am God. I have all power. I am the beginning and the end. I created everything through my only Son. In the beginning, I created your earth and its heaven.
2 At first there was nothing on earth but a dark ocean. My Spirit moved on the water's surface.
3 I said, "I want there to be light." So there was.
4 I saw that the light was good. I separated the light from the darkness.
5 I called the light "day." I called the darkness "night." I did this through my Son. He did it just the way I told him to. This was the first day.
6 Then I said, "I want a space to run through the middle of the water, to split it up." This happened just like I said.
7 I made a space to split up the water. Some water was above the space and some water stayed below it, just like I had said.
8 I called the space "sky." This was the second day.
9 Then I said, "I want all the water under the sky to come together into one place, so that dry land comes up." This happened just like I said.
10 I called the dry land "earth." I called the place where the water came together "sea." I saw that everything I had made was good.
11 I said, "I want grass, plants, and fruit trees to grow on the earth. Each plant and tree should have seeds that will grow into the same kind of plant or tree." This happened just like I said.
12 The earth grew grass, plants, and fruit trees. Each plant and tree had seeds that would grow into the same kind of plant or tree. I saw that everything I had made was good.
13 This was the third day.
14 Then I said, "I want there to be lights in the sky. They will separate the light from the darkness. They will be used to measure seasons, days, and years.
15 "They will light up the earth." This happened just like I said.
16 I made two large lights. The larger one shone during the day. The smaller one shone at night. The stars were also made the way I commanded.
17 I put these lights in the sky to light up the earth.

Moses

18 The sun lit up the day, and the moon lit up the night. They separated the light from the darkness. I saw that everything I had made was good.

19 This was the fourth day.

20 Then I said, "I want there to be animals living in the water. I want there to be birds flying in the sky."

21 So I created whales and all other kinds of water animals. I created birds. Each kind of animal could have babies of the same kind. I saw that everything I had made was good.

22 I blessed the water animals and the birds. I told them, "Have many babies. Fill the earth and sea."

23 This was the fifth day.

24 Then I said, "I want there to be animals on the land. I want there to be farm animals, wild animals, and animals that crawl on the ground." This happened just like I said.

25 I made all kinds of land animals. Every kind of animal could have babies of the same kind. I saw that all this was good.

26 Then I said to my only Son, "Let's make human beings to look like us. We will put them in charge of the fish, the birds, and the animals." All this happened just like I had said.

27 I made human beings to look like me and my only Son. I made both men and women.

28 I blessed the human beings. I told them, "Have many children, so the earth is filled with people. Learn to use the earth's goods. Take charge of the fish, the birds, and the animals."

29 I said to the human beings, "I give you every kind of plant and fruit for food.

30 "All the animals and birds I have created will eat plants, too." This happened just like I said.

31 I saw that everything I had made was very good. This was the sixth day.

CHAPTER 3

1 That is how I, God, finished creating the earth and sky and everything in them.

2 I finished the Creation on the seventh day. I rested from all my work. I saw that everything I had created was very good.

3 I blessed the seventh day. I made it holy, because that was the day I rested from the work of the Creation.

4 This is the order in which I created the spirits of the things that live on the earth and in the sky.

5 Every plant was created before it grew. That is because I made the spirits of all the things I have talked about before I made their bodies. The plants could not have been growing yet in their bodies, because I had not yet made it rain on earth. There was no one on earth yet to help the plants grow. I had created the spirits of all the people who would live on earth. But those spirits were in heaven. There were no people or animals on earth with bodies.

⁶ Instead of rain, I made a mist come up out of the earth to water the ground.
⁷ Then I formed a man. I made him from the same matter the ground was made of. I breathed into the man's nose to make him come to life. He became the first man. He was the first living thing on earth with a body. I had already created everything. But I had created their spirits, not their bodies.
⁸ I planted a garden in Eden, to the east. I put the man in the garden.
⁹ I made all kinds of trees grow out of the ground. The man could see the trees. He could see how beautiful they were. I had already created the trees' spirits. But now they became living things. The man saw that I had made the trees so that he could use them for food. In the middle of the garden, I planted the Tree of Life and the Tree of Knowing Good and Evil.
¹⁰ I made a river flow out of Eden to water the garden. Then it split into four smaller rivers.
¹¹ I named the first river Pison. It runs around Havilah, where I created a lot of gold.
¹² The gold there was good. There were perfume and jewels there, too.
¹³ I named the second river Gihon. It runs around Ethiopia.
¹⁴ I named the third river Hiddekel. It runs east of Assyria. The fourth river was the Euphrates.
¹⁵ I put the man in the Garden of Eden to take care of it.
¹⁶ I told the man, "You may eat fruit from every tree in the garden.
¹⁷ "But I do not want you to eat fruit from the Tree of Knowing Good and Evil. You are free to choose for yourself whether or not to eat its fruit. But I command you not to. If you eat that fruit, you will have to die."
¹⁸ Then I told my only Son that it was not good for the man to be alone. I said, "I will make a proper companion for him."
¹⁹ I formed all kinds of animals and birds. I made them from the same matter the ground is made of. I commanded them to go to Adam so he could name them. They were living things now. That is because I had created bodies for their spirits and brought them to life.
²⁰ Adam named all the animals and birds. But none of these was a proper companion for Adam.
²¹ So I made Adam fall sound asleep. While he was asleep, I took a bone out of his side. Then I closed the skin back up.
²² I made the bone into a woman. I brought her to Adam.
²³ He said, "This is one of my bones—part of my own body. I will call her 'woman,' because she was taken out of man."
²⁴ That is why men and women leave their parents and come together to form one body when they are married.
²⁵ Adam and his wife were both naked. But they did not feel shame.

MOSES

CHAPTER 4

¹ *I, the Lord, said to Moses:* Satan—the one you told to go away from you— existed before the Creation. He came to me and said, "Send me to be your Son. I will save every single person. No one will be lost. Give me your glory."
² But my dear Son was the one I had chosen from the beginning. He said, "Father, I will do whatever you want. The glory will always be yours."
³ Satan turned against me. I gave people the freedom to make their own choices. But Satan tried to take that freedom away. He tried to make me give him my power. So I had to send him away from heaven. I did it through my only Son's power.
⁴ That is how Satan became the devil. He is the father of all lies. He tricks people. He keeps them from seeing the truth. He turns everyone who refuses to listen to me into his slaves. He makes them do whatever he wants.
⁵ Now, the snake was the most clever of all the animals I had made.
⁶ Satan had gotten many spirits to follow him. He used the snake to trick Eve. He was trying to destroy the world, because he did not understand God's plan.
⁷ Satan said to the woman, "Is it true that God has said you cannot eat fruit from all the trees in the garden?" Satan was talking to Eve through the snake.
⁸ The woman said to the snake, "We can eat fruit from the trees in the garden.
⁹ "But God has told us not to eat fruit from the tree you see there in the middle of the garden. He told us that if we eat its fruit, or even touch it, we will have to die."
¹⁰ The snake said to the woman, "You won't have to die!
¹¹ "God knows that if you eat that fruit, you will come to know good and evil. Then you will be like gods."
¹² The woman saw that the fruit was good to eat and beautiful to look at it. She saw that it would make her wise. She saw that this would be a good thing. So she ate the fruit. She gave some to Adam. He ate it, too.
¹³ Then Adam and Eve knew that they were naked. They sewed fig leaves into aprons to cover themselves.
¹⁴ In the evening, when it was cool, they were walking through the garden. They heard the Lord's voice. They ran away to hide from him in the trees.
¹⁵ I shouted after Adam, "Where are you going?"
¹⁶ He said, "When I heard your voice, I became frightened. I went to hide because I saw I was naked."
¹⁷ I said to Adam, "Who told you you were naked? Have you eaten the fruit I told you not to eat so you would not die?"
¹⁸ Adam said, "I did eat the fruit. My wife gave it to me—the woman you told me to stay with."
¹⁹ I said to the woman, "What have you done?" She said, "I ate the fruit because the snake tricked me."
²⁰ I said to the snake, "You will be

MOSES

punished for what you have done. You will be more worse off than any animal. You will crawl on your stomach and eat dirt all your life.

21 "You and the woman will be enemies. Your descendants and her descendants will hate each other. They will stamp on your head. You will bite them on the heel."

22 I said to the woman, "Because of what you have done, you will be able to have many children. But it will be very hard and painful for you. You will want your husband. He will rule over you."

23 I said to Adam, "Because you obeyed your wife and ate the forbidden fruit, the earth will change. It will become harder for you to grow food. You will have to work very hard all your life.

24 "Thorns and weeds will grow along with the plants you need to eat.

25 "You will have to work very hard to get food until the day you die—and it is certain now that you will die. When you die, you will go back to the ground you came from. Your body was made from the same matter the ground is made of. It will break up into that matter again when you die."

26 Adam named his wife Eve, because she was the first woman. All people on earth are her descendants. I always name the first woman on earth Eve. Since there are many earths, there are many Eves.

27 I gave Adam and Eve clothing made of animal skins.

28 Then I said to my only Son, "Now Adam and Eve have become like us. They know good and evil. We need to keep them from eating fruit from the Tree of Life, or they will live forever."

29 So I sent Adam and Eve away from the Garden of Eden to grow their own food.

30 I did this because my words must come true. Everything must happen the way I have said.

31 So I made Adam and Eve leave the Garden of Eden. At the east end of the garden, I put an angel with a fiery sword to guard the path to the Tree of Life.

32 (This is what I told Moses. Now you have heard it, too. I have revealed as much truth here as I want to. Do not show this to anyone who does not believe, until I tell you differently. Amen.)

CHAPTER 5

1 After I, the Lord, sent Adam and Eve away from the Garden of Eden, they started to plant crops. They began to keep farm animals. They began to work for their food, as I had commanded them.

2 Adam and Eve had sons and daughters. They began to fill the earth with people.

3 Their sons and daughters married each other. They set up their own homes throughout the land. They planted crops and kept farm animals. They had children of their own.

4 Adam and Eve prayed to the

Lord. They heard his voice speaking to them from the direction of the Garden of Eden. But they could not see him, because they were not able to be with God anymore.

5 God commanded them to worship him. He commanded them to sacrifice animals to him. Adam obeyed the Lord.

6 Many days later, an angel appeared to Adam. The angel asked, "Why do you make sacrifices to the Lord?" Adam replied, "I do not know. All I know is that God told me to."

7 The angel said, "The sacrifices you make are to remind you of the sacrifice God's only Son will make.

8 "You should do everything in the Son's name. You should repent and pray to God in the Son's name forever."

9 That same day, Adam received the Holy Ghost. It testified to him about the Father and the Son. It said, "The Father chose me to be his only Son from the beginning. You have fallen. But through me you can be saved. So can everyone else who wants to be."

10 Then Adam was filled with the Spirit. The Spirit showed him what was going to happen to everyone on earth in the future. He said, "Praise be to God! Because I ate the forbidden fruit, now I know good and evil. God will give me joy while I am alive. I will see him again after I come back from the dead."

11 When Eve heard all this, she was happy, too. She said, "If we had not eaten the forbidden fruit, we would not have been able to have children. We would not have known good and evil. We would not have known the joy of being saved, or the eternal life God gives to those who obey him."

12 Adam and Eve praised God. They taught everything they had learned to their children.

13 But Satan appeared to their children. He said, "I am also God's son." He told Adam and Eve's children not to believe what their parents taught. They did what he told them. They loved Satan more than God. From that time on, people started caring about earthly things more than spiritual things. They became like Satan.

14 The Lord sent the Holy Ghost to tell everyone, everywhere, to repent.

15 God made an law that everyone who believed in the Son and repented of their sins would be saved. Those who refused to believe or repent could not be saved.

16 Adam and Eve kept praying to God. They had another son named Cain. Eve said, "The Lord has given me another son. Maybe this one will obey him." But Cain refused to listen to what his parents taught. He said, "What do I care about the Lord?"

17 Eve had another son named Abel. Abel obeyed the Lord. Abel kept sheep. Cain worked in the fields.

18 Cain loved Satan more than God. Satan told Cain, "Make a sacrifice to the Lord."

19 So when his crops grew, Cain brought some of them for a sacrifice.

20 Around the same time, Abel brought his best lambs for a sacrifice. The Lord accepted Abel and his sacrifice.

21 He did not accept Cain and his sacrifice. This made Satan happy. But Cain became very angry.

22 The Lord said to Cain, "Why are you so angry?

23 "If you do good, I will accept you. If you do not do good, you will fall into Satan's power. Unless you keep my commandments, Satan will be able to do whatever he wants with you. At the same time, you will rule over him.

24 "From now on you will be the father of his lies. You will be called Perdition, because you also existed before the Creation.

25 "Someday people will say, 'All these terrible sins started with Cain, because he refused to listen to God's advice.' That is what will happen to you if you do not repent."

26 But Cain just stayed angry. He refused to listen to the Lord. He refused to listen to his righteous brother, Abel.

27 Adam and Eve were filled with sorrow because of Cain and his brothers.

28 Cain married one of his brothers' daughters. They loved Satan more than God.

29 Satan said to Cain, "Swear by your throat to keep what I tell you a secret. If you tell it, you will die. Make your brothers swear the same thing. Make them swear by their heads and by God. That way Adam will not find out. If you do this, I will give you power over your brother Abel."

30 Then Satan swore to Cain that he would do whatever Cain told him. All this was done in secret.

31 Cain said, "Now I am Mahan, the master of this great secret. Now I can commit murder and get rich." That is why Cain was called Master Mahan. He was proud of his wickedness.

32 Cain went to the fields to talk to Abel. While they were there, Cain killed Abel.

33 Cain was proud of what he had done. He said, "I am free. Now my brother's sheep will be mine."

34 The Lord said to Cain, "Where is Abel?" Cain said, "I don't know. Is it my job to take care of him?"

35 The Lord said, "What have you done? I hear your brother's blood calling to me from the ground.

36 "Because you spilled Abel's blood on the earth, the earth will no longer support you.

37 "The crops you plant will not grow. You will have to wander all over the earth, hiding because of your crime."

38 Cain said to the Lord, "Satan tempted me to kill Abel so I could get his sheep. I also did it because I was angry that you accepted his offering but not mine. You are punishing me too hard!

39 "You are forcing me to hide from you and your people. Whoever finds me as I am wandering will kill me for what I have done. I know now that it is impossible to hide my sins from the Lord."

40 I said to him, "Whoever kills you will have to pay for it seven times." I put a mark on Cain so that no one who found him would kill him.

MOSES

⁴¹ Cain was not able to live with the Lord anymore. He, his wife, and many of his brothers moved to Nod. Nod was east of Eden.

⁴² Cain and his wife had many children. They had a son named Enoch. Cain built a city. He named the city Enoch, after his son.

⁴³ Enoch had many children. One of his children was named Irad. One of Irad's children was named Mahujael. One of Mahujael's children was named Methusael. Methusael had a son named Lamech.

⁴⁴ Lamech had two wives, Adah and Zillah.

⁴⁵ Adah had two sons, Jabal and Jubal. Jabal's descendants lived in tents and kept cows. Jubal's descendants played harps and pipes.

⁴⁶ Zillah had a son named Tubal Cain. He taught people how to make things out of brass and iron. Zillah also had a daughter named Naamah.

⁴⁷ Lamech said to Adah and Zillah, "Listen, my wives. I have been wounded killing a young man.

⁴⁸ "If someone has to pay seven times for killing Cain, then surely the one who hurt me will have to pay for it 77 times."

⁴⁹ Lamech said this because he had made a promise with Satan, the way Cain did. Because of that promise, Lamech became Master Mahan. He was master of the same secret Satan had taught to Cain. Irad, Enoch's son, knew about this secret. He began to tell Adam's family about it.

⁵⁰ This made Lamech angry, so he killed Irad. This was different from Cain killing Abel. Cain killed Abel to get rich. But Lamech killed Irad to protect the secret.

⁵¹ From Cain's time on, there was a secret group of men who did wicked things. They had secret ways of knowing who else belonged to their group.

⁵² The Lord punished Lamech, his family, and everyone else who had made promises with Satan. God was unhappy that these people did not keep his commandments. He was not able to teach or bless them. Their secret sins began to spread throughout the land. But they spread only among men.

⁵³ Women were not allowed to learn the secret. That was because after Lamech told his wives the secret, they turned against him. They started telling everyone about the secret. They did not care what might happen to Lamech.

⁵⁴ Because of what they did, Lamech was hated and thrown out. He had to hide from everyone, to keep from being killed.

⁵⁵ This is how most of the men on earth became wicked.

⁵⁶ Because of what they did, they could not receive God's blessings. Everyone on earth began to suffer, because they would not keep God's commandments.

⁵⁷ They would not listen to God, who created them. They would not believe in his only Son, who had been chosen before the Creation to come to earth.

⁵⁸ From the very beginning of the world, God taught people the gospel. He taught them through angels. He taught them through his own voice. He taught them through the gift of the Holy Ghost.

⁵⁹ All things were confirmed to

Adam by a holy ordinance. God promised that the gospel would be preached on earth until the end of the world. He kept that promise. Amen.

CHAPTER 6

1 Adam listened to God. He told his sons to repent.
2 Adam and Eve had another son, named Seth. Adam praised God. He said, "God has given me another son to take the place of Abel, who was killed by Cain."
3 God revealed himself to Seth. Seth did not turn against God. Like Abel, he made a sacrifice God could accept. Seth had a son named Enos.
4 These men began to pray to the Lord. The Lord blessed them.
5 A record was kept in Adam's language. Everyone who prayed to God was given the Spirit, so they would know what to write.
6 They taught their children to read and write. Their language was pure and holy.
7 "This same priesthood, which existed in the beginning, will still be on earth at the end of the world."
8 This was something Adam taught while he was filled with the Holy Ghost. God's children kept a list of their descendants in a book. This is what the book said. When God created human beings, he made them to look like him.
9 The bodies of men and women look like God's body. God called the first man Adam. He created Adam's body and brought it to life.
10 When Adam was 130 years old, he had a son named Seth. Seth looked just like Adam.
11 After Seth was born, Adam lived 800 years more. He had many other children.
12 When Adam was 930, he died.
13 When Seth was 105, he had Enos. Seth was a prophet all his life. He taught Enos to follow God. Enos became a prophet, too.
14 After Enos was born, Seth lived 807 years more. He had many other children.
15 They were many people on earth. Satan had power over them. He made them angry with each other. There were wars. There were men who killed their own family members. People did things in secret, trying to get power.
16 When Seth was 912, he died.
17 When Enos was 90, he had Cainan. Enos and the rest of God's people moved away from the land of Shulon to a promised land. Enos named the promised land Cainan, after his son.
18 After Cainan was born, Enos lived 815 years more. He had many other children. When he was 905, he died.
19 When Cainan was 70, he had Mahalaleel. He then lived 840 years more. He had other children. When he was 910, he died.
20 When Mahalaleel was 65, he had Jared. He then lived 830 years more. He had other children. When he was 895, he died.
21 When Jared was 162, he had

Enoch. He then lived 800 years more. He had other children. Jared taught Enoch to always follow God.

22 This is the list of Adam's descendants. Adam was God's son. God himself talked with Adam.

23 These men were prophets. They taught others to be righteous. They told all people, everywhere, to repent. They taught people to have faith.

24 When Jared was 962, he died.

25 When Enoch was 65 years old, he had Methuselah.

26 One day Enoch was travelling among the people. God's Spirit came down from heaven and stayed with him.

27 He heard a voice out of heaven say, "Enoch, my son, talk to this people for me. Tell them to repent. Tell them I am very unhappy with them. They will not open their hearts. They do not listen. They are blind.

28 "For many years now, ever since I created them, they have disobeyed me. They have made their own secret, wicked plans. They have committed murder. They have not kept the commandments I gave to Adam.

29 "By making promises with Satan, they have brought death on themselves. If they do not repent, they will be in Satan's power after they die. They will suffer terribly.

30 "This is a law which I myself spoke when the world began. My servants, your ancestors, taught people about this law. It will go out to the whole world."

31 When Enoch heard this, he bowed down on the ground. He said to the Lord, "Why have you chosen me to do this? I am just a boy. Everyone hates me because I cannot speak well. Why have you made me your servant?"

32 The Lord told Enoch, "If you do what I have commanded you, no one will hurt you. When you go to speak, I will give you things to say. I control every living thing. I will do what I think best.

33 "Tell these people—choose to serve the Lord, who created you.

34 "You have my Spirit. I will back up everything you say. Mountains will run away from you. Rivers will change direction. I will always be with you. So walk with me."

35 The Lord said to Enoch, "Put clay on your eyes. When you wash it off, you will be able to truly see." Enoch did this.

36 He was able to see all the spirits God had created. He saw things that other people cannot. From then on, the news spread, "The Lord has sent a seer to his people."

37 Enoch went around among the people. He stood on hills and other high places. He testified loudly about the people's sins. He said harsh things about everyone.

38 They came to the high places to hear him. They told their servants, "Stay here and watch over the tents, while we go to see the seer. There is something strange in the land. A crazy man has come here."

39 No one who came to hear Enoch could arrest him or hurt him. They were too frightened, because he walked with God.

40 A man named Mahijah came to him and said, "Tell us clearly

MOSES

now—who are you? Where do you come from?"

41 Enoch answered, "I came from the land of Cainan, where my ancestors live. The people there are still righteous. My father taught me to always follow God.

42 "While I was travelling from Cainan, near the east sea, I had a vision. I saw heaven. I heard the Lord talk to me. He commanded me to come say what I am telling you now."

43 Enoch said, "The Lord who spoke with me is God. He is my God and your God. You are my brothers and sisters. Why do you make wicked plans together? Why do you turn away from God?

44 "He made the heavens. He owns the earth. He created it and brought many people to live on it.

45 "Some of our ancestors have died. Still, we know them. We even know the very first man, Adam.

46 "We know this thanks to the record we have. It is written in our own language, the way God himself first wrote it with his finger."

47 While Enoch taught God's words, the people shook. They could not keep standing in front of him.

48 *Enoch said to them:* We exist because Adam fell. We also have to die and suffer because he fell.

49 Satan has come among us. He tempts people to worship him. People have come to care more about earthly things more than spiritual things. They have become like Satan. They cannot live with God.

50 God taught our ancestors that everyone needs to repent.

51 He said to Adam, "I am God. I created the world. I created the spirits of all people."

52 He said to Adam, "Listen to me. Have faith. Repent of all your sins. Be baptized in the name of my only Son. Then you will receive the gift of the Holy Ghost. My only Son is Jesus Christ. He is full of love and truth. People can be saved only through his name. You will receive everything you ask for in his name."

53 Adam asked the Lord, "Why do people need to repent and be baptized?" The Lord said, "I have forgiven you for disobeying me in the Garden of Eden."

54 That is how people learned that God's Son has paid the price for Adam's having disobeyed God. This means that children cannot be punished for their parents' sins. Children are innocent from the very beginning.

55 The Lord said to Adam, "Because your children are born into a sinful world, they become sinful as they grow up. They taste what is bitter, so they can learn to value what is good.

56 "Because they know good and evil, they are able to make their own choices. That is why I have given you this new commandment.

57 "Teach your children that everyone, everywhere, must repent in order to live in God's kingdom. Nothing unholy can live with God in his kingdom. That is because God is holy. His name (in Adam's language) is Holy Man. The name of God's only Son is Son of Man. He is Jesus Christ. He is the righteous judge who will come to earth in the future.

Moses

58 "I command you to teach this to your children. This is what you will tell them.

59 "Because of sin came the Fall. Because of the Fall came death. When you were born, there was water, blood, and spirit. (I mean the spirit God put into you to bring you to life.) In the same way, for you to be born into God's kingdom, there must be water, Spirit, and blood. (I mean the blood which my only Son will sacrifice so that all your sins can be washed away.) Then you can enjoy the words of eternal life in this world and eternal life in the next.

60 "You keep my commandment by being baptized. Your sins are forgiven through the Spirit. You are made holy through Christ's blood.

61 "Then you are able to receive the Holy Ghost. It comes from heaven to testify to you. It brings you God's peace. It teaches you all truth. It gives life to all things. It knows all things. It has all power. Everything it does is done in wisdom, truth, mercy, and justice.

62 "This is the plan of salvation for all people. The plan depends on the sacrifice of my only Son. He will come to earth in the future.

63 "Everything is like something else. Everything has been created to testify about me—earthly things and spiritual things, things in heaven and things on earth, things up high and things down below. Everything testifies about me."

64 After the Lord said this, Adam prayed. The Spirit picked him up. It carried him into the water. It laid him down under the water. Then it brought him back out of the water.

65 That is how Adam was baptized. After he was baptized, God's Spirit came down to him. That is how he was born again. That is how he was changed inside.

66 He heard a voice from heaven say, "You are baptized with fire and the Holy Ghost. This is the testimony of the Father and the Son.

67 "You belong to the order of the One who has no beginning and no end.

68 "You are united to me. You are a son of God. In the same way, all people can become my children. Amen."

CHAPTER 7

1 Then Enoch said, "Adam taught all this to his descendants. Many of them believed. They became God's children. Those who did not believe died without having their sins forgiven. Now they are afraid and in pain. They are waiting for God's punishments.

2 Enoch told the people, "While I was travelling, I came to the place called Mahujah. I prayed to the Lord. A voice from heaven told me, 'Go climb Mount Simeon.'

3 "So I did. On the mountain, I had a vision. I was covered with glory.

4 "I saw the Lord standing in front of me. He talked with me face-to-face, the way people talk to each other. He told me, 'Look, and I will show you the future.'

MOSES

5 "I saw the valley of Shum. I saw a great people, living there in tents. These were the Shumites.

6 "The Lord told me again, 'Look.' I looked north. I saw the Canaanites. They also lived in tents.

7 "The Lord told me, 'Speak.' So I opened my mouth. This is what the Spirit told me to say. The Canaanites will start a war with the Shumites. The Shumites will be completely destroyed. Then the Canaanites will split up and take over the Shumites' land. Nothing will grow in the land. No one but the Canaanites will live there.

8 "The Lord will cause the land to become very hot. Nothing will ever be able to grow in it again. A blackness came over the Canaanites. Everyone hated them.

9 "The Lord said to me, 'Look.' When I looked, I saw the lands Sharon, Enoch, Omner, Heni, Shem, Haner, and Hanannihah. I saw the people who lived in those lands.

10 "The Lord told me, 'Go tell these people that if they do not repent, they will die."

11 "He commanded me to baptize people in the name of the Father, and of the Son, and of the Holy Ghost."

12 Enoch kept preaching to all the people, except the Canaanites. He told the people to repent.

13 He led God's people. He had so much faith that when their enemies came to fight them, he was able to command mountains to move. He made rivers change direction. People heard lions roaring in the desert. The whole world was afraid. Enoch was able to make all this happen because of the power of the words God gave him.

14 A land came up out of the ocean. The enemies of God's people were so afraid that they all ran onto it.

15 The giants of the land also ran away. Terrible things happened to those who fought against God.

16 From that time on, there were wars and killing among the wicked. But the Lord came to live with his righteous people.

17 The whole world was afraid because of the glory the Lord gave his people. The Lord blessed his people's land. They grew strong in the mountains and highlands.

18 The Lord called his people Zion, because their hearts and minds were one. They lived righteously. None of them were poor.

19 Enoch kept preaching to God's people. He built a city called the City of Holiness, or Zion.

20 One day Enoch said to the Lord, "Surely Zion will be safe forever." But the Lord said, "It is true I have blessed Zion. But the rest of the people will suffer."

21 The Lord showed Enoch everyone on earth. Enoch saw the future. He saw Zion being taken up into heaven. The Lord said, "Zion will be my home forever."

22 Enoch saw the rest of the people on earth. They were a mixture of all the families descended from Adam except Cain's. That is because Cain's descendants were black. No one would let Cain's descendants live with them.

23 After he saw Zion taken up into heaven, Enoch saw all the countries of the world.

24 He watched many years pass. He

watched this from high in the air, with the Father and the Son. Below, he saw the earth in Satan's power.

25 He saw angels going down from heaven. He heard a voice shout, "Terrible things are coming to the people of earth!"

26 He saw Satan holding a huge chain. The chain covered the whole earth with darkness. Satan looked up and laughed. His angels rejoiced.

27 Enoch saw angels going down from heaven. They testified about the Father and the Son. Many people received the Holy Ghost. They were lifted up into Zion by God's power.

28 God looked down on the people and cried. Enoch saw God crying. He said, "How is it that heaven cries, dropping tears like rain on the mountains?"

29 Enoch said to the Lord, "How can you cry? You are holy and eternal.

30 "If it were possible to count every speck of dust on earth, or on millions of earths like this one, that number would not begin to come close to the number of your creations. Yet there you are, full of justice, mercy, and kindness.

31 "Out of all your creations, you have taken Zion to be with you forever. You sit on a throne of peace, justice, and truth. Your mercy never ends. How, then, can you cry?"

32 The Lord said, "These people are your brothers and sisters—my children. I created them. I made them intelligent. In the Garden of Eden, I gave them the power to make their own choices.

33 "I commanded them to love each other. I commanded them to choose to follow me, their Father. But they have no love. They hate even their own families.

34 "Because of their sins, they will suffer. A giant flood will destroy them.

35 "I am God. I am named Holy Man, Wise Man, Endless, and Eternal.

36 "I can hold all my creations in my hands. I can see through them with my eyes. Nowhere in the universe has there ever been a people as wicked as this one.

37 "It is their parents' fault for teaching them to be so wicked. They will become Satan's children. They will suffer with him. Everyone in heaven, and everything I have created, will cry to see them suffer. Shouldn't I cry, too?

38 "The people you see are going to die in the giant flood. I will put their spirits in a prison I have prepared.

39 "My Chosen One has begged me to save them. He suffers for their sins. If they repent, they can be saved when he comes back to me. But until then, they will suffer.

40 "That is why everyone in heaven and everything I have created will cry."

41 Then the Lord told Enoch about all the wicked things people do. Enoch saw how much people suffer. Then Enoch cried, too. He was filled with love for the whole universe. He stretched out his arms as if to hug them all. When he did this, the universe shook.

42 Enoch saw that Noah and his family would be saved from the giant flood.

43 Enoch watched Noah build an ark. The Lord protected Noah's ark. But all the wicked were drowned in the flood.
44 When Enoch saw this, he became very bitter. He cried for the people who died. He told the Lord, "I refuse to be comforted." But the Lord said, "Be happy. Look."
45 When Enoch looked, he saw Noah's descendants filling the earth with people again. Enoch asked, "When will the Lord's day come? When will the Righteous One sacrifice his blood, so that everyone who repents can become holy and receive eternal life?"
46 The Lord said, "That will happen halfway through the earth's history. It will be a wicked time."
47 Enoch saw God's Son come to be born on earth. When he saw it, he was filled with joy. He said, "The Righteous One is lifted up high—the one who was chosen before the Creation to sacrifice his life to save people. Because of faith, I am with the Father. Zion is with me."
48 Enoch heard a voice come out of the earth. It said, "How I suffer—I, the mother of all people! My children's wickedness has worn me out. When will I be able to rest? When will I be washed clean? When will my Creator make me holy, so I can rest? When will righteousness finally last on earth?"
49 When Enoch heard how sad the earth was, he cried. He asked the Lord, "Won't you be merciful to the earth? Won't you bless Noah's descendants?"
50 Enoch kept praying. He said, "Lord, in the name of your only Son, I ask you to show mercy to Noah's descendants. Never again cover the earth with a flood."
51 The Lord could not refuse. He promised Enoch that he would never again cover the earth with a flood. He promised to reveal himself to Noah's descendants.
52. He promised that his descendants would never be entirely destroyed.
53. The Lord said, "Blessed is the one into whose family the Messiah will be born! I am the Messiah. I am Zion's king. I am the Rock. Whoever comes to me will be safe forever. They will be blessed. They will come singing songs of never-ending joy."
54 Enoch said to the Lord, "When the Son is born on earth, then will the earth rest? Please show me these things."
55 The Lord said, "Look." Enoch looked and saw the Son nailed to a cross.
56 He heard a loud voice. He saw the sky turn black. All creation was filled with sorrow. There was a terrible earthquake. The righteous came back from the dead. They stood at the Son's right hand wearing crowns of glory.
57 The people in spirit prison also came back from the dead. They too stood at God's right hand. The rest of the spirits had to wait until the Last Judgment to come back from the dead.
58 Enoch cried again. He asked the Lord, "When will the earth rest?"
59 Enoch saw the Son going up to the Father. He called to the Lord, "Won't you come back to earth? I know you. You are the God who created me. You commanded me to

Moses

pray in the name of the Son. You have promised to let me sit on your throne. You have promised it not because I earned that right, but because of your love. So I ask you—will you come back to earth?"

⁶⁰ The Lord said, "When the world is coming to its end, I will come back. It will be a wicked time. I will come to keep the promise I made to you about Noah's descendants.

⁶¹ "Someday, the earth will rest. But before that happens, the sky will turn black. The earth will be covered with darkness. Earth and sky will shake. There will be great trouble among the people of the world. But I will keep my people safe.

⁶² I will send righteousness down from heaven, and truth up out of the earth. I will send the world a testimony of my only Son. I will testify about his coming back from the dead—about everyone's coming back from the dead. Righteousness and truth will cover the earth like a flood. The righteous will come together out of every part of the world. I will prepare a place for them to build a holy city. It will be called Zion, a New Jerusalem. There they will get ready for the Second Coming."

⁶³ The Lord said to Enoch, "Then you and the people of your city will come to meet them. We will all hug and greet each other.

⁶⁴ "I will make Zion my home, out of the whole creation. Then the earth will rest for 1000 years."

⁶⁵ Enoch saw the Second Coming. He saw the Son come down to earth to live for 1000 years. He saw that everyone living during that time was righteous.

⁶⁶ But before that happened, he saw great suffering among the wicked. He saw terrible storms on the ocean. People gave up hope. They waited in fear for God to judge them.

⁶⁷ The Lord showed Enoch all these things. He showed Enoch the end of the world. Enoch saw the righteous being saved. He saw them receive full joy.

⁶⁸ Enoch's Zion was on earth for 365 years.

⁶⁹ Enoch and all his people walked with God. God lived in Zion. In time, God took Zion up into heaven. That is why people say, "Zion has run away."

CHAPTER 8

¹ Enoch lived on earth 430 years.

² Enoch had a son named Methuselah. Methuselah was not taken into heaven with Zion. He was left behind so that Noah would be a descendant of Enoch's, as the Lord had promised.

³ Methuselah knew that Noah would be his descendant. He became proud. He preached that every king on earth would be descended from him.

⁴ A terrible famine came because of people's sins. Many people died.

⁵ When Methuselah was 187, he had Lamech.

⁶ After Lamech was born, Methuselah lived 782 years more. He had other children.

⁷ When he was 969, Methuselah died.

MOSES

8 When Lamech was 182, he had a son.
9 He named his son Noah. He said, "Because of the Fall, we have had to work hard. We have suffered. But this son of mine will comfort us."
10 After Noah was born, Lamech lived 595 years more. He had other children.
11 When he was 777, Lamech died.
12 When Noah was 450, he had Japheth. 42 years later, he and Japheth's mother had Shem. When he was 500, he had Ham.
13 Noah and his sons listened to the Lord. They were called God's sons.
14 In time, these men had children of their own. They had beautiful daughters. Their daughters married men who did not follow God.
15 The Lord said to Noah, "Your sons' daughters have sold themselves by marrying men who refuse to listen to me."
16 Noah was a prophet. He taught the things of God, just as they had been taught in the beginning.
17 The Lord said to Noah, "My Spirit cannot be with people if they will not receive it. In the end, everything that lives must die. People have 120 years to live. If they do not repent, a giant flood will come to destroy them.
18 There were giants on earth in those days. They tried to kill Noah. But the Lord's power was with him. It kept him safe.
19 The Lord gave Noah the priesthood. He commanded Noah to preach the gospel to people, like Enoch did.
20 Noah warned the people to repent. But they would not listen.
21 They said to him, "We are God's sons. We eat, and drink, and get married. Our wives give us sons who grow up to be powerful men, like those famous men who lived long ago." So they would not listen to Noah.
22 God saw that the people of the world had become very wicked and proud. Everyone's thoughts were evil, all the time.
23 Noah kept preaching to the people. He said, "Listen to me!
24 "Have faith. Repent of your sins. Be baptized in Jesus Christ's name, the way our ancestors were. Then you will receive the Holy Ghost. It will reveal everything to you. Unless you do all this, you will be destroyed in a giant flood." Still, the people refused to listen.
25 Noah became very sad. He felt sorry that the Lord had ever created human beings.
26 The Lord said, "People have become so wicked that Noah is sorry they were ever created. They have tried to kill him. But they are the ones who will be destroyed, along with every other living thing on earth."
27 The Lord was kind to Noah, because Noah was righteous. Noah walked with God. So did his three sons, Ham, Shem, and Japheth.
28 Everyone else on earth was wicked. The earth was filled with killing and fighting. People used force to get what they wanted. They did terrible, harmful things.
29 God saw how much wickedness there was on earth. He saw that nothing on earth was the way it was supposed to be.
30 God said to Noah, "The end has

Moses

come for life on earth. There is nothing more I can do. Because of the terrible, harmful things people are doing, every living thing on earth is going to be destroyed."

ABOUT THE BOOK OF ABRAHAM

While Joseph Smith was living in Kirtland, a man named Michael Chandler brought four mummies over from Egypt. Along with the mummies came some little books called papyri. The papyri were written in a kind of picture writing. The church decided to buy the mummies and the papyri.

Through the Lord's power, Joseph started to translate the papyri. He found that they included a record written by Abraham. Joseph translated part of Abraham's record. After he moved to Nauvoo, he published the part he had translated. He promised church members that he would translate more of the record as soon as he could. But he was killed before he could finish.

After Joseph was killed, his wife Emma sold the papyri. Then they disappeared. A hundred years later, a few small pieces of the papyri were found and given to the LDS Church. No one knows where the rest of the papyri are today.

The Book of Abraham is the part of Abraham's record that Joseph translated and published before he was killed. The pictures in the Book of Abraham are copies Joseph made of pictures from the papyri. Papyri found buried with other Egyptian mummies have pictures that look a lot like the pictures in the Book of Abraham.

THE BOOK OF ABRAHAM
CHAPTER 1

1 I, Abraham, was living in my ancestors' home in Chaldea. I saw that I needed to move somewhere else.
2 I wanted to receive my ancestors' blessings. I knew those blessings would bring me more happiness and peace. I wanted to be ordained so I could give others those same blessings. I was already righteous. I had tried to learn a lot. But I wanted to become more righteous and learn even more. I wanted to have many descendants. I wanted to be a prince of peace. I wanted to learn and keep God's commandments. So I became a high priest. I received the same rights and promises my ancestors did.
3 I received the priesthood through my ancestors. It was passed down among them from even before the Creation. Adam held the priesthood. He was the first man. It came down through his descendants to me.
4 I received the priesthood in keeping with the laws God gave my ancestors about their descendants.
5 My ancestors became wicked. They stopped keeping God's commandments. They started worshipping false gods. They refused to listen to me.
6 Their hearts were set on doing evil. They worshipped the gods of Elkenah, Libnah, Mahmackrah, and Korash. They also worshipped the god of Pharaoh, king of Egypt.
7 They sacrificed their children to idols. Instead of listening to me, they tried to have me killed by the priest of Elkenah. The priest of Elkenah was also the priest of Pharaoh.
8 Back then, the priest of Pharaoh used to sacrifice men, women, and children to idols. He sacrificed them on an altar in Chaldea.
9 He made sacrifices to the god of Pharaoh and the god of Shagreel, the way the Egyptians did. The god of Shagreel was the sun.
10 The priest sacrificed a child on the altar by Potiphar's Hill, on the plain of Olishem. He did this to show thanks to his gods.
11 Once, the priest sacrificed three young women on this altar. The women were the daughters of Onitah. Onitah belonged to a royal family descended directly from Ham. Onitah's daughters were sacrificed because they were righteous. They would not worship idols. So they were killed on this altar, the Egyptians' way.
12 The priests tried to sacrifice me on the altar, too, like they sacrificed those young women. I have put a picture of the altar at the beginning of this record, to show you what it was like.
13 It looked like the kind of bed the Chaldeans used. It stood in front of the idols of Elkenah, Libnah, Mahmackrah, Korash, and an idol like Pharoah's.
14 I have put pictures of these gods at the beginning of this record. The Chaldeans call pictures like these "Rahleenos." The Egyptians use these pictures to write.
15 While the priests were getting ready to sacrifice me, I prayed to the Lord. The Lord answered my

Abraham

prayer. He gave me a vision. I saw his angel standing next to me. The angel untied me.

16 He said to me, "Abraham, my name is Jehovah. In answer to your prayer, I have come to save you. I will lead you away from your father's house and from all your relatives. I will lead you into a land you know nothing about.

17 "I will do this because your relatives have started worshipping idols instead of me. They will be punished for this. The man who tried to kill you will be destroyed.

18 "I myself will lead you. I will give you my authority—the priesthood, which your father holds. My power will protect you.

19 "You will be like Noah. Thanks to your teachings, the people of the world will know about me forever. I am your God."

20 Potiphar's Hill was in Ur of Chaldea. The Lord tore down the altar there. The idols were destroyed, and the priest died. The Chaldeans were filled with sorrow. So were Pharaoh and everyone who helped him rule.

21 Pharaoh was a descendant of Ham. This meant he was descended from the Canaanites.

22 All the Egyptians descended from Ham. That is how it ended up that the Canaanites had descendants still living after the giant flood.

23 Ham and Egypt had a daughter. She was the one who discovered Egypt. "Egyptus" in Chaldean is "Egypt," which means "forbidden."

24 When this woman discovered Egypt, it was underwater. After the water drained away, she moved to Egypt with her sons. That is how Ham's descendants came to live in that land. Ham's descendants were not able to receive certain blessings.

25 Ham's daughter was named Egyptus (like her mother). Her oldest son was Pharaoh. He set up Egypt's first government. It was based on Ham's government, in which power was passed down from father to son.

26 Pharaoh was a righteous man. He set up his kingdom and ruled his people wisely and fairly all his life. He tried very hard to copy the governments set up by Adam and Noah. Noah was Ham's father. Noah blessed Ham with wisdom and earthly goods. But Noah also said that Ham would not be able to hold the priesthood.

27 Pharaoh could not hold the priesthood because was a descendant of Ham. But the Pharaohs said they had received the priesthood from Noah, through Ham. That is how my father was tricked into worshipping their idols.

28 Later, I will try to outline the history going back from me to the Creation. I now own the records which tell this history.

29 After the priest of Elkenah died, there was a famine in Chaldea. The Lord had told me this was going to happen.

30 The famine spread through all of Chaldea. My father suffered very much because of the famine. He repented of trying to kill me.

31 The Lord kept my ancestors' records safe with me. Those records tell who is allowed to hold the priesthood. Through those records, I have learned what my ancestors

were taught about the Creation, the planets, and the stars. I will try to write some of those things in this record, to help my descendants.

CHAPTER 2

1 The famine in Ur became so bad that my brother Haran died. My father Terah kept living in Ur.
2 I married Sarai. My brother Nahor married Milcah, Haran's daughter.
3 The Lord had said to me, "Abraham, get out of this country. Leave your relatives and your father's house. Go to a land I will show you."
4 So I left Ur, in Chaldea, to go to the land of Canaan. I took my nephew Lot and his wife. I also took my wife, Sarai, and my father. We went to a land we named Haran.
5 The famine began to go away. There were many sheep in Haran. So my father stayed there. He started worshipping idols again.
6 Lot and I prayed to the Lord. The Lord appeared to me. He said, "Take Lot with you away from Haran. I am sending you to teach people in another land about me. Your descendants will own that land forever if they obey me.
7 "I am the Lord, your God. I live in heaven. I have all power over the earth. The ocean obeys me. I ride on wind and fire. If I tell the mountains, 'Go away,' they are carried off at once by a whirlwind.
8 "My name is Jehovah. I knew everything that would happen in the world even before it was created. I will protect you.
9 "I will make your descendants into a powerful people. I will give you more blessings than you could count. People all over the world will honor you. Your descendants will be blessed because of you. Like you, they will be my servants. They will take the priesthood to the whole world.
10 "I will bless the world through you. Everyone who accepts my gospel will be counted as your descendants. They will think of you as their ancestor.
11 "Those who accept you will be blessed. Those who reject you cannot be blessed. All the families on earth will be blessed through the priesthood which you and your descendants hold. The priesthood will bring all families the blessings of the gospel. It will bring them salvation and eternal life."
12 When the Lord finished talking to me, he disappeared. Then I prayed in my heart, "I am your servant. I truly looked for you. Now I have found you.
13 "You sent your angel to save me from being sacrificed to idols. I know that what you have told me is for my good. So let me leave this place in peace."
14 I left Haran, like the Lord told me to. Lot went with me. I was 62 at the time.
15 I took Sarai and Lot. We took all the food we had gathered. We took all the people who had joined us in

Haran. We started travelling to Canaan. On the way, we lived in tents.

16 God watched over us as we travelled. He kept us safe. On the way from Haran to Canaan, we came to Jershon.

17 In Jershon, I built an altar. I made sacrifices to the Lord. I prayed that my father's family would be saved from the famine.

18 Then we went to Sechem, on the plains of Moreh. By this time, we were in Canaan. I made sacrifices there on the plains of Moreh. I prayed very hard to God, because now we were in the land of a people who worshipped idols.

19 The Lord answered my prayers by appearing to me. He said, "I will give this land to your descendants."

20 From the place where I had built the altar, I travelled to a mountain east of Bethel. I camped between Bethel and Hai. I built another altar and prayed to the Lord.

21 Then I kept travelling south. The famine was still very bad there. So I decided to go stay in Egypt.

22 When I got close to Egypt, the Lord said to me, "Your wife Sarai is a very beautiful woman.

23 "When the Egyptians see her, and when they know she is your wife, they will kill you so they can take her for themselves. So do this—

24 "Have Sarai tell the Egyptians she is your sister. Then you will not be killed."

25 I told Sarai everything the Lord had said to me. "Please," I told her, "tell them you are my sister. By doing this, you will save my life."

CHAPTER 3

1 I had the Urim and Thummim which the Lord gave me in Ur.

2 I saw how large and powerful the stars were. I saw the star closest to God's throne. There were many other large, powerful stars near it.

3 The Lord said to me, "These are the ruling stars. The one closest to me is called Kolob. I have given Kolob power over all the stars and planets belonging to the same group as your earth."

4 The Lord told me that time is measured on Kolob the same way the Lord measures time. For the Lord, one day is the time it takes Kolob to move around in a circle. That is the same as 1000 years on earth. The Lord told me this through the Urim and Thummim.

5 The Lord said to me, "The moon has longer days than the earth does. That is because it turns more slowly than the earth. There are fewer days, months, and years on the moon than there are on earth during the same amount of time.

6 "Now, Abraham, you can see two facts. You know how time is measured on earth, on the sun, and on the moon.

7 "You also know that a day on the moon is longer than a day on earth.

Abraham

8 "If you know these two facts, you can know another. There will be another planet or star where days are even longer.

9 "So you will have one planet or star after another, with days getting longer on each one, until you get to Kolob, where time is measured the Lord's way. Kolob is close to God's throne. It rules all the planets and stars which belong to the same group as your earth.

10 "I am going to teach you how time is measured on all the stars, from here all the way to God's throne."

11 I was talking with the Lord face-to-face, the way people on earth talk to one another. He told me about his creations.

12 He said to me, "My son, I will show you all these creations." As he said this, he reached out and put his hand over my eyes. Then I saw his many creations. There were so many of them, they seemed to go on forever.

13 He said to me, "This is Shinehah (the sun). This is Kokob (which means 'star'). This is Olea (the moon). This is Kokaubeam (which means 'stars' or everything that shines in the sky)."

14 It was night-time when the Lord said to me, "I will give you as many descendants as there are stars or grains of sand."

15 The Lord said, "Abraham, I am showing you all this before you go to Egypt so you can teach people there what I have told you.

16 "If there are two things, one above the other, there will be greater things above them. Kolob is the greatest of all the Kokaubeam you have seen, because it is closest to me.

17 "If there are two things, one above the other—like the moon is above the earth, because its days are longer—then there could be another planet or star above that, with even longer days. And there is nothing the Lord decides to do that he does not do.

18 "So there will, in fact, be another planet or star above the first two. The same is true of spirits. One spirit can be more intelligent than another. Even so, both spirits have always existed and always will exist. They are *gnolaum* (eternal)."

19 The Lord said to me, "If there are two spirits, one more intelligent than another, then there will be another spirit even more intelligent. I, the Lord, am more intelligent than all the spirits.

20 "The Lord sent his angel to save you from the priest of Elkenah.

21 "I live among all the spirits. I have come down to tell you about my creations. The fact that I created them proves that I am wiser than all the spirits. I am the all-wise ruler of heaven and earth. I rule over all the intelligent spirits you have seen. I came down among all those spirits before the Creation."

22 Earlier, the Lord had shown me the intelligent spirits that were formed before the Creation. Many of the great ones were there.

23 God saw how good these spirits were. As he stood in the middle of them, he said, "I will make these spirits my rulers." He said to me, "You were one of those spirits, Abraham. I chose you before you were born."

24 One of the spirits standing there was like God. He said to the other spirits with him, "We will go down to that space there. We will take this matter and make an earth for these spirits to live on.
25 "We will do this to test them, to see if they will do everything the Lord commands them.
26 "Those who pass their first test will receive more glory. Those who do not pass their first test will not be able to go to the same kingdom as those who do. Those who pass their second test will receive more and more glory forever."
27 The Lord said, "Who will I send?" The one who was like God said, "Send me." Someone else said, "No, send me." The Lord said, "I will send the first one."
28 This made the second one angry. He did not pass his first test. Many spirits followed him.

CHAPTER 4

1 Then the Lord said, "Let's go down." So the Gods went down in the beginning. They organized the matter that was there to form the earth and sky.
2 After it was formed, the earth was empty. There was nothing living on it, because the Gods had not formed anything but the planet itself. There was nothing but a dark ocean. The Gods' Spirit floated above the ocean.
3 The Gods said, "We want there to be light." So there was.
4 The Gods could see the light, because it was bright. They made it so that the light would be separate from the darkness.
5 The Gods called the light "day" and the darkness "night." That was how what they called "day" and "night" began.
6 Then the Gods said, "We want a space to run through the middle of the water, to split it up."
7 So the Gods set up a space to split up the water. Some of the water went above the space and some of the water stayed below it, just the way they had ordered.
8 The Gods called this space "sky." They did this during the second period of time they called "night and day."
9 Then the Gods said, "We want all the water under the sky to come together in one place, so that dry land comes up." This happened just like they ordered.
10 The Gods called the dry land "earth." They called the place where the water came together "great waters." The Gods saw that they were obeyed.
11 The Gods said, "Let's get the earth ready to grow grass and other plants. All the different plants and trees will have seeds. The seeds will grow into the same kind of plant or tree." All this happened the way they ordered.
12 The Gods organized the earth so that grass, plants, and fruit trees could grow on it. All the different plants and trees would grow seeds which could grow into the same kind of plant or tree. The Gods saw that they were obeyed.

13 This was the third period of time the Gods called "night and day."

14 Then the Gods organized lights in space. They set these lights up to separate day from night. They also set the lights up to measure seasons, days, and years.

15 The Gods set them up to give light to the earth. Everything happened the way the Gods wanted.

16 The Gods organized the sun and moon. They made the sun shine during the day. They made the moon shine at night. They made the stars shine at night, too.

17 The Gods put these lights in space to give light to the earth day and night, and to keep the light separate from the darkness.

18 The Gods watched the things they had ordered until they obeyed.

19 This was the fourth period of time the Gods called "night and day."

20 Then the Gods said, "Let's get the water ready to put animals in. Let's get ready to put birds on earth."

21 The Gods prepared the water so that whales and all other kinds of water animals could live in it. They also got the earth ready to put all kinds of birds on. The Gods saw that they would be obeyed. They saw that their plan was good.

22 The Gods said, "We will bless the water animals and birds. We will make it so they can have babies. The ocean will be filled with animals. There will be many birds on the land."

23 This was the fifth period of time they called "night and day."

24 Then the Gods got the earth ready to put all other kinds of animals on—farm animals, wild animals, and animals that crawl on the ground. Everything happened the way the Gods said.

25 The Gods organized the earth so that all the different kinds of animals could live on it. They made it so that the animals could have babies. The Gods saw that the animals would obey.

26 Then the Gods made plans together. They said, "Let's go down and form human beings to look like us. We will put them in charge of all the fish, birds, and land animals."

27 So the Gods went down to organize human beings. They had decided they would form both men and women. Men and women would look like the Gods.

28 The Gods said, "We will bless the human beings. We will make them so they can have many children and fill the world with people. They will learn how to use the earth's goods. They will be in charge of all the fish, birds, and land animals.

29 "We will give them all the plants and fruit trees. Plants and fruit are what they will eat.

30 "All the animals and birds on earth will eat plants. That is how we will organize these things."

31 The Gods said, "We will organize everything the way we have said. Everything will do what we have ordered." This was the sixth period of time they called "night and day."

Abraham

CHAPTER 5

1 The Gods said, "This is how we will finish creating the earth and sky and everything in them."
2 Then the Gods said, "During the seventh period of time, we will finish all the work we have planned. We will rest."
3 The Gods make the seventh period of time holy, because that was the time they decided to rest from the works. These were the things they decided when they planned together to form the earth and sky.
4 Then the Gods came down to carry out their plans. This is the order in which they formed the earth and sky and everything in them.
5 They made their plans before there were any plants growing on earth. This is because the Gods had not yet made it rain on earth. They had not yet formed anyone to help the plants grow.
6 Instead, a mist came up out of the earth to water the ground.
7 When they came down to carry out their plans, the Gods formed a man. They formed him from the same matter the ground was made out of. Then they put the man's spirit into him. They breathed into the man's nose to bring him to life.
8 The Gods planted a garden in Eden, to the east. They put the man in the garden.
9 The Gods made every kind of tree grow out of the ground. They grew trees that are beautiful to look at and trees that are good to eat. In the middle of the garden, they made the Tree of Life grow. They also made the Tree of Knowing Good and Evil grow.
10 A river ran out of Eden to water the garden. It then split up into four smaller rivers.
11 The Gods put the man in the Garden of Eden so he could take care of it.
12 They told him, "You may eat fruit from any tree in the garden.
13 "But do not eat fruit from the Tree of Knowing Good and Evil. If you eat fruit from that tree, you will die that same day." I, Abraham, saw that this meant a day on Kolob. The Gods had not given Adam his own way of measuring time yet. So time was still measured on earth the Lord's way.
14 The Gods said, "It isn't good for the man to be alone. Let's make a proper companion for him."
15 The Gods made Adam fall sound asleep. While he was asleep, they took a bone out of his side. Then they closed his skin back up.
16 The Gods used Adam's bone to form a woman. They brought the woman to him.
17 Adam said, "This was one of my bones—a part of my own body. Now I will call her 'woman,' because she was taken out of man.
18 "Man and woman were once part of one body. So men and women will leave their parents and come together to form one body again when they are married."
19 Adam and his wife were both naked. But they did not feel shame.
20 The Gods formed every kind of animal and bird. They formed them out of the same matter the

ground was made of. They brought the animals and birds to Adam so he could name them.

21 Adam named all the animals and the birds. But the woman was his proper companion.

JOSEPH SMITH—MATTHEW

Joseph Smith—Matthew is part of Joseph's translation of the Bible. It is his translation of Matthew 23:39-24:51. If you want to read more about Joseph Smith's translation of the Bible, read "About the Book of Moses."

In Joseph Smith—Matthew, Jesus tells his followers how they can know that the Second Coming is near. Early church members were very interested in Joseph Smith—Matthew, because they believed that the Second Coming might happen during their own lives. Church members today are still getting ready for the Lord's coming.

1 "You will not see me anymore. You will not know that I am the one the prophets wrote about until the time comes when you say: Blessed is the One who comes in the Lord's name. Blessed is the One who comes down through the sky with all the angels!" Then Jesus' followers understood that he would come back to earth after he had gone up to heaven to rule at God's right hand.

2 After Jesus left the temple, his followers came to him and said, "Master, tell us what you meant when you said that the temple buildings would be torn down and completely destroyed."

3 Jesus answered, "Don't you understand, even after everything you have seen? There is not a single stone in this temple that will not be torn down."

4 Jesus left his followers and went to the Mount of Olives. While he was sitting there, his followers came to him privately and said, "Tell us when the temple and the Jews will be destroyed, like you said. How will we know when you are coming back? How will we know when the world will end. In other words, how will we know when the wicked will be destroyed?"

5 *Jesus said to them:* Do not let anyone fool you.

6 Many people will come who say they are Christ. They will fool many people.

7 They will arrest you and hurt you. They will even kill you. The whole world will hate you because you are my followers.

8 Many people will lose their faith. They will turn against each other and hate each other.

9 There will be many false prophets fooling people.

10 There will be so much wickedness that many people's love will turn cold.

11 But those who stay strong and do not give in will be saved.

12 The prophet Daniel wrote about a terrible sin that causes destruction. When you see that terrible sin, go stand in the holy place. (Readers should understand what this means.)

13 Those in Judea should run away into the mountains.

14 If you happen to be on your roof, do not even go back down to get anything out of the house.

15 If you happen to be working in the fields, do not even go back to get your clothes.

16 Women who are pregnant or who have small children will have a very hard time.

17 So pray to the Lord that you will

Joseph Smith—Matthew

not have to run away during the winter or on the Sabbath.

18 The Jews and the people in Jerusalem will have terrible troubles then. Their troubles will be worse than anything the Israelites have ever suffered. They will be worse than anything the Israelites will ever suffer again.

19 All the terrible things that have happened to them so far are just the beginning of the troubles they are going to have.

20 If I did not cut their troubles short, none of them would live through it. But I will cut their troubles short, because of the promises I have made to them.

21 I have told you what will happen to the Jews. After these terrible things have happened to Jerusalem, do not believe anyone who tells you that Christ has come back.

22 At that time there will be false Christs and false prophets. They will do amazing miracles. They will try to fool my chosen people.

23 I say this to help my chosen people. Do not be upset when you hear about wars. Everything I have just told you about must happen. But it will not be the end of the world.

24 I repeat what I said before.

25 If they tell you, "Christ is in the desert," do not go. If they tell you, "Christ is in this secret place," do not believe it.

26 When the sun comes up in the east, it covers the whole earth with its light. That is what it will be like when God's Son comes.

27 Now I will tell you something with a hidden meaning. Wherever there is a dead body, that is where the eagles will gather. That is what it will be like when my chosen people gather together from all over the world.

28 They will hear about wars, and talk of wars.

29 Different countries will fight each other. There will be famine and sickness. There will be earthquakes in many places.

30 Again, there will be so much wickedness that people's love will turn cold. But those who do not give in will be saved.

31 Again, my gospel will be taught in every country of the world. Then the end of the world, or the destruction of the wicked, will come.

32 Again, the things Daniel wrote about the terrible sin that causes destruction will come true.

33 Right after the troubles of that time, the sun and moon will stop shining. The stars will fall out of the sky. The powers of heaven will shake.

34 Before all the people who see this happen have died, everything else I have told you will come true.

35 Even though earth and heaven might someday come to an end, my words will stand forever. They will all come true.

36 After the troubles of that time, and after the powers of heaven shake, then the Son's sign will appear in the sky. All the peoples of the world will be filled with sorrow. They will see God's Son coming down through the sky. He will come with power and glory.

37 Those who hold on to my word will not be fooled. The Son will come, just as he said. First his angels will come, with the sound of a

Joseph Smith—Matthew

trumpet. They will gather the rest of God's chosen people from every part of the world.

38 Now listen to what I tell you about the fig tree. When the tree's branches are still soft, and just beginning to grow leaves, then you know it is almost summer.

39 In the same way, my chosen people will know that the Second Coming is almost here when they see the things I have told you about.

40 No one but my Father knows exactly when it will happen. Not even the angels know.

41 The Second Coming will be like the flood in Noah's time.

42 Before the flood, people ate and drank and held weddings. They did this right up to the time Noah went into the ark.

43 Before they knew it, the flood came and took them all away. That is what the Second Coming will be like.

44 Then what was written about the end of the world will come true. Two people will be working together in the field. One will be taken. The other will be left.

45 Two people will be grinding flour at the mill. One will be taken. The other will be left.

46 I say this to one and all—be on the lookout. You do not know when the Lord will come.

47 If the owner of a house had known when a thief was going to come, he would have been on the lookout. He would have been ready. Then his house would not have been broken into.

48 You need to be ready. God's Son will come when you are not expecting it.

49 Listen to this story. Then ask yourself—what kind of servant are you? A master goes away on a journey. He leaves one of his servants in charge of his house. The servant is in charge of feeding everyone in the house.

50 If the master comes home and finds the servant carrying out his duties, he will bless the servant. He will make that servant ruler over everything he has.

51 But a wicked servant will say, "It will be a while before my master comes."

52 He will begin to treat the other servants in the house badly. He will spend his time eating and drinking with people who like to get drunk.

53 Suddenly, when he is not expecting it, his master will come home.

54 The master will throw that servant out of his house, because the servant has only pretended to be righteous. The servant will cry, and howl, and grind his truth.

55 That is how the wicked meet their end. Just like Moses said, they will not be able to live with God's people. But even then it will not be quite time for the earth to end.

JOSEPH SMITH—HISTORY

As the restored church grew, people spread false stories about Joseph Smith. Joseph decided that he needed to write down his history. Then people would know the truth about him and how he restored the church.

He started writing the history in 1838. It was published four years later, while the church members were living in Nauvoo.

Joseph Smith's history tells about his very first visions. It tells about his vision of the Father and the Son. It tells about his being visited by the angel Moroni. It tells how he got the gold plates and began to translate the Book of Mormon. It tells how he and Oliver Cowdery received the Aaronic priesthood from John the Baptist.

What is most important about Joseph Smith—History is that it tells about all these things in Joseph Smith's own words. It is Joseph's own testimony of how God used him to carry out his work.

Why This History Was Written

1 Wicked people have spread many stories about the The Church of Jesus Christ of Latter-day Saints, trying to make it look bad. So I have decided to write this history. That way everyone will know the facts. As far as I know, everything I write here about myself, and about the church, is true.

2 In this history, I will tell the truth about what has happened in this church. The church was organized eight years ago [in 1830].

Joseph Smith's Family

3 I was born on December 23, 1805 in Sharon, Vermont. I was named after my father. My father moved from Vermont to Palmyra, New York, when I was about 10. Four years after my father moved to Palmyra, he moved his family to the nearby town of Manchester.

4 There were eleven people in my family. There was my father, Joseph Smith, and my mother, Lucy Mack Smith. There were my brothers Alvin, Hyrum, Samuel Harrison, William, and Don Carlos. There were my sisters Sophronia, Catherine, and Lucy. And there was me. Alvin died on November 19, 1823. He was 26 years old.

The First Vision

5 Two years after we moved to Manchester, the people in our area became very excited about religion. It all started with the Methodists. But soon all the other churches in the area were excited, too. Huge groups of people from all over gathered in the different churches. The people became divided. Some argued in favor of the Methodist church, some for the Presbyterian church, others for the Baptist church.

6 The people joining the different churches talked a lot about how much love they had. The preachers of the different churches said they didn't care which church people joined, just as long as they were "converted." But when people began going off to different

churches, it became clear that the preachers and converts didn't really feel as friendly towards each other as they said they did. They began to argue with each other. This caused a lot of unfriendly feelings.

7 This happened while I was 14. At that time, four members of my family joined the Presbyterian church. They were my mother, Hyrum, Samuel Harrison, and Sophronia.

8 All this excitement caused me to think very hard. I felt very worried. But I didn't join any of the churches. I had strong feelings, though, and I went to the different churches' meetings whenever I could. Over time, I began to feel I might like to join the Methodist church. But the churches argued so much that it was impossible for someone as young as I was to decide who was right.

9 They argued so much that sometimes I became very upset. The Presbyterians, Methodists, and Baptists were all certain that they were right. They all had ways to make people think that the other churches were wrong.

10 During all this arguing, I often asked myself, "What should I do? Which church is right? Or are they all wrong? If one of them is right, how will I know?"

11 One day, while I was trying to figure out what to do, I read James 1:5. "Anyone who needs wisdom should ask God. He gives freely to everyone. He does not become angry when people ask him things. He will give everyone the wisdom they need."

12 This scripture touched my heart very strongly. I thought about it over and over. I knew that I needed wisdom from God. Unless I got more wisdom, I would never know what to do. The preachers of the different churches explained the scriptures so differently that I could never decide what to do just by reading the Bible.

13 Finally I decided that the only way to get an answer was to do what James said—ask God. If God gave wisdom freely to whoever needed it, without getting angry, then I could dare to ask.

14 So on a beautiful spring morning in 1820, I went alone to the woods. It was the first time in my life I had ever tried to pray out loud.

15 After I reached the place I had chosen, I looked around to make sure I was alone. Then I knelt down and started praying. As soon as I started praying, some strange power came over me. I couldn't speak. It became dark all around me. I felt like I was about to be destroyed.

16 Gathering all my strength, I begged God to save me from this strange power. I wasn't just imagining this. I really felt that some person I couldn't see was about to destroy me—someone with more power than I'd ever felt before. Just when I was about to give up hope, a column of light appeared right over my head. It was brighter than the sun. It slowly came down on top of me.

17 As soon as it appeared, I felt free of the power that was trying to destroy me. When the light came down on top of me, I saw two people standing in the air above me. It would be impossible to describe

how bright and glorious they were. One of them called me by my name. He pointed to the other, and said, "This is my dear Son. Listen to him!"

18 As soon as I could talk again, I asked these two people the question I had come to ask. Which church was right and which should I join? (I had never even thought that they might all be wrong.)

19 I was told not to join any of them, because none of them were right. The person talking to me said that all the churches had beliefs that were wrong. He said that all their preachers had gone wrong. He said, "They say they are close to me. But their hearts are far away from me. The doctrines they teach have been made up by people. They do some things the way God wants. But they do not have his power."

20 He told me again not to join any of the churches. He said many other things, but I cannot write them all now. The next thing I knew, I was lying on my back, looking up into heaven. After the light left, I was completely helpless. But soon I got enough strength back that I could walk home. My mother saw me leaning against the fireplace. She asked what was wrong. I said, "Don't worry, I'm all right." Then I said, "I've learned for myself that the Presbyterian church isn't true." Satan must have known early on that someday I would make trouble for his kingdom. Why else would he have used his power against me? Why would so many people have made trouble for me from the time I was still nearly a child?

21 A few days later, I was talking with a Methodist preacher about religion. I decided to tell him about my vision. To my surprise, he told me that my vision was from the devil. He said God had stopped giving people visions and revelations after the time of the apostles. He said God would never give such things to anyone again.

22 I soon learned that a lot of preachers were against me because of my vision. People began to give me more and more trouble. I was only 14 years old. There was no reason to believe I would ever amount to anything. But powerful men felt the need to turn people against me. They made my life very hard. All the churches came together against me.

23 I have often thought it strange that the most powerful churches of the time would feel they needed to speak out against a 14-year-old farmboy. But, strange as it is, that is exactly what happened. This often made me very sad.

24 But it was true that I had seen a vision. I felt like Paul defending himself to King Agrippa. When he told the king about his vision—the light he had seen and the voice he had heard—few people believed him. Some said he was lying. Others said he was crazy They all made fun of him. But this didn't make his vision any less real. It didn't matter how much trouble people caused him. It didn't matter if they killed him. Paul knew he had seen a light and heard a voice, and nothing could change that.

25 That is how it was with me. I really saw two people standing in

257

that light. They really talked to me. Even though people hated me and made my life hard because I said I'd seen a vision, I knew it was true. All the time people were making fun of me and saying terrible, false things about me, I thought, "Why do you hurt me for telling the truth? I really saw a vision. How can people think they can make me say I didn't?" I knew I had seen a vision. I didn't dare say I hadn't, because I knew God would punish me.

26 I now knew that instead of joining any of the churches, I should wait for more directions. I had learned that James' testimony is true. If people ask God for wisdom, he will give it to them.

Moroni's Visits

27 All sorts of people, both in and out of the churches, kept making trouble for me because I still said I had seen a vision. At the same time, I kept working as usual until September 21, 1823.

28 During that time, I didn't join any of the churches. People who should have been my friends—people who should have helped me if they thought I was wrong—made my life hard. I spent time with all sorts of people. I made a lot of foolish mistakes, like many young people do. I committed some sins. They weren't terrible sins, because I've never been the sort of person who would do such things. But I didn't always act as seriously as someone who had been called by God should have. This won't surprise anyone who remembers me as a young man or who knows how cheerful I tend to be.

29 I often felt guilty for my weaknesses and mistakes. So after going to bed on September 21, I asked God to forgive my sins. I asked him to let me know how I stood with him. I had complete faith I could receive a vision like I had before.

30 While I was praying, a light appeared in my room. It grew brighter and brighter until it seemed like noon. Suddenly a man appeared in the air next to my bed. His feet didn't touch the floor.

31 He wore a loose robe. It was whiter than anything I'd ever seen. I don't think anything on earth could be made that white. His hands, feet, and part of his arms and legs were bare. So were his head and neck. The robe was open at the chest, so I could see that the man wasn't wearing anything else.

32 Not only was his robe white, his whole body shone in a way I can't describe. His face was like lightning. The whole room was very bright. But it was brightest right around the man. When I first saw him, I was afraid, but not for long.

33 He called me by my name. He told me he was an angel sent from God. He said his name was Moroni. He told me God had a work for me to do. He said that people all over the world would say both good and bad things about me.

34 He said there was a book buried nearby. It was written on gold plates. It told the history of the ancient peoples of America and where they came from. The complete gospel was in the book, the

Joseph Smith—History

way the Savior taught it to people in America long ago.

35 He said there was something called the Urim and Thummim buried with the plates. It was made up of two stones in silver bows connected to a breastplate. The people who were called "seers" long ago were people who owned and used these stones. God prepared them so I could translate the book.

36 Then the angel started quoted scriptures from the Old Testament. First he quoted parts of Malachi, chapters 3 and 4. But he quoted them differently from the way they are in our Bible. This is how he quoted Malachi 4:1.

37 "Soon the proud and wicked will be burned up like dead straw. Those who come will burn them up. There will be nothing left of them. They will have no descendants."

38 He quoted Malachi 4:5-6 this way. "Before the Second Coming, I will reveal the priesthood to you through the prophet Elijah.

39 "Elijah will remind people of the promises made to their ancestors. People's hearts will turn to their ancestors. If this did not happen, the whole world would be destroyed during the Second Coming."

40 He also quoted Isaiah, chapter 11. He said the things written in that chapter were about to come true. He quoted Acts 3:22 23 just like it is in our Bible. He said that the prophet the scripture talked about was Christ. He said that the part which says "those who will not listen to that prophet will not be able to live with God's people" hadn't come true yet. But it would come true soon.

41 He quoted Joel 2:28-32 and said that it would soon come true. He said that it was almost time for the gospel to go from the Gentiles back to the Jews, like it says in Romans 11:25. He quoted and explained many more scriptures than I can talk about here.

42 He told me that I wouldn't be given the plates for a while. He said that when I got them, I shouldn't show them to anyone unless the Lord told me to. I shouldn't show anyone the Urim and Thummim either. If I did, I would be destroyed. While he was talking about the plates, I saw in my mind the place where they were buried. I saw it so clearly that I knew the place when I went there later.

43 When the angel finished his message, the light in the room gathered close around him until the rest of the room was dark again. Suddenly, a gateway opened into heaven. The angel went up into it and disappeared. The room was left the way it had been before the light appeared.

44 I lay in bed thinking. I was amazed by what the angel had told me. Suddenly, the room began to get bright again. The angel appeared a second time next to my bed.

45 He repeated everything he had said before, word for word. Then he told me about the famines, wars, and diseases that would come to the people of today because of their sins. When he finished, he went back up into heaven.

46 By now, I was too amazed to sleep. So I lay in bed thinking about what I had just seen and heard. To my surprise, the angel appeared a third time. He again repeated his message. Then he warned that because my family was so poor, Satan would tempt me to sell the gold plates. The angel commanded me not to do this. He said that if I tried to use the plates for anything except helping to build God's kingdom, I wouldn't be allowed to have them.

47 After his third visit, the angel went back up into heaven. I was left thinking about how strange this all was. Almost as soon as the angel disappeared the third time, the rooster crowed. The angel's visits had taken all night.

48 A little later I got up and went to work in the fields as usual. But I was too tired to work. My father saw that something was wrong. He told me to go home. I started back towards the house. But while I was trying to climb over a fence, I fainted.

49 The next thing I remember was a voice calling my name. I looked up and saw the angel standing over my head. He was surrounded by light, just like before. He repeated everything he had said the night before. Then he told me to go tell my father about my vision.

50 I went back to my father and told him everything. He believed that the vision was from God. He told me to go do what the angel commanded me. I left our farm and went to the place where the plates were buried. I knew the place as soon as I saw it because of the vision I'd had earlier.

51 Near Manchester there is a fairly large hill. It is the largest hill in the area. The plates were buried near the top of the hill's west side. They were buried in a box under a large stone. The top of the stone was thick and round in the middle, but the edges were thin and covered with dirt.

52 I removed the dirt and managed to lift the stone up with a stick. Looking inside, I saw the plates and the Urim and Thummim, just like the angel had said. The box they were buried in was made of stones stuck together with cement. Two more stones had been laid across the bottom of the box. The plates and other things were on top of these two stones.

53 I tried to take them out, but the angel told me not to. He told me that I would have to wait four years before I could take them. He told me to meet him again in that same place every year, on that same day, until it was time for me to take the plates.

54 I met the angel there every year. He taught me how the Lord was going to run his kingdom during the time just before the end of the world.

Joseph Smith Gets Married

55 Because my father was poor, we had to hire ourselves out to work for other people whenever we could, in order to live comfortably. This meant that sometimes we were at home and sometimes we were in other places.

56 In 1823, my oldest brother Alvin died. In October 1825, I went to

Joseph Smith—History

work for an old man named Josiah Stoal. He was trying to find an old silver mine which he had heard some Spaniards had dug in what is now Harmony, Pennsylvania. He took me and the rest of his workers to dig around, looking for the mine. We worked for a month but didn't find anything. Finally I told Mr. Stoal to give up. That is why a lot of people say I used to dig for treasure.

57 While I was working for Mr. Stoal, I lived with a man named Isaac Hale. There I met his daughter Emma. On January 18, 1827, Emma and I were married. I was still working for Mr. Stoal at the time.

58 People still made trouble for me because I said I had seen a vision. So Emma's parents didn't want us to get married. We had to leave Harmony and get married in New York. I then returned to my father's home to work on his farm.

Joseph Gets the Gold Plates

59 Finally it was time for me to receive the plates and the Urim and the Thummim. On September 22, 1827, I went as usual for my yearly meeting with the angel. He gave me the plates and warned me to take good care of them. He said that if I let them get lost, I would be punished. But if I did everything I could to protect them until the angel came to take them back, they would be kept safe.

60 I soon learned why the angel gave me this warning and why said he would come back for the plates. As soon as people heard that I had the plates, they did everything they could think of to take them away from me. My life became even harder than before. Huge groups of people were always trying to get the plates. But God helped me keep them safe until I had done everything I was supposed to with them. Then I gave them back to the angel. He has the plates to this day (May 2, 1838).

61 People spread enough stories and lies about me and my family to fill books. The trouble became so bad that finally Emma and I had to move from Manchester back to Pennsylvania. We were very poor. But as we were getting ready to move, a man named Martin Harris gave us $50 to help us. Martin was a respected farmer from Palmyra, New York.

Martin Harris Goes to See Dr. Anthon

62 Thanks to Martin's help, I was able to move to Pennsylvania. There I lived in Isaac Hale's house. As soon as I had moved, I started copying symbols from the plates. After I had copied a lot of symbols, I used the Urim and Thummim to translate some of them. I did this from December to February.

63 Sometime during February, Martin Harris took the symbols I had copied to New York City. I now quote from his own record of what happened there.

64 "In New York City, I showed the symbols to Charles Anthon, a well-known professor. I also showed him Joseph's translation. Dr. Anthon said that the translation was

correct. He said it was better than any Egyptian translation he had ever seen. Then I showed him the symbols that hadn't been translated. Dr. Anthon said that they were real Egyptian, Chaldaic, Assyriac, and Arabic symbols. He gave me a letter telling all this to the people of Palmyra. I put the letter in my pocket and started to leave. Dr. Anthon called me back and asked how Joseph found out there were gold plates buried in the hill. I said that an angel had told him where they were.

65 "Dr. Anthon said, 'Let me see that letter.' When I gave it back to him, he ripped it up. He said that angels didn't visit people anymore. He said that if I brought him the plates, he would translate them. I told him that part of the book was sealed shut and I wasn't allowed to bring it. He said, 'I cannot read a sealed book.' Then I went to see Dr. Mitchell. Dr. Mitchell agreed with what Dr. Anthon had said about the symbols and the translation."

Oliver Cowdery Meets Joseph Smith

66 On April 5, 1829, I met Oliver Cowdery for the first time. He came to my house. He told me that he had been working as a schoolteacher in my father's neighborhood. He had lived with my father's family for a while. They told him about how I had gotten the plates. So he came to me to learn more.

67 Two days after Oliver arrived (April 7), I started translating the Book of Mormon. Oliver wrote down the translation for me.

John the Baptist's Visit

68 We kept working on the translation. In the translation, we read about people being baptized to have their sins taken away. In May 1829, we went into the woods to ask the Lord about baptism. While we were praying, an angel came down from heaven in a bright cloud. He put his hands on our heads and said:

69 "In the name of Messiah, I give you, my fellow servants, the Aaronic priesthood. It gives you the power to receive visits from angels. It gives you the authority to teach people to repent. It also gives you the authority to baptize them, to take away their sins. This priesthood will stay on the earth until the Levites again make a righteous sacrifice to the Lord."

70 The angel said that the Aaronic priesthood did not have the power to give people the gift of the Holy Ghost. He said we would receive that power later. Then he commanded us to be baptized. I should baptize Oliver. Then Oliver should baptize me.

71 We baptized each other the way the angel commanded. Then I put my hands on Oliver's head and ordained him to the Aaronic priesthood. He did the same to me. The angel commanded us to do this.

72 The angel who gave us the Aaronic priesthood said he was John the Baptist. He said he had been sent to us by Peter, James, and John. He said that those three were in charge of the Melchizedek priesthood. Later, he told us, we would receive the Melchizedek

Joseph Smith—History

priesthood. Then I would serve as first elder in the church. Oliver Cowdery would serve as second elder. We were ordained by the angel and baptized on May 15, 1829.

73 As soon as we were baptized, Heavenly Father gave us many glorious blessings. As soon as I baptized Oliver, the Holy Ghost came over him. He was able to tell about things that would happen in the future. As soon as Oliver baptized me, the Holy Ghost came over me, too. I was able to tell about the setting up of the church in the future. I said many things about the church and about the people of today. We were filled with the Holy Ghost. We were very happy that God had saved us.

74 From then on, we were able to understand, for the first time, what even the hardest scriptures really mean. But we had to keep our having been ordained and baptized a secret, because of the trouble people were already causing in the neighborhood.

75 Mobs tried to hurt us now and then—mobs led by preachers. The only reason they couldn't actually do what they wanted is that Emma's family promised to protect us. Thanks to God, Emma's family had become very friendly to me. They believed it was wrong for people to form mobs. They felt I should be able to keep working on the translation. They promised to do everything they could to protect me.

This is what Oliver Cowdery said about John the Baptist's visit:

I will never forget that time. I was thankful to be able to serve as the prophet's scribe. Day after day, he used the Urim and Thummim to translate the Book of Mormon out loud. I wrote down what he said.

Some time later, I will say more about the Book of Mormon. Right now, I am going to talk a little about how the church was started. Thousands of people have joined the church. They did it even though others told them they were making the wrong choice. What I am going to say should interest them.

Joseph and I were translating the things the Savior taught the Nephites about how to start his church. The things he taught have been changed by people over time. That is why everyone these days is so confused. While we were translating the Savior's teachings about baptism, we wanted to be baptized. We wanted to show God that we were willing to obey him.

After we translated the part about the Savior's visit to America, we could see that what Isaiah wrote had come true. Darkness covered the minds of the people on earth. Everyone argued about religion. But no one had authority from God to perform gospel ordinances. How can someone who doesn't believe in modern revelation have Christ's authority? A testimony of Christ is a revelation. Christ's church has always been based on revelation, throughout history. We now knew the truth, which wicked people long ago had hidden. We were only waiting for God to command us to be baptized.

We didn't have to wait long. The Lord always answers humble people's prayers. When Joseph and I went off alone to pray, he answered us. Suddenly, we heard the Savior's voice say, "Peace." We saw a angel come down, covered in glory. He told us what we had been waiting to hear. He gave us the authority to baptize. What joy! What amazement! At that moment millions of people were confused about religion. But we saw and heard an angel in broad daylight! He spoke softly, but his voice made us shake. He said, "I am God's servant, just like you." Then we stopped being afraid. We listened and looked in wonder! It was an angel's voice, giving us a message from God! We felt God's love as we saw this vision. We knew for certain that he is real.

Think how happy and surprised we must have been when we knelt down to be ordained by the angel. He said, "In the name of Messiah, I give you, my fellow servants, this priesthood. It will remain on earth so that the Levites can once again make a righteous sacrifice to the Lord."

I won't try to describe how we felt. But believe me when I say that no one on earth has ever spoken as powerfully as the angel. Everything he said, through the Spirit's power, gave us joy, peace, and wisdom. People can fool each other. People can teach the whole world to believe lies. But one revelation from the Savior is enough to wipe away those lies forever. We knew we had seen an angel. We knew we had heard Jesus' voice. We knew God had revealed the truth to us. I will be thankful for the Savior's love all my life. I hope to worship him in heaven forever.

ARTICLES OF FAITH

While Joseph Smith was living in Nauvoo, he received a letter from a man named John Wentworth. Mr. Wentworth ran a newspaper in Chicago. He wanted Joseph to tell him about the church. Joseph wrote a letter back to Mr. Wentworth. In the letter, he told about the First Vision and other important happenings in church history.

At the end of his letter, Joseph made a list of some of the basic beliefs of church members. Today we call that list the Articles of Faith.

1 We believe in God, our Heavenly Father. We believe in his Son, Jesus Christ. We believe in the Holy Ghost.

2 We believe that people will be punished for their own sins. They will not be punished for Adam's having eaten the forbidden fruit.

3 We believe that all people can be saved through Christ's Atonement if they obey God's laws and receive gospel ordinances.

4 We believe that to start living the gospel, people need to do these things. (1) Have faith in Jesus Christ. (2) Repent. (3) Be baptized completely underwater to have their sins forgiven. (4) Receive the gift of the Holy Ghost by the laying on of hands.

5 We believe that before people can preach the gospel or perform gospel ordinances, they need to be called by God, through his servants on earth. They also need to be ordained by church leaders, by the laying on of hands.

6 We believe the church should be organized the same way it was in New Testament times—with apostles, prophets, bishops, teachers, patriarchs, and so on.

7 We believe in the gifts of the Spirit. We believe the Spirit can tell people things to say. We believe it can give them revelations or visions. We believe people can be healed through the Spirit. We believe the Spirit can make people speak or understand other languages.

8 We believe that the Bible is God's word. But we also believe that the Bible has not always been translated correctly. We believe the Book of Mormon is God's word, too.

9 We believe everything God has revealed in the past. We believe everything God reveals now. And we believe God will reveal many important things about his kingdom in the future.

10 We believe that the Israelites will be gathered together to their homeland again. We believe that the lost ten tribes will come back. We believe that Zion (the New Jerusalem) will be built in America. We believe that Christ will rule personally on earth. We believe that the earth will become like the Garden of Eden.

11 We believe that everyone should be able to worship God in whatever way they feel is right. They should be able to worship however, wherever, and whatever they want.

12 We believe in obeying kings, presidents, rulers, and judges. We believe in keeping, respecting, and supporting the law.

13 We believe in being honest, true, pure, kind, and righteous. We be-

Articles of Faith

lieve in doing good to everyone. We can say that we do what Paul taught in Philippians 4:8. We believe all things. We hope all things. We have suffered many things. We hope to be able to endure to the end, no matter what happens. We look for whatever is righteous or beautiful. We look for whatever people talk well about, or whatever is worthy of praise.

WORDS TO KNOW

Here are the meanings of some of the words used in *The Easy-to-Read Doctrine and Covenants* and *The Easy-to-Read Pearl of Great Price*. They are listed in a-b-c order. When you see a word written like *this*, it means that word is also listed in the "Words to Know" pages.

Aaronic priesthood: the *authority* God gave to Aaron and his *descendants* in Bible times. Today, people who hold the Aaronic priesthood can *baptize* and give the *sacrament* to church members.

adultery [commit adultery]: to have sex with someone other than your husband or wife. Someone who commits adultery is breaking the promise they made to their *spouse* when they got married.

agent: someone who does business for someone else.

alcohol: a drink that can make you drunk. Wine and beer are examples of alcohol.

amber: a kind of stone. It is yellow and see-through. People use amber to make jewelry.

Amen: a word meaning "may it be." We say "Amen" at the end of prayers. Most of the *sections* in Doctrine and Covenants end with the word "Amen."

ancestors: family members who lived before you. Your parents, grandparents, great-grandparents, and so on, are your ancestors.

ancient: something from long ago.

anoint: to put oil on someone, normally on their head. In the *restored* church, we anoint people who are sick when we bless them. People are anointed in the *temple* as part of the *endowment*.

apostle: a special *witness* of Jesus Christ. Jesus chose twelve apostles in Bible times to help him teach the people of the world. There are apostles in the *restored* church today. They have the same *calling* the apostles did long ago.

armor: what people wear to protect their bodies in battle. Armor might be made out of thick animal skins or metal plates.

ark: the giant ship Noah built to save his family and the animals from the flood.

ark of the covenant: a special box where the Israelites kept the stones that God wrote the Ten Commandments on. The Old Testament said that anyone who touched the ark of the covenant without permission would die.

ashery: a kind of factory where ash is turned into things people can use, like soap.

atonement: the work Jesus Christ did to help people come back to God. Jesus suffered and died to pay for the *sins* of those who *repent*.

authority: the power or the right to do something. The *priesthood* gives people the authority to perform *gospel ordinances* or to give blessings. The *restored* church has the authority to help people go back to live with God.

baptism [baptize]: being put all the way underwater and then being

267

taken out of the water again. When we are baptized, we promise God that we will keep the *commandments*. God promises to take away our *sins*.

baptism for the dead: being *baptized* for someone who died without having the chance to be *baptized* into the *restored* church. If the person accepts the baptism while they are in *spirit prison*, they can enter the *celestial kingdom* as if they themselves had been *baptized*.

Baptists: one of the churches Joseph Smith attended when he was a boy. Baptists believed that only adults should be *baptized*, not children. They believed that people should be *baptized* all the way underwater.

barley: a kind of grain.

bishop: a church leader who is in charge of meeting people's earthly needs.

bishopric: a *bishop*, plus two *counselors*.

born again: to be *converted* to the *gospel*. It is called being born again because it is like starting your life over.

brag: to tell people how great you are. People who brag are too proud of themselves.

branch: a group of church members living in the same place. Normally, it means people living away from most of the other members.

breastplate: a metal plate you wear over your chest to protect you in battle.

calling: something God has asked you to do to help carry out his work.

caretaker: a person who takes care of something for someone else.

celestial kingdom: the part of heaven where the most *righteous* people will go to live with Heavenly Father forever.

certificate: a piece of paper which proves that you've done something.

church court: a meeting held to decide if someone who has committed a serious *sin* can still be a member of the church.

circumcise: to cut off a tiny piece of a baby boy's skin. The Israelites circumcised their baby boys in Bible times so they would remember the promises God had made with them. After Jesus came, the *apostles* taught church members that they didn't need to circumcise their boys anymore.

claim: when someone has a claim to a piece of land, it means the land belongs to them.

commandments: things God tells us to do. God gives us commandments so we will know how to carry out his work, and how to be happy.

company: in Doctrine and Covenants, a group of people travelling together.

confess: to admit that you have done something wrong.

confirm: to give someone the *gift of the Holy Ghost*. It can also mean to give more proof of something, or to make something stronger.

Congress: part of the United States government. The Congress is a large group of people, a few from each state, who go to Washington D.C. to make laws for the whole country.

constitution: a written plan for running a government. The United States is run by a constitution.

convert: to change your life. In Doctrine and Covenants, converts are people who join the *restored* church.

counselor: someone who helps you decide what to do. In the *restored* church, a *president* always has counselors, so there isn't just one person making all the decisions.

county: a small part of a state. A county usually has several towns in it.

covenant: a holy promise. Normally, it means a promise God makes to people on earth. But it can also mean a holy promise made between two people, like marriage.

curse: something bad that happens. After Adam and Eve ate the *forbidden fruit*, the land was cursed. That meant it became harder for people to grow food.

deacon: one of the *offices* in the *Aaronic priesthood*. Deacons pass the *sacrament*.

debt: owing money to someone.

dedicate [dedication]: setting something apart to be used for a special purpose. When a *temple* is dedicated, a prayer is read to make it *holy*. After that prayer has been said, the *temple* is used only for God's work.

descendants: family members who will live after you. Your children, grandchildren, great-grandchildren, and so on, are your descendants.

doctrine: church teachings or beliefs. Different churches have different doctrines. The *scriptures* tells us we shouldn't argue with people about doctrines.

donate [donation]: to give money or property to a good cause. Early church members were told to donate everything they had to the church, so that all the members could be taken care of.

doubt: wondering if something is true. Sometimes people doubt that God is real, or that his promises are really going to come true.

duty: something a person is supposed to do.

Egyptians: one of the peoples who lived in Africa long ago. The Egyptians buried people as *mummies*. They wrote in pictures. In Joseph Smith's day, no one knew how to read Egyptian writing.

elder: an *office* in the *Melchizedek priesthood*. Elders go on *missions* and help lead the church.

endowment: a special gift. It is also the name of an *ordinance* done in the *temple* to teach people about the plan of *salvation* and to help them go back to live with God.

Endowment House: a building in Salt Lake where church members could perform *temple ordinances* before the *temple* was finished.

endure to the end: to live the *gospel* all the rest of one's life. Enduring to the end can be hard because of the troubles we may have when we live the *gospel*.

envy: wanting what belongs to someone else. When you feel angry at someone who has more than you do, or when you wish you could have what they have, you are feeling envy.

eternal: something that has to do with God. For example, "eternal life" means the kind of life God has. "Eternal" can also mean something that never ends.

exalt [exaltation]: to lift up. In the *restored* church, we use the word "exaltation" to mean going back to live with Heavenly Father in the highest level of the *celestial kingdom*.

exist: to be. When we say that God exists, we mean that God is real. When we say that something has always existed, we mean it has always been around.

faithful: having faith, or doing the right things.

Fall: what happened when Adam and Eve ate the *forbidden fruit*. Because of the Fall, people couldn't live with God anymore. Jesus Christ's *atonement* undoes the Fall.

famine: a time when there isn't enough food or water for people to live.

fast [fasting]: to go without food for a time. Church members fast to become more *humble*, and to feel closer to the Spirit.

First Presidency: the *president* of the church, plus two *counselors*. Together, they lead the whole *restored* church.

fold: a place where sheep are kept.

font: the special pool where people are *baptized*.

footstool: a little stand or pillow for someone to rest their feet on.

foot-washing: an *ordinance* in which a church leader washes other members' feet, the way Jesus washed the *apostles'* feet during the Last Supper.

forbidden fruit: the fruit Adam and Eve ate in the Garden of Eden. By eating the fruit, they made it possible for people to be born on earth and to die.

forgive [forgiveness]: to stop holding someone's mistakes against them. Jesus taught that we should forgive people when they do things that hurt us. If we *repent*, God will forgive our *sins*.

general conference: a special meeting the *restored* church holds every six months. When the church was first formed, general conference was a time for members from different *branches* to come together to decide how to run the church.

Gentile: a person who is not an *Israelite*. Most people in the world are Gentiles.

gift of the Holy Ghost: having the Holy Ghost with us always. We receive the gift of the Holy Ghost after we are *baptized*. Little by little, as we try to do what is right, the Holy Ghost teaches us and makes us holy.

Godhead: the Father, the Son, and the Holy Ghost.

gods: the word can mean two very different things. It can mean false gods or *idols*. Or it can mean *righteous* people who live with God and share his power.

gospel: a word meaning "good news." The gospel is God's message for the world. Jesus and the *prophets* teach us the gospel.

gossip: to tell stories or secrets about other people. The stories might be true or false, but they are normally mean.

grace: God's love, or the help we receive from him. Grace gives us the strength to keep the *commandments*. It is the power that takes our *sins* away. We receive grace through Jesus Christ's *atonement*.

guilty: someone who has done something wrong is guilty.

harsh: being angry with someone, or saying things that make them feel bad. Sometimes people who love us are harsh with us when they see us doing something wrong.

hell: the place where Satan lives. Wicked people will be in hell after they die. They will suffer because they did not do the things that would have made them happy.

herbs: plants used as medicine.

high council [high councilor]: a group of twelve *high priests* who help lead a *stake*.

high priest: an *office* in the *Melchizedek priesthood*. High priests play a big part in leading the church. A *bishop* or *stake president*, for example, must be a high priest.

Hosanna: a word people shout to praise God. It means "God save!"

humble: the opposite of "proud." People who are humble know they need God's help. They do not think they are better than other people.

idol: a statue of a false *god*. Anything people *worship* besides God can be called an idol.

immortal: having a body that will live forever. After people come back from the dead, they will be immortal.

innocent: not *guilty* or not to blame.

inspire: when the Spirit tells us what to do, we say that it inspires us.

intelligence: being wise. Sometimes it means the power God gave us to think.

Ishmaelites: in the Book of Mormon, the people who were *descendants* of Ishmael, who travelled with Lehi in the desert. The Ishmaelites were counted among the *Lamanites*.

Israelites: the people God gave the Ten Commandments to.

Jacobites: in the Book of Mormon, the people who were *descendants* of Nephi's brother, Jacob. The Jacobites were counted among the *Nephites*.

Jew: a member of the tribe of Judah. Jews are *Israelites*. Jesus was a Jew. Christians have done terrible things to the Jews throughout history, because they said the Jews were the ones who killed Jesus.

Josephites: in the Book of Mormon, the people who were *descendants* of Nephi's brother, Joseph. The Josephites were counted among the *Nephites*.

Junior: a man who has the same name as his father is called Junior, to tell the two apart. Joseph Smith was called Joseph Smith, Junior, because his father was also named Joseph.

justice: what is right and fair.

Lamanites: one of the peoples talked about in the Book of Mormon. In Doctrine and Covenants, *Native Americans* are called Lamanites.

Last Judgment: the time at the end of the world when everyone will receive the reward or punishment they have earned, based on their works.

Latter-day: having to do with the time just before the end of the world. Members of the *restored* church are called Latter-day *Saints*, because we believe the end of the world is not far off.

Law of Moses: the laws God gave the *Israelites* to follow during Old Testament times.

laying on of hands: putting your hands on someone else, normally on their head. In the restored church, we use the laying on of hands to give people blessings, the *gift of the Holy Ghost*, and the *priesthood*.

Lemuelites: in the Book of Mormon, the people who were *descendants* of Nephi's brother, Lemuel. The Lemuelites were counted among the *Lamanites*.

Levites: the family who was in charge of running the *temple* and making *sacrifices* in Bible times.

Liahona: in the Book of Mormon, the brass ball God gave Lehi so he would know which way to lead his family through the desert.

license: written permission to do something.

lust: wanting to have sex with someone. Lust is a natural feeling. But we need to learn to control it, so it doesn't lead us to do things that are wrong.

matter: what all things are made out of. People, animals, plants, dirt, water, air, and stars are all made of matter.

Melchizedek priesthood: the *authority* God gave Melchizedek in Bible times. People who hold the Melchizedek priesthood today have the power to give people the blessings they need to live with God again.

mercy [show mercy]: being kind to people. God shows mercy when he helps us or when he *forgives* our *sins*.

Messiah: another name for Christ. The *prophets* of the Old Testament said that the Messiah would come to save the *Israelites* from their enemies.

Methodists: one of the churches Joseph Smith attended when he was a boy. Methodists believed in building strong *relationships* and working to become perfect. Joseph almost decided to join the Methodists.

mission: a special work God gives you to carry out. In the *restored* church, being called on a mission normally means being sent somewhere to teach the *gospel*.

missionary: someone who goes out to teach the *gospel*.

mummy: a person's body, treated

in a special way so it won't rot. The Egyptians buried people as mummies long ago. They wrapped the person's body in cloth and buried it in a dry place. Today, thousands of years later, people look for mummies so we can use them to learn about *ancient* Egypt—and because the mummies were often buried with treasure.

Native Americans: the tribes who lived in America before white people arrived. When the white people came, they fought with the Native Americans. They forced the Native Americans to move farther and farther away, so they could take over the Native Americans' land.

Nephites: one of the peoples talked about in the Book of Mormon. The Nephites were destroyed because they became wicked.

office: a *calling* with its own special set of *duties*. *Deacon, teacher, priest, elder,* and *high priest* are all offices in the *priesthood*.

olive: a small green or black fruit. A lot of olives were grown in the part of the world where Jesus lived.

ordain: to give someone the *priesthood,* or a special *calling*. When you are ordained, people lay their hands on you.

ordinance: a special action such as *baptism* or the *endowment*. When we perform ordinances, we show that we want to be with God, and we open ourselves up to receive God's blessings.

organize: to put things in order.

papyri: a type of book used by the *Egyptians* long ago. Papyri did not open up with lots of pages, the way books do today. Instead, they were written on long sheets of paper and then rolled up.

palms: big leafy branches from a kind of tree that grows in the part of the world where Jesus lived. People wave palms as a way of praising God.

patriarch: an *office* in the *Melchizedek priesthood*. The word "patriarch" means "father." A patriarch gives church members a special blessing to help them know what God wants them to do with their lives.

perdition [children of perdition]: people who are so wicked that they can't live in any part of heaven. They will have to go live with Satan instead. The word "perdition" means "lost."

plates: thin sheets of metal. The Book of Mormon was written on gold plates.

Pharaoh: the title of the king of Egypt.

plural marriage: when a man who is a member of the *restored* church has more than one wife at the same time. The church no longer performs plural marriage.

preach: to teach people the *gospel*. Preaching normally means speaking in front of whole groups of people.

Presbyterians: one of the churches Joseph Smith attended when he was a boy. Presbyterians believed that the church should be run by *elders*. In New Testament times, *elders* were called "presbyters."

president: in the *restored* church, the leader of a *quorum* or other church group.

presidency: in the *restored* church, a *president* and two *counselors*.

priest: one of the *offices* in the *Aaronic priesthood*. Priests bless the *sacrament*.

priesthood: the power to do certain things to help God's work. People need the priesthood before they can *baptize*, pass the *sacrament*, or give blessings.

printer: someone who makes books.

printshop: a store where books are made.

proclamation: a special writing. People make proclamations when they want to tell something important to the world.

professor: someone who has studied a lot. Professors often teach at colleges.

prophet: someone who speaks for God. God gives *revelations* to prophets, so they can teach people what God wants them to do.

publish: to make something into a book, so many people can read it.

pulpit: the stand that a person stands behind to *preach*.

quorum: a group of people who meet together. *Deacons*, *teachers*, *priests*, and *elders* all have their own quorums.

quote: to repeat something someone else has said. The angel Moroni quoted, or repeazted, parts of the *scriptures* when he visited Joseph Smith.

recommend: a note someone writes to show other people they trust you or think well of you. People who go to the *temple* need to take a recommend to show that their *bishop* and *stake president* feel they are *worthy* to enter.

record: a written history.

reject: the opposite of "accept."

relationship: sharing your life with another person in some way. We have relationships with our family members, our friends, our *spouses*, and so on.

repent [repentance]: to turn away from *sin*. Someone who repents stops doing things that are wrong. They ask God to *forgive* them. If they have hurt other people, they try to make up for it.

restore [restoration]: to bring something back after it has been lost or taken away.

revelation [reveal]: a message from God. God teaches people by sending them revelation.

righteous [righteousness]: doing what is right.

rod: another word for "pole."

rudder: the part of a ship that makes it turn.

rye: a kind of grain.

Sabbath: the day God set aside to be holy. We rest from our work and go to church on the Sabbath.

sacrament: the bread and water people take to remember Jesus Christ's body and blood. When we take the sacrament, we show that we are still trying to follow Jesus.

sacrifice: giving up something you want. In Bible times, it meant killing an animal as a *symbol* of Jesus giving his life to save us.

saints: people who have been made holy. The members of Christ's church are called saints because they have the *gift of the Holy Ghost*.

salvation: freedom from death and from the pain of *sin*. We receive salvation through Jesus Christ's *grace*.

Savior: someone who saves people. Jesus Christ is our Savior, because he saves us from death and *hell*.

scribe: a person who writes things down for someone else. When Joseph Smith was *translating* the Book of Mormon, Oliver Cowdery wrote down what Joseph said. So Oliver was Joseph's scribe.

scriptures: the books where we read God's word. In the *restored* church, we use four books of scripture—the Bible, the Book of Mormon, Doctrine and Covenants, and the Pearl of Great Price.

seal [sealing]: to stick something tightly together or tightly closed. In the *restored* church, a sealing is a marriage done in the *temple*. A sealed marriage lasts forever, not just while the husband and wife are alive.

Second Coming: the time when Jesus will come back to rule the earth. No one knows when the Second Coming will be.

section: a part of something. The different *revelations* in Doctrine and Covenants are called sections.

seer: a *prophet* who has power from God to see special things.

Senior: when a man has a son with the same name, the man is called Senior, to keep the two apart. Joseph Smith's father was called Joseph Smith, Senior.

seventy: an *office* in the *Melchizedek priesthood*. Seventies help do *missionary* work and lead the church.

Shakers: a religious group of Joseph Smith's day. Shakers believed in living simply. They did not believe in getting married. They got their name from the way they used to dance during their meetings.

share: a part of a business. When someone is trying to start a business, they may sell shares in order to raise the money they need. People who buy shares get a certain part of the money the business makes.

shield: a piece of thick wood or metal you hold in front of you to protect yourself in battle.

sin [sinner]: breaking God's *commandments*. We all have sins, because we all do things that are wrong.

soul: in D&C 88, the word "soul" means a body and a spirit together. In other parts of the *scriptures*, a soul is the same as a spirit.

spirit prison: the place where the spirits of people go who didn't accept the *gospel* while they were alive.

spiritual: things that have to do with God or the *gospel*. The *scriptures* teach that spiritual things are more important than earthly things. That is because earthly things end, but spiritual things go on forever.

spouse: a husband or wife.

stake: a tent peg. In Doctrine and Covenants, groups of church members living outside *Zion* are called stakes. The idea is that as more and more groups of members are formed, the church becomes bigger and stronger, like a tent does when you add more stakes.

stake president: the person in charge of leading a *stake*.

state seal: the *symbol* of a state. The state seal often appears on the state's flag.

stock: a part of a business. (See *share*.)

stockholder: someone who buys *shares* in a business. Stockholders get part of the money the business makes.

storehouse: a building where goods are kept safe for people to use later.

Supreme Court: in the United States, nine judges who have the right to decide if a law is in keeping with the *constitution*.

symbol: something which stands for something else. For example, a flag is a symbol of a country. The bread we eat during the *sacrament* is a symbol of Christ's body.

tannery: a kind of factory where animal skins are gotten ready to be made into shoes or clothes.

teacher: an *office* in the *Aaronic priesthood*. Teachers get the *sacrament* ready to be blessed.

telestial kingdom: the part of heaven where the people who are least *righteous* will go after they come back from the dead.

temple: God's house on earth. In the *restored* church, temples are used for special *ordinances*, like *baptism for the dead* and *sealings*.

tempt [temptation]: to try to get people to do something wrong. Satan tempts us because he wants us to *sin*. He wants to keep us from being able to live with God.

terrestrial kingdom: the part of heaven where people will go who are *righteous* enough to live with Jesus, but not with Heavenly Father.

testify: to tell other people what you know is true.

testimony: a way to know that something is true or right. If we live the *gospel*, the Spirit will make us feel that it is true. That is a testimony.

tithing: money or other goods given to God. The words means "ten percent."

traitor: someone you think you can trust, but who turns against you or tries to hurt you.

translate [translation]: to take words in one language and change them into another language, so people can understand them. Joseph Smith had to translate the Book of Mormon into English, because no one around him could understand the language it had been written in.

treasury: a place where treasure or other important things are locked up.

United Order: a special group of church members who shared everything they owned. The United Order ran church property and helped take care of the poor.

Urim and Thummim: a special stone or pair of stones. God can show people things by having them look into the stones. Joseph Smith used a Urim and Thummim to *translate* the Book of Mormon.

Utah Commission: a special group formed in the 1800s to report to the United States government about what was going on in Utah.

vision: seeing something through God's power. For example, Joseph Smith had a vision of the *celestial kingdom*. That meant he was able to see the *celestial kingdom* through God's power.

witness: a person who sees something with their own eyes. Witnesses are able to tell other people about what they saw.

worldly: caring more about earthly things than about *spiritual* things. Sometimes when the *scriptures* talk about "the world," they mean the people who haven't accepted the *gospel*.

worship: to show our love for God. When we worship, we meet with other people to pray, sing, read the *scriptures*, and learn about God's *commandments*.

worthy: we say that someone is worthy when they are ready to receive a certain kind of blessing, like a *gospel ordinance*. When we say that someone is not worthy, we mean that they cannot receive God's blessings, because they are not doing the right things.

Zion: a group of people who live in peace and share all they have. Enoch built a city called Zion. In Doctrine and Covenants, Zion almost always means a city that church members were building in Missouri. Zion can also mean the *restored* church.

Zoramites: in the Book of Mormon, the people who were *descendants* of Nephi's friend, Zoram. The Zoramites were counted among the *Nephites*.

WHERE DO I FIND . . . ?

Here are some important people, stories, and teachings found in the Easy-to-Read Doctrine and Covenants and the Easy-to-Read Pearl of Great Price. They are in a-b-c order.

People, Stories & Teachings	Scripture Reference	Page
AARONIC PRIESTHOOD		
Restored by John the Baptist	D&C 13; JS-H 1:68-72	18, 262
Duties of priests	D&C 20:46-52	27
Duties of teachers	D&C 20:53-59	27
Duties of deacons	D&C 20:57-59	27
Lesser priesthood	D&C 107:1-20	150-151
ABRAHAM *Bible prophet*		
Almost sacrificed	Abr. 1:8-20	241-242
Received the priesthood	Abr. 2:10-11	243
Learned about the stars	Abr. 3:1-21	244-245
Saw the premortal life	Abr. 3:22-28	245-246
Has been exalted	D&C 132:29-32	190
ADAM *first man on earth*		
Created by God	Moses 3:7; Abr. 5:7	223, 248
The Fall	Moses 4; A of F 2	224-225, 265
Offered sacrifice	Moses 5:5-8	226
Baptized by the Holy Ghost	Moses 6:64-68	232
Adam-ondi-Ahman	D&C 107:53-57; 116	153, 165
ALVIN SMITH *Joseph Smith's brother*		
In the celestial kingdom	D&C 137	201-202
ANGELS		
Visited Joseph Smith	D&C 128:20-21	184-185
How to tell if they're real	D&C 129	185-186
Where they live	D&C 130:4-7	186
ATONEMENT (look under JESUS CHRIST)		
BAPTISM		
How to baptize	D&C 20: 37, 71-74	26, 28
In another church	D&C 22	30
When 8 years old	D&C 68:27	87

People, Stories & Teachings	Scripture Reference	Page
BAPTISM FOR THE DEAD		
Done in temples	D&C 124:28-32	174-175
Joseph Smith taught about	D&C 127-128	182-185
BATH-SHEBA *one of David's wives*		
Exalted without David	D&C 132:39	190-191
BOOK OF MORMON		
Proves Bible true	D&C 20:8-12	25
The Saints must study	D&C 84:54-58	107
Floods the earth with truth	Moses 7:62	236
Word of God	A of F 8	265
BRIGHAM YOUNG *2nd church president*		
President of the Twelve	D&C 124:127	179
Accepted by the Lord	D&C 126	181
Led the Saints west	D&C 136	199-201
CAIN *Adam and Eve's son*		
Killed Abel	Moses 5:16-41	226-228
Started secret combinations	Moses 5:49-55	228
CHILDREN		
Blessed in church	D&C 20:70	28
Saved by Atonement	D&C 29:46-47; 74	37-38, 92
Should go to school	D&C 55:4	68
Will not die during Millennium	D&C 63:51	80-81
In the celestial kingdom	D&C 137	201-202
Sealed to their parents	D&C 138:48	204
CHURCH		
Only true church on earth	D&C 1:30	4
Arguing with other churches	D&C 18:20	21
Name of Christ's church	D&C 115:4	164
COMMANDMENTS		
Given to help us	D&C 82:8-10	103
Lead to blessings	D&C 130:20-21	187
DAVID *Israelite king*		
Lost his exaltation	D&C 132:38-39	190-191

People, Stories & Teachings	Scripture Reference	Page
DAVID WHITMER *early Church member*		
Book of Mormon witness	D&C 17	20
EARTH		
We must take care of	D&C 59:18-20; Moses 2:28	74, 222
Will become celestial kingdom	D&C 88:18-20	114
There are other earths	Moses 1:29-35	220
Created by God	Moses 2-3; Abr. 4-5	221-223, 246-249
EDWARD PARTRIDGE *first LDS bishop*		
Called to be bishop	D&C 41:9-11	48
Warned to repent	D&C 85	111
EGYPTUS *Noah's granddaughter*		
Discovered land of Egypt	Abr. 1:23-25	242
ELIJAH *Bible prophet*		
Brought priesthood keys	D&C 2; 128:17-18	5, 184
Appeared in Kirtland Temple	D&C 110:14-16	160
EMMA SMITH *Joseph Smith's wife*		
Married Joseph Smith	JS-H 1:57-58	261
A chosen woman	D&C 25	32-33
Should accept plural marriage	D&C 132:51-56	191-192
ENOCH *Bible prophet*		
Became a seer	Moses 6:26-38	230
Built Zion	Moses 7:12-19, 68-69	233, 236
Saw the future	Moses 7:20-67	233-236
EVE *first woman on earth*		
Created by God	Moses 3:21-23; Abr. 5:15-17	223, 248
The Fall	Moses 4; 5:11	224-226
A glorious woman	D&C 138:38-39	204
FAITH		
Can make miracles	D&C 84:65-72	108
Enoch's moves mountains	Moses 7:13	233
In Jesus Christ	A of F 4	265

People, Stories & Teachings	Scripture Reference	Page
FAMILIES		
Parents should teach children	D&C 68:25-26; Moses 6:6	87, 229
How to support	D&C 83	104-105
Church leaders warned about	D&C 93:40-50	126-127
Eternal families	D&C 132:19-20; 138:48	189, 204
FORGIVENESS		
How to be forgiven	D&C 1:31-32	4
Forgive everyone	D&C 64:8-11	82
GOVERNMENT		
Church beliefs about	D&C 134	196-197
Saints must respect	A of F 12	265
HEAVENLY FATHER		
Christ does his will	D&C 19:2, 24	23, 24
We can live with	D&C 76:50-70	96-97
Has a body	D&C 130:22	187
We are in his image	Moses 2:26-27; 5:8-9	222, 226
We lived with before	Abr. 3:21-28	245-246
HEAVENLY MOTHER		
All Gods will be known	D&C 121:28	169
Exalted women are Gods	D&C 132:19-20	189
Gods make the earth	Abr. 4-5	246-249
Women in God's image	Abr. 4:26-27	247
HOLY GHOST		
Makes us feel what's right	D&C 9:8-9	12
How to confirm	D&C 20:68	28
Spiritual gifts	D&C 46	58-59
Does not have a body	D&C 130:22-23	187
HYRUM SMITH *Joseph Smith's brother*		
Called to learn God's word	D&C 11:20-21	17
First patriarch	D&C 124:91-96	177-178
Killed in Carthage jail	D&C 135	197-199
JESUS CHRIST		
Suffers so we won't have to	D&C 19:15-19	23
Defends us to the Father	D&C 45:3-5	55
Appeared in Kirtland Temple	D&C 110:1-10	160
Visited spirits in prison	D&C 138	202-205

People, Stories & Teachings	Scripture Reference	Page
JESUS CHRIST (*continued*)		
His work and glory	Moses 1:39	220
Created the world	Moses 2-3	221-223
Atonement saves us	A of F 3	265
JOHN TAYLOR *3rd church president*		
Called to be apostle	D&C 118:6	167
Saw Joseph Smith die	D&C 135	197-199
JOSEPH SMITH *1st church president*		
The First Vision	JS-H 1:5-20	255-257
Moroni's visits	JS-H 1:27-54	258-260
Restored the Church	D&C 20-21	25-29
Testified of Jesus Christ	D&C 76:22-24	94-95
In Liberty Jail	D&C 121-123	168-173
Killed in Carthage Jail	D&C 135	197-199
Moses knew about	Moses 1:41	221
JOSEPH F. SMITH *6th church president*		
Vision of spirit world	D&C 138	202-205
LEARNING		
Study best books	D&C 88:118	119
Lasts and goes on after death	D&C 130:18-19	187
LOVE		
Needed to do God's work	D&C 4:5	6
God wraps us in love	D&C 6:20	9
Wrap yourselves in love	D&C 88:125	120
Love everyone	D&C 121:45	170
Enoch filled with love	Moses 7:41	234
LUCY MACK SMITH *Joseph Smith's mother*		
The First Vision	JS-H 1:20	257
In the celestial kingdom	D&C 137:5	201
MARRIAGE		
Love your spouse	D&C 42:22	49
Part of God's law	D&C 49:15-17	61
Eternal marriage	D&C 131:1-4; 132:15-20	187-188, 189
Become one body	Moses 3:24-25; Abr. 5:18-19	223, 248

People, Stories & Teachings	Scripture Reference	Page
MARTIN HARRIS *early Church member*		
Visited Dr. Anthon	JS-H 1:64-65	261-262
Lost 116 pages	D&C 3; 10	5-6, 13-16
Book of Mormon witness	D&C 17	20
MELCHIZEDEK PRIESTHOOD		
Restored by Peter, James, John	D&C 27:12-13	34
Calling of an elder	D&C 53:3	67
Oath and covenant	D&C 84:33-40	106-107
Greater priesthood	D&C 107:1-20	150-151
How to lead	D&C 121:34-46	170
MISSIONARIES		
How to serve	D&C 4	6
Worth of souls	D&C 18:10-16	21
Teach by the Spirit	D&C 50:13-24	62-63
Tell our neighbors	D&C 88:81	117
MOSES *Bible prophet*		
Visions of God and Satan	Moses 1	219-221
Had Melchizedek priesthood	D&C 84:19-25	106
Appeared in Kirtland Temple	D&C 110:11	160
NEW JERUSALEM (look under ZION)		
NOAH *Bible prophet*		
Preached Christ's gospel	Moses 8:12-24	237
Was sorry God made people	Moses 8:25-30	237-238
OLIVER COWDERY *early Church member*		
Received Aaronic priesthood	JS-H 1:68-73	262-263
Tried to translate	D&C 8-9	11-12
Book of Mormon witness	D&C 17	20
PARLEY P. PRATT *early Church member*		
Mission to the Lamanites	D&C 32	39-40
Preached to Shakers	D&C 49	60-62

People, Stories & Teachings	Scripture Reference	Page
POOR		
Everyone should be equal	D&C 49:20; 78:6-7	61, 101
The rich should share	D&C 56:16-19; 104:14-18	69, 144
Saints should help	D&C 58:8-11; 105:3-4	71, 147-148
No one poor in Zion	Moses 7:18	233
PROPHETS		
Listen to prophets	D&C 1:14	3
Joseph Smith a prophet	D&C 21	29
Only one at a time	D&C 28; 43:1-3	34-35, 52
REPENTANCE		
What it means	D&C 58:42-43	72
Parents teach children how	D&C 68:25-26	87
SABBATH (SUNDAY)		
Sabbath activities	D&C 59:9-14	74
Seventh day holy	Moses 3:3; Abr. 5:3	222, 248
SACRAMENT		
Prayer over the bread	D&C 20:77	28
Prayer over the water	D&C 20:79	28
SARAI *Abraham's wife*		
Kept God's commandments	D&C 132:34	190
Saved Abraham's life	Abr. 2:22-25	244
SATAN		
Thrown out of heaven	D&C 76:25-27; Moses 4:1-4	95, 224
Tempted Eve	Moses 4:5-12	224
Moses sent him away	Moses 1:12-22	219-220
Tried to stop God's work	D&C 10	13-16
Has power over water	D&C 61:14-19	76-77
SECOND COMING		
Signs of the times	D&C 45; JS-M 1	54-58, 251
What will happen	D&C 29; 88:87-116; 133	35-38, 117-119, 193-196

People, Stories & Teachings	Scripture Reference	Page
SIDNEY RIGDON *early Church member*		
Helped Joseph translate	D&C 35:20	42
Vision of degrees of glory	D&C 76	94-99
In First Presidency	D&C 90:6	112
SPENCER W. KIMBALL *12th church president*		
Blacks and the priesthood	OD 2	210-211
TEMPLES		
Saints should build	D&C 88:119-120	119
Kirtland Temple	D&C 109-110	156-160
Temple ordinances	D&C 124:28-41	174-175
Temple marriage	D&C 131:1-4; 132:15-20	187-188, 189
TITHING		
Why pay tithing	D&C 64:23	83
How much to pay	D&C 119	167
VIENNA JACQUES *early Church member*		
Servant of the Lord	D&C 90:28-31	123
WILFORD WOODRUFF *4th church president*		
Called to be an apostle	D&C 118:6	167
Ended plural marriage	OD 1	207-209
WORD OF WISDOM		
Revealed to Joseph Smith	D&C 89	121-122
ZION (NEW JERUSALEM)		
Built by Enoch	Moses 7:18, 69	233, 236
Will come again	Moses 7:62-64	236
In America	A of F 10	265
In Jackson County	D&C 57	69-70
Law of consecration	D&C 42:29-36	49-50
Saints failed to build	D&C 101; 103; 105	135-139, 142-143, 147-149

ABOUT THE AUTHOR

John C. Duffy is the first member of his family born into the Church of Jesus Christ of Latter-day Saints. He served a full-time proselyting mission in the Dominican Republic. He holds a bachelors degree in English from Brigham Young University and a masters in English from the University of Utah, where he now teaches writing.